THE LAST BLACKROBE

OF INDIANA AND THE

POTAWATOMI TRAIL OF DEATH:

REVEREND BENJAMIN PETIT

AND THE

POTAWATOMI INDIANS OF INDIANA

OTHER BOOKS BY JOHN MCMULLEN:

Pour Souls
Defector from Hell
2084: Tomorrow is Today
Utopia Revisited: Political Intrigue, Human Sexuality,
* and Religious Liberty Collide*

First Edition Paperback – November, 2006
ISBN 0-9791304-0-9
Cover art – Julia Stilchen
Interior layout – Roger Hunt
Editor – Rennell Brunclik

Printed in the United States of America

Readers may contact John McMullen at:
jmcmullen@materdei.evansville.net

Published by Charles River Press, Inc.
541 Long Lane.
Casper, Wyoming 82609

10   9   8   7   6   4   3   2   1

To the Potawatomi People
and
All Those Who Remember the Trail of Death

The Last Blackrobe of Indiana is a historical novel based in large part on *The Trail of Death: Letters of Benjamin Marie Petit* by Irving McKee, Indiana Historical Society Publications, volume 14, number 1 (Indianapolis: Indiana Historical Society, 1941), which is used here by permission. The text of Petit's letters is somewhat revised and modernized.

Another source used with permission was the book *Potawatomi Trail of Death—Indiana to Kansas* by Shirley Willard and Susan Campbell, eds., 2003, published by Fulton County Historical Society, Rochester, Indiana.

ACKNOWLEDGMENTS

A very special thank you goes to Susan Campbell and Shirley Willard for their invaluable editorial advice in the writing of this book.

"The utmost good faith shall always be observed toward Indians; their lands and properties shall never be taken from them without their consent; and in their property, rights, and liberty, they shall never be invaded or disturbed, unless in just and lawful war authorized by Congress; but laws founded in justice and humanity shall from time to time be made, for preventing wrongs done to them, and for preserving peace and friendship with them . . . ."

—From the Northwest Ordinance of 1787

"The Americans grew from the scum of the great water when it was troubled by an evil spirit and the froth was driven onto the American shores by a strong east wind. They are numerous and I hate them. They are unjust; they have taken away your lands which were not made for them."

—Tenskwatawa, the Shawnee Prophet,
(the brother of Chief Tecumseh),
in a sermon to his followers.

You have been told, O man, what is good,
And what the Lord requires of you:
Only to do justice, to love tenderly,
and to walk humbly with your God.

—Micah 6:8 (New American Bible)

"I stood there at midnight, the moon shone in all its splendor with nothing to break the stillness of the night save the occasional hooting of an owl or the call of the whip-poor-will, when I heard the footfall of the hoofs of a horse as he came galloping down the hill. I heard him as he splashed through the creek, and as he passed by, I saw whom he carried . . . it was the Blackrobe Father Benjamin Petit, hastening on to comfort his people and to counsel them . . . .

"Of all the names connected with this crime, there is one, Father Benjamin Petit, the Christian martyr, which stands like a star in the firmament, growing brighter and it will shine on through ages to come."

—Benjamin Stuart

"For American Indians the scars of injustice inflicted upon them in the past are deep, painful, and, tragically, are inherited from one generation to the next. Those injustices have become ghosts in the cultural memory of a people crying out for justice. We must fully disclose the past in order to deal with the many years and generations of unresolved grief and distrust."

—Thomas Hamilton, Warsaw, Indiana,
descendant of Abram Nanweshmah Burnett
and member of Citizen Potawatomi Nation, Shawnee, Oklahoma.

Prologue

Bayonets

4 September 1838

In spite of his fever and the physician's insistent warning for him to remain in bed, Benjamin Petit mounted his steed. With great haste, Petit rode south for the mission at Chief Menominee's village.

He soon arrived and found himself surrounded by armed horsemen. The soldiers refused him entry and guarded him with bayonet-tipped rifles, but his collar, cassock, and the cross about his neck indicated his purpose. Dismounting his ride, he tied the reins at the hitching post and entered the former chapel now reduced to a barn. More than a hundred of his people were corralled in the building.

The natives' faces were devoid of color and emotion. Their desperate question of why this was happening weighed upon his conscience. Nanweshmah approached him. "Chichipé Maketakônia, the doctor said—"

"Never mind me," Petit replied, shaking his head. "I must be here with all of you. I am your father."

The sight of all the people squeezed together like animals, nothing more than penned up livestock amid a plague of flies, infuriated Petit. The specter of such injustice made it tempting to hate the Americans.

Together the Indians began to chant their prayers in the Potawatomi tongue. He felt as if he was presiding over a Requiem Mass; the entire people a corpse about to be laid to rest. Yet this people had no burial ground; they were being ripped from their lands.

Petit was painfully aware that he would likely never see any of them again. Gazing at his dying mission and hearing the heartrending sobs of women and children, his tears choked off his words as the dusky faces of his people prayerfully looked to heaven.

Their prayers of supplication were interrupted by Colonel Pepper's voice. "The time for removal has come, Reverend."

"This is unspeakable," Petit said as he turned around.

"Spare me the drama, Reverend," Colonel Pepper said. "You and your people are moving west." Pepper placed his hand on his revolver. "Take it up with Governor Wallace and General Tipton!"

"This is a crime against justice—in a country which prides itself upon liberty!"

Pepper stood speechless as did all the Indians.

Suddenly gunfire rang out and Pepper nodded to a decorated officer entering the chapel. It was General Tipton. The terror of not knowing what was to happen next was agonizing, especially for the children.

More and more of the Potawatomi people were pushed inside the chapel. While the American soldiers guarded the door, Petit and the Potawatomi all began to realize their impending fate.

General Tipton's first act was to take Chief Menominee prisoner. He placed his rifle's bayonet at Menominee's neck.

"How could any people have allowed things to come to this?" Chief Menominee dejectedly asked, though loud enough for all to hear—even above the cruel laughter of the volunteer soldiers.

"There are over a hundred militiamen surrounding the village," Tipton announced. "It will go well if everyone cooperates."

How could they have done otherwise? They had no further

recourse; this was the end. The orders were clear: Tipton's men were to shoot the first Indian resistor.

The general then gloated that he and his men had discovered a cache of weapons hidden in the cornfield and adjacent woods. All of the weaponry has been collected and placed under guard in a covered wagon.

"Forty rifles in the corn and twenty more in the woods near the river—you people were going to ambush us, weren't you?" Tipton looked at Menominee.

None answered.

When Petit exited the chapel, he saw over one hundred armed soldiers with bayonets and guns surrounding his children.

The patriotism of the American citizens was such that in order to secure the white citizens from violence and all-out war with the Indians at Menominee's village, the last remnant of the Potawatomi tribe in Indiana had to be removed.

"I have lived too long to see my people come to an end such as this," Menominee declared to Petit. "The flap of the wigwam of my life is opening to the better land beyond. Soon I shall enter into the wigwam of the Great Spirit, and there I shall stand firm and beseech Him to grant our people a future of hope. I shall plead with Him to protect my people from the great destroyer of your children and ours, the great dragon." Menominee continued, "Yet I fear that, in time, our race shall disappear. Generations yet to be born will likely hear of our race and ask 'Where have they gone?' Civilized man considered our races savage and yet he has treated us most savagely."

He sighed and adjusted his turban. "The only way for a man to know the heart of an Indian is for that man to become an Indian. What white man has ever done that?"

Petit said nothing as Menominee's chocolate-brown eyes glistened with sorrow.

"Only our beloved Catholic blackrobes have done so. Your eyes speak truthfully, *Maketakônia Chichipé*," Menominee said firmly. "You have become one of us. You are Potawatomi."

"I am no longer French; I was never an American," Petit declared. "I am Potawatomi. *Maketakonia Chichipé* is my name."

O Lord, who will speak on behalf of the Indians? Who will be their advocate in the face of all the wrongs committed upon their people? His unspoken questions, indeed prayers of lament, remained unanswered.

He was frozen and weary. What could he do? *Will my people despise me knowing that I am to remain behind while they go off to an unknown land alone?* Some of the Indian converts lamented, "Has the God of the Blackrobes abandoned us?" Others questioned, "Where is God, Father Chichipé." Worst of all were the children's plaintive cries, "Maketokonia Chichipé, why are these bad men making us leave? Where are they taking us? What did we do wrong?" they clutched him tightly in fear. One of the newly baptized asked: "Where is Jesus?"

Petit knew where He was: He was about to be led away as once before to Golgotha. *Lord, have mercy. How had it come to this? Had he come this far only for it all to end this way?*

His thoughts returned to the first day he ever considered becoming a priest.

CHAPTER 1

A CHANGE OF PLANS

My life seemed perfectly in order until the missionary bishop of Vincennes, Indiana, Simon Bruté, visited France.

In 1835 Benjamin Petit was in Rennes, France, practicing law as an advocate. He had graduated from the law school at the University of Rennes in 1832 when he was but twenty-one and had practiced law rather successfully for three years.

Rumors were abounding throughout Brittany that the saintly Bishop Bruté, native of Rennes and missionary to the United States, had returned to his boyhood home for a visit. He was exhorting seminarians and priests throughout Europe to join him in the missionary fields of the American West; he was also inviting men to enter priestly studies so as to become missionaries. It was to this purpose that Benjamin Petit believed God placed Bishop Bruté in his path.

Bruté never spoke of himself, yet nearly every Breton knew the story of how he had once been a bright, young physician full of promise when Napoleon Bonaparte appointed him head physician of the First Dispensary in Paris. Bruté rejected Bonaparte's offer and entered the Seminary of Saint-Sulpice. Bruté's reputation was nearly legendary. By no means was Petit legendary in his field; nonetheless, he and Bruté did share something in common: neither of them had originally intended to be priests.

The call of the Lord intervened, and, by a strange twist of events, Benjamin Petit came face to face with the man he had grown up hearing about. The bishop was small of stature and stooped over from rheumatism and a perpetual hernia condition. At fifty-six, he was toothless and his smile was as wide as his face, yet his large, gray eyes were alive with enthusiasm and seemed to penetrate Petit's soul.

Bruté had a magnetic personality; however, not everyone seemed to think so. Petit's mother was not impressed with him. She had heard him say Mass at Rennes and believed he represented a pre-revolution church that no longer existed.

Yet the former president of the United States John Quincy Adams said that Bishop Simon Bruté was the most learned man in the United States.

Having grown up in Rennes, Petit knew well the near legendary accounts of how young Simon Bruté had graduated magna cum laude at the College of Rennes and entered the prestigious medical school at the University of Paris where he finished first out of a class of eleven hundred students. He came to the attention of Bonaparte who offered him the post of Court Physician and head of the First Dispensary in Paris, but Bruté turned down the offers and enrolled in the esteemed Seminary of Saint-Sulpice in order to become a priest of God so as to deliver men from the ravages of diseases of their souls.

As a seminarian, Bruté witnessed the famous coronation of Bonaparte by Pope Pius VII. Bruté's brilliance and holiness attracted the attention of the pope who granted him a private audience. After Bruté was ordained, Bonaparte offered to make him Chaplain of the Imperial Court. And again he refused the emperor. Bruté returned to Rennes where he taught theology until he heard the voice of the Lord, in the person of Benedict Joseph Flaget, the newly ordained Bishop of Bardstown, calling him to the New World in 1810.

At the invitation of Bishop Flaget, Bruté agreed to visit America. Once there, he soon canceled plans to return to

France. He was named President Rector of Mount Saint Mary's Seminary & College in Emmitsburg, Maryland, where he labored until 1834. At that time, His Holiness Pope Gregory XVI elevated Vincennes, Indiana, to an Episcopal see and named Bruté the first bishop of the city.

The zealous Bishop Bruté went to work immediately after arriving in Vincennes, making a pastoral visit on horseback to every corner of the diocese in just six months time. When Bruté arrived in Vincennes in November of that same year, there were only two other priests in the entire diocese, three with himself included! Oh, the sacrifices of missionary life! The long hours, the meager diet, fasting, and prayer.

Like Benjamin Petit's mother, his older brother, Paul, was also unimpressed with Bruté. Paul couldn't understand why Bruté would or could abandon everything and leave for America, a land of savages and barbarians. Little did Benjamin's mother and brother know that Bruté had convinced him to abandon the law of man for the Law of God. Bruté pointed to the work Petit did in legally defending the disadvantaged and poor as a sign that God may well be calling him to be their spiritual advocate as well. He reasoned that if Petit was defending common men against law breakers, how much more good would he accomplish by defending men and women against the wickedness and tyranny of the devil. What better way to be engaged in the spiritual battle between good and evil than to become a priest?

Admittedly, Petit felt the desire to be a priest since he was a boy, but as he grew older and became a young man, he suppressed the idea of a religious vocation out of a desire to live his life on his own terms and also from a sense of duty to his family to make good in life. A career as a churchman was not in vogue. Bishop Bruté had merely confirmed the Lord's calling in Petit's heart; the missionary bishop's invitation was that of the Lord.

Now Petit had returned to the life of devotion where he first felt God calling him to be priest: daily Mass and daily rosary.

With Bishop Bruté in Europe collecting funds and priests and seminarians for his fledgling missionary diocese, Petit decided to abandon his law career for the priestly life. That August he left the Rennes Tribunal and entered the Seminary of Saint-Sulpice in Paris. Exactly how he came to leave the legal profession so easily only Providence can fathom.

His brother, Paul, opposed the idea. He distrusted the Church for its past alliance with the monarchists and recent denunciation of republican principles. He was wont to point out the scoundrel priests who kept mistresses, entertained prostitutes, or lived luxuriously while the poor of their parishes languished.

Petit's mother purposely avoided the subject of her son's entering the seminary. With a distinguished legal position, she hoped her son would soon marry and have children. She feared he was gambling away his education and career on a capricious whim. Petit's deceased father had left sufficient funds that provided for his son's formal education; he always wanted Benjamin to follow in his footsteps as a lawyer.

The day Benjamin Petit left Rennes for Saint-Sulpice in Paris his mother embraced him and bid him adieu. Paul wrote to tell him that she wept for a week. He was convinced Benjamin would return to Rennes in a fortnight.

Eventually their mother came to accept the reality that her youngest son, Benjamin Marie Petit, was to become a priest. She then began to pray fervently for the day when Benjamin would return to Rennes, serve as the rector of the cathedral, be named a monsignor, and eventually be consecrated a bishop.

Vanity of vanities; all is vanity. Regardless of what his mother desired, he would be obedient wherever his superiors sent him.

CHAPTER 2

INVITATION

Leave Paris? Leave France? Leave Europe? Leave every-thing? Leave all.

In the spring of 1836, Bishop Bruté, still in Europe, had made Saint-Sulpice Seminary in Paris his temporary quarters before his departure to America. He had been throughout Europe and met with the heads of state, superiors of religious communities, bishops, and the pope to secure financial aid, sacred vessels, books, and most importantly, missionary clergy for the Diocese of Vincennes. From all accounts Bruté was out of place in the presence of such opulence, preferring instead the humble inn and homes of friends. His life was a witness to the power of self-sacrifice and humility. Bruté spoke of nothing but the missions. He was convinced that he was called to spend himself for the salvation of souls.

On a Monday evening in May, the day after Pentecost, the rector of the seminary invited Benjamin Petit to join him and a few of the other seminarians for dinner. They gathered along the *Rive Gauche* at an outdoor café on *Rue Saint-Severin* in the shadow of the eight-hundred-year-old church built over the saint's tomb. It was there that Petit was to meet Bruté.

The rector of the seminary had recommended Petit for the mission field. Petit had prayed about leaving France as a missionary for some time. He thought about going to China or Africa, but he believed he was being called to America.

As Petit sat at the table awaiting the distinguished prelate's arrival, he thought of his youth and inexperience. The first time he had mentioned the idea of becoming a missionary to his family no one was supportive. His mother said she would prevent it. She and his brother, Paul, had argued that Benjamin was too young and unfamiliar with worldly ways to ever become a missionary. Benjamin kept his anxiety in check as he sat at the table.

The sound of the café conversations were accompanied by clopping horses and rattling carriages on the stone street.

The rector of Saint-Sulpice made eye contact with Petit and smiled. It was the same rector who had encouraged him to embrace the life of a missionary. Petit recalled a conversation with the rector earlier in the week.

"Madame Chauvin Petit has written me again," he said as he held a letter postmarked from Rennes. Benjamin Petit's mother and brother had written Petit in order to dissuade him from committing to such a foolhardy adventure. "I must ask, if you should depart with Bishop Bruté, are you aware of the difficulties and challenges that await?"

"Oui."

"Even death?"

Petit paused before answering. "Oui."

Petit's attention returned to the moment as he studied the half-filled wine carafe in the middle of the table surrounded by three priestly birettas. He reached for his glass and took a sip. As he set the glass down, he ran his right index finger along its rim. In the glass, he saw the reflection of purple raiment. Before he could turn, his companions and the rector were on their feet. It was Bishop Bruté. His eyes were alive and his step quick; he seemed younger and more alive than his stooping figure betrayed. Bruté greeted each of the men individually; his attention so focused it seemed each man was the only person in the entire world.

Bruté eschewed any comparisons between the lives of the saints and himself, even though he was following in the steps of the French missionaries, the famous blackrobes, of which he was the last of a dying breed. As for comparison, he did compare himself to the disappearing bison of the American West. He said something about the disappearing American Indian, but his toothless pronunciation rendered the words lost to the sounds of the street and café.

This was not merely a social gathering. No, this was an invitation not unlike the invitation Ignatius of Loyola had extended to Francis Xavier in 1540 to take the Gospel to India. For Petit's part, he was being invited to Indiana. The slight-framed bishop folded his hands in prayer and glanced up at the Church of Saint-Severin as the steeple bells tolled the Angelus.

The moment finally arrived when the bishop asked the question Petit was expecting: "Have any of you men considered the missions?" It had only been a year since Petit entered the seminary, but already he was ready and willing to renounce all for the sake of the Gospel.

The bishop continued, "I have no doubt that some of you will leave with me." It was bold of him to proclaim, yet he already had at least twelve volunteers. "I know that not all of you are skilled woodsmen or aspire to be rugged frontiersmen, but I believe one or more of you shall sail with me to America."

The rector gave a toast to the missions of the New World and to all who had left everything for the sake of the Gospel. The call of Christ was clear: "Go, sell all that you have and give to the poor and you will then have treasure in heaven. Leave all things you have and come and follow me. Everyone who has given up home, brothers or sisters, father or mother, wife or children or property for my sake will receive many times as much and inherit eternal life."

The words of Christ both comforted and challenged Petit.

The truth at last forced its way to Petit's conscious mind. Indeed he was about to embark upon a most uncertain mission—yet not one without hope.

A parish priest of Paris stopped at their table. He was from the privileged class, and he looked at Bruté in much the way Petit's brother did. This priest was one who, in Petit's opinion, would not likely volunteer for the missionary life. He addressed the bishop, "Father, we have read the newspaper accounts of life in the American West. It is a land of lawlessness. Unless you are good with a rifle and are prepared to do battle with the savages, not to mention bears and wolves, then these recruits of yours will not likely survive their first year. The United States is nothing but a land of ruffians. Many of its immigrants are European troublemakers; the rest of the native-born Americans are greedy land-grabbers."

"The true native-born American is the Indian—the so-called savage—and he is fast being displaced from his ancestral homeland," Bruté answered. "The New World is very much like the Old World, more so than the Americans—and others—care to admit."

"Not in every respect," the priest replied. "One must not forget that much of the American prosperity has been made on the backs of slave labor."

"The holy Father has condemned the slave trade and has exhorted us to send missionaries to the United States. By the example of our lives and through our preaching, we might hope and pray to change the hearts of the slave-owning Americans."

"But why would you even want to live in a country that regards a goodly number of its people as noncitizens and mere property?"

"For the same reason that Christ humbled himself to share in our humanity: to love others so that they in turn can learn to love God."

8

"Simplistic answers are for children, Father."

"We are all called to be as simple as children, Father Bovinet."

"How do you know me?"

"Our blessed Lord was chastised for eating and drinking with prostitutes and publicans, was he not?" Bruté replied without answering the priest's question.

"Yes, but a nation whose wealth depends upon slave labor . . . ?"

"Did not our ancestors endure the ruin of the barbarians, as well as the wrath of the Revolution and the Reign of Terror?"

"We have also endured corrupt popes and bishops," Father Bovinet snorted.

". . . and corrupt kings and governments," Bruté finished his sentence, hinting at the ongoing debate between Gallicanism, a movement initially among the French clergy that believed papal control over the Church should be more limited, and Ultramontanism, the position that ultimate authority in the Church was "beyond the mountains" and vested with the pope of Rome.

Father Bovinet abruptly ended the conversation when two fashionably dressed, well-to-do ladies came out of one of the shops and approached him. They were familiar with him and he engaged them in conversation.

Bruté resumed his thoughts aloud, directing them to those at the table. "Do not think that simply because you are attached to your home and family that you would not make a missionary. I think you would be surprised at how well you could amalgamate with the western pioneers.

"Your bishops have all indicated to me that they are willing to release you from your commitments to your respective dioceses should you volunteer—and be accepted—for the missions."

Silence followed.

"A priest is never his own, gentlemen." Bruté nodded and glanced at each of the men. "As Saint Paul wrote: 'Faith is assurance of things hoped for and conviction about those things that are unseen. Hope is not hope if its object is seen. Hoping for what one cannot see means awaiting it with patience and endurance. Who or what will separate us from the love of Christ? Trial, or distress, or persecution, or hunger, or nakedness, or danger, or the sword? If God is for us, who can be against us? Is it possible that He who did not spare His own son will not grant us all things?'

"Our Lord reminds us: We are in the world, but not of the world. We must be as wise as serpents but innocent as doves. Nothing can separate us from the love of God that comes to us through Christ our Lord."

The church bell rang eight o'clock and Bruté stood. His conviction was compelling and his purpose was clear.

Benjamin Petit was to meet with the visiting missionary bishop again the next morning. At that time, Bruté would present him with a formal invitation to become a missionary. In anticipation of that meeting, Petit excused himself and decided to pray. He entered the Church of Saint-Severin and made his way to the front pew. He gazed upon the sanctuary lamp and rested in the Lord's presence for nearly an hour. He nodded off at one point and caught himself falling off the *prie-dieu*. He stood, genuflected, blessed himself at the holy water font, and left the church.

The three-quarters moon was modestly covered by wispy clouds. A streak of lightning splintered several directions and etched a trail in the slate blue clouds of the western sky. The rumble of far away thunder reverberated off the buildings, streets, and bridges. The wind began to gust and a static mesh of fiery, blue-white fingers reached through the clouds and stretched across the approaching storm, eerily lighting the Seine

Valley and the Cathedral of Notre Dame. Large drops of rain fell like cannon fire on a battlefield, scattering the Parisians.

Petit held his biretta on his head and hurried back to the seminary while the rain cleansed the cobblestone of the horse dung and evening dust. As he ran along with his cassock whipping in the wet wind, he looked like a raven about to take flight.

CHAPTER 3

DECISION

I am not worthy of the priesthood, yet Bishop Bruté has asked me to join him in America as a missionary.

The next morning the peal of church bells awakened Petit. It was still drizzling, and a thick fog from the cool night air enveloped Paris. The great spire of Saint-Sulpice was lost in the low clouds of dawn as the early morning worshipers filed in for morning Mass. When the priests processed up the aisle and ascended the altar steps Bishop Bruté was the main celebrant. He was robed in brilliant green, gold-trimmed vestments as two deacons serving as acolytes held up the ends of his chasuble, the long, sleeveless vestment meant to resemble the seamless garment of Christ. It seemed a great dichotomy: such a humble man dressed in such a lavish mantle.

All during Mass, Petit thought of the impending meeting with the rector and Bishop Bruté. There were a hundred things to consider if he were to leave for America: how would he tell his mother and brother; how would he live in the New World wilderness; to whom would he minister?

The Gospel reading of the day was from Matthew: At the sight of the crowds, Jesus' heart was moved with pity. They were lying prostrate from exhaustion, like sheep without a shepherd. He said to his disciples, "The harvest is plenty, but laborers are few. Beg the harvest master to send out laborers to gather his harvest."

After receiving communion, he returned to his pew and knelt in prayer. He remained kneeling when the Mass was over and prayed the rosary. There was such a surge within him, his heart felt large within his breast as he thought of the opportunity that lie before him: to take the Gospel to an unenlightened race of the New World.

He moved to the side aisle of the church, blessed himself at the holy water font, slowly marked the sign of the cross over his chest, and exited out the side door into the courtyard of the seminary.

Petit's professors had told him that with his knowledge of Latin, Greek, and law, he could be a professor of philosophy and theology, a life of prestige and honor within the Archbishop's court—just as he had distinguished himself as a lawyer in Rennes. It was a worldly temptation. Petit knew he wasn't even worthy of the priesthood.

No one is worthy of the priesthood. And he knew what leaving Paris for life as an American missionary would mean. *Foxes have dens, birds have nests, but the Son of Man has nowhere to lay his head.* He continued to discern God's will for his life.

He entered the seminary building and climbed the stairwell to the rector's office where the meeting with Bishop Bruté was to take place. The wooden floor of the hallway creaked underfoot as he made his way. Rich tapestries and vivid Renaissance artwork adorned the walls. As he sat in one of the high-backed tapestried chairs, the rector's door opened.

"Benjamin Petit," the rector said as he motioned him inside. "Entre."

"Monseigneur." Petit stood and the rector escorted him in.

Bishop Bruté was standing just inside the door. "Bishop Bruté," the rector began, "I believe you remember our lawyer from Rennes, Benjamin Petit."

"Ah, *mais oui, mon petit Benjamin.* Of course, my little

Benjamin." The bishop was dressed in a red-buttoned black soutane with a purple silk cape over his shoulders. A four-cornered purple biretta sat atop his head. There was an aura of strength and peace about his presence—an aura hard to describe but real nonetheless. It caused the hair on Petit's arm to rise.

"Your Excellency." Petit nodded and genuflected to kiss the bishop's signet ring.

"My son. Please, have a seat." Bruté raised him up and led him to a chair off to the side. The bishop and rector sat next to one another and Petit sat opposite them. Bruté's grasp seemed that of a larger man, not one from such a diminutively framed individual.

The bishop removed his biretta from his head to reveal a balding head with gray hair above his ears. The tabs of his abbreviated frock came down from his collar and draped over the front of his black soutane to the third button. His simple silver crucifix, which served as a pectoral cross, was attached to the third button while the chain hung down along both arms of the cross. Bruté's thin fingers grasped the cross as he looked up at Petit. "Benjamin, your professors here, as well as those at the University of Rennes and the law school there, have all given you the highest of recommendations. If you choose to accept the mantle of a missionary, you would be following in the tradition of Saint Francis Xavier who left Europe to go to the people of India. In your case, you would be leaving Europe for the people of Indiana.

"However, my son, as the Saint Benedict states in his holy rule, the novice who truly seeks God and shows an eagerness for the works of God must be told of the hardships, trials, and difficulties of obedience that will lead him to God.

"Therefore, I will tell you that the wilderness of Indiana is fraught with dangers and uncertainty: illness, fevers, pox, pests and pestilence, horrid summers, dreadful winters, bears, wildcats, and wolves. The sacrifices one has to make will often border on the heroic. In the American West there are no paved thoroughfares; the forests are so thick and towns so few and distant that one can travel for days without seeing another human soul.

"Unfortunately, the religious prejudice against Catholics and the hatreds for the Church and her sacraments, the Blessed Mother, and the Holy Father have found their way into the thick forests of the New World. The land hailed as a beacon of religious freedom has shown little tolerance for Catholicism.

"There is even the possibility of martyrdom amidst some of the more war-like Indian tribes. Then there is also the fear of being martyred by some of the fanatical Protestants who call themselves *natives*, who insist that one must be born in America in order to be an American.

"In my own See City of Vincennes, many of the people are reluctant to take religious instruction, and with American traders all too eager to ply the Indians with whiskey, oftentimes the Indians are too intoxicated to pray. The Indians are called savage, but the Americans themselves can be quite savage. Two years ago a frenzied mob of drunken Protestants burnt an Ursuline convent in the state of Massachusetts. Thankfully no one was killed.

"The hostility to the Gospel remains the same and the hostility to the Catholic immigrant and his faith regrettable, yet our mission remains our own. We shall tirelessly proclaim the Gospel, administer the sacraments, hear confession, say Mass for the faithful, and provide the last rites and Eucharistic Viaticum for the dying.

"Wherever you serve Christ and His Church, you will spend yourself in the field of the kingdom. But in this era of emphasis upon worldly wealth and possessions, people have forgotten

Christ and His Church. They have abandoned the traditions and witness of the early Church. Yet, I myself am guilty of some of these same things. I myself am not worthy to be a missionary or a bishop, yet that is what I am by the grace of God. Is God calling you to the same life?"

Petit wasn't sure whether it was a rhetorical question or if the bishop expected him to answer it. In Petit's hesitation Bruté spoke again, "Do you have any questions?"

"No," he answered as he thought of the extreme risks of sailing the Atlantic Ocean.

"You have considered the priesthood for some time," Bruté interrupted the momentary daydream. "Therefore I will give you the week to think and pray—especially pray. You would do well to recall the words of the founder of the Company of Jesus, Ignatius Loyola: 'He who forgets himself for God's service may be sure that God will not forget him.' Let us continue to pray for the missions. And I shall pray especially for you, mon petit Benjamin."

With that Bruté rose. "*Dominus vobiscum*" (The Lord be with you).

Petit rose and bowed his head. "*Et cum spiritu tuo*" (and with your spirit).

Bruté raised his hand over Petit's head and invoked a blessing. "*Benicat vos omnipotens*," he said as he traced the sign of the cross in the air, "*Deus, Pater, et Filius, et Spiritus Sanctus*" (May almighty God bless you in the Name of the Father, and the Son, and the Holy Spirit).

"Amen," Petit answered as he looked up into the eyes of the smiling, toothless bishop.

"I shall discuss this matter with you in one week, Benjamin." Bruté clasped Petit's hand firmly. "I will leave for America two weeks from today. I pray you may be in our company. Join me in the western missions, my son."

Within the week Petit had made his decision. He would be leaving France for America in the company of Bishop Bruté and several other priests and seminarians on the first of June.

He prepared to leave for Rennes to inform his family of his decision to enter the missionary field. It was easier said than done.

CHAPTER 4

MISSIONARY

I sincerely believe God is calling me to become a missionary.

—•◇●◇•—

Petit secured a horse and made the day-long journey north wondering if this might be the last time he would ever make the trip home. This horse was unlike his horse, *Bijou*, but then no horse could compare with her. He patted the borrowed horse's mane, squeezed his legs into its sides, and pulled the right rein. As the horse turned, he eased his heels into the flank, allowing the reins to dangle as the horse achieved a trot along the cobblestones.

His mind drifted back to his church history class, recalling the words of the professor, "The gift of poverty has given the Church the grace of destitution. That is the spirit of reform we must pray for: the freedom from all tyranny, particularly political and economic tyranny." The words called to mind the ongoing tension between Protestants and Catholics in Prussia and the surging hostility in the Papal States. He worried that the unrest could trigger reactionary measures throughout Europe.

The conflict that triggered much of the unrest and that caused so much anxiety in recent years centered on the question of mixed marriages between Protestants and Catholics. In 1830, Pope Pius VIII forbid the clergy from witnessing mixed marriages unless the Protestant partner signed a written promise that any offspring of the union would be raised as Catholics. The Prussian government asserted that in situations of mixed marriages, the male offspring should follow the religion of their father and the female offspring should follow the religion of the mother. In May of 1836, the Archbishop of Cologne refused to follow the Prussian law and ordered his priests to violate the legislation. There was mounting fear that the government intended to subdue the Catholic Church altogether throughout the region, especially when the king threatened to order that all children of mixed marriages be raised as Protestants.

The Church had once again been humbled back to its beginnings as a church under siege, the age of apostles and martyrs, and the era of persecution. Again, his seminary professor's words came to mind, *"Did you not know that the Church, the Bride of Christ, must also suffer and be put to death? But she, like her Lord, will rise again."*

Petit knew that some of the Enlightenment thinkers believed that the Catholic Church must be crushed. Rousseau's philosophy was that the right to govern comes not from God, but from man. Both philosophies were shared by many Europeans and Americans. The argument was that the Church could no longer operate as a monarchy, and it must embrace the ideals of Republicanism.

The conflict between the adherents of Gallicanism (the French Catholic nationalists) and the Ultramontanism (the traditionalist Catholics who looked *beyond the mountains* into Italy for sole authority coming from the pope) was never ending. Both sides of the argument had valid points and Petit couldn't help but view the arguments through his lawyer mind. He tended to come down on the side of the Ultramontanes, for he did believe that there was no Christianity without the authority of the Church of Rome.

Yet the French priest Feli de Lamennais had made a bold stand in his brand of Liberal Catholicism. Many of his adherents argued that much of what he proposed, such as freedom of the press and freedom of religion, had served the Catholic Church well in the United States. Nevertheless, the pope and his cardinal advisers did not see things in the same way. Lamennais and Liberal Catholicism had been squelched even though Bishop Simon Bruté was a close friend to Lamennais.

As Petit made his way to Rennes, all the sights, sounds, and smells along the way gave him a feeling of consolation, but at the same time, a marked sense of disquietude kept jolting him back into reality.

What must it be like, oh Lord, to leave all of this behind forever? To go to the New World where nothing is familiar? When I am an old man, if it is your holy will that I live that long, will I lie awake at night and try to remember these houses, these streets, these villages, these faces? Will I remember the faces of my homeland, my beloved Brittany?

He longed to share with his father the joy of being called to become a missionary for the Lord and his Church.

Before dying, Petit's father asked, "Benjamin, are you still thinking of becoming a priest?"

"As a young man I considered the call, but I have chosen law as my career."

"As I near death I know some things," his father said between coughs as he gazed at the crucifix on his bedroom wall. "Perchance I should not have discouraged you from becoming a priest."

"*Father,* you didn't discourage me."

"Oui, but I certainly didn't encourage you." He turned and looked intently at his son.

"You have been a good father." The memory faded as he arrived at his family home.

Passing by the apple orchard and vineyard, he loped down the lane and headed for his family's livery stable and carriage house. There he saw Bijou. She was a beautiful caramel-colored beauty with a black mane. Bijou was different from other horses, an intelligent breed. He didn't give her mere commands: she understood him. He dismounted the borrowed ride and led the horse into the stables next to his treasured companion.

"Well, if it isn't my old friend Bijou. It's too bad you cannot go with me to the New World." He stroked her head and patted her mane. "I cannot imagine ever loving another as I love you," he chuckled to himself, kissing the horse. "There I go again, talking as if it has all been decided! Oh, such difficult decisions we humans must make, Bijou. Perhaps you could give me some advice." Leaning into the horse's face, he asked, "What do you think I should do? Should I go to the New World, or should I stay here with you?" Bijou neighed loudly, nodding her head up and down. "So you think I should stay with you? Well, I am sorry to say that I must leave you for now, but only until tomorrow. My brother would be angry to know you were the first family member I greeted upon my return. I shall see you again in the morning and we shall have a long ride. Goodnight, my dear. Sleep well." He patted her one last time and turned to walk up the lane.

His youngest sister, Jeanne, a vivacious seventeen-year-old, eyed him as she rounded the corner of the house. "Benjamin, Benjamin! You are home!"

She was a beautiful young woman and was even more beautiful than the last time he saw her.

"Jeanne, how many beaus have come to call on you today?" He removed his black straw hat and bowed to her.

"Oh, brother," she blushed, brushing her dark braided hair aside.

"Do you remember the day when you would run to me and I would pick you up and toss you in the air?"

They warmly embraced. She took his left hand in her right and they walked up the hill to the house.

"Benjamin, why have you returned this time? Usually you write to tell us you are coming. This is an unexpected surprise."

"I have a matter to discuss with Mother, and then I must return to Paris."

"I must return to the seminary in a few days," Jeanne said, lowering her voice to a deeper, more nasal, yet serious tone, imitating him.

"Is that what I really sound like?" he asked, laughing.

"Yes, and you still laugh like a duck."

He swatted at her with his straw hat.

"Is it true that when you become a priest, you will return to Rennes as pastor of our beloved Saint-Germaine?"

"That's not for me to decide, dear. A priest goes where his bishop or superior sends him."

"So, the prodigal son returns," a voice called out.

He looked up. It was his brother, Paul. He was standing at the stone gate at the end of their lane staring in Benjamin's direction. He returned his hat to his head and walked toward Paul and their boyhood home.

Benjamin kissed Paul on the cheeks.

"So, are you home for good this time?" Paul smiled as if expecting Benjamin to respond in the affirmative.

Paul hesitated for a moment then continued on his way without an answer. "Well, are you?" Paul persisted, turning to catch his eyes.

"Am I what?" Benjamin asked with full knowledge of exactly what he was asking.

"Have you left the seminary?"

"You ask me that every time I come home for a visit."

"Yes and your answer is always the same. You truly are taken up with this idea of becoming a priest, aren't you?"

"Why, yes, brother. I am." He dared to wonder how Paul would respond to his leaving France altogether.

"Yes, of course. Our sister, Jeanne, here has convinced Mother that when you are finished with your studies and ordained as priest, you will come back here to Rennes. I think otherwise. You'll never return, will you, brother?"

"A priest makes a vow of obedience to his bishop. Where I will be sent is to his discretion."

"Drop the theological language and the Parisian accent. I'm your brother."

"Where is Mother?" Petit asked, intentionally changing the subject.

"How long are you staying this time?" Jeanne interrupted.

"Two days," he answered, looking at her.

"Can't you stay any longer?" Paul made no attempt to hide his disappointment. "If you do, then you will please Mother and the girls." *The girls.* Just the phrase made Benjamin realize how crushed Anne and Jeanne would be once they would learn of his missionary plans.

"I am to become a priest. I no longer live here." He couldn't help but feel for his family. His mother had lost her brother in the war with Austria and his father had not been dead quite five years.

"Father spent a fortune on you and your education. How could you so easily cast it to the wind?"

Benjamin had no reply.

As the elder brother, Paul had tried to shield his younger brother from the realities of life. Benjamin knew he meant well. He always had. He knew Paul loved him. He loved him too. However, if Benjamin were to go through with his plan, neither he nor his mother—or anyone for that matter—was going to make him feel guilty for becoming a missionary priest or cause him to regret his decision to leave for the New World.

As they approached the door to the house, Benjamin's weariness briefly subsided as he grinned at Jeanne.

"Anne is in the kitchen preparing dinner," Jeanne said. "She was in the middle of burning some bread when you arrived or she would have come out with me to greet you."

"So, our poor Anne is still learning to cook." Petit laughed.

"Yes, but please don't say anything," she whispered. "You know how she bursts into tears over the least little thing. And she'll make me cook if I complain."

"Jeanne, you must not be so harsh with her. It's Anne's sensitive nature that makes us love her so."

"That's easy for you to say. You do not live with her every day."

Benjamin stiffened his jaw to keep from laughing at her candor.

Jeanne went ahead of him and he followed her through the back door. They were greeted by Anne, their nineteen-year-old sister.

She greeted Benjamin with great enthusiasm, nearly knocking him over as she embraced and kissed him at once. Then she went back to work in the kitchen. The house was alive with female chatter, a sound which Benjamin had not heard in a long time, and one that was becoming increasingly unfamiliar to him. He shook his head and smiled, recalling the way his sisters always seemed to talk at the same time yet heard every word each was saying.

All of his senses were overwhelmed with the girls' conversation, the sight of the familiar furniture, and the smell of potatoes, vegetables, meat, and burnt bread. He leaned against the wall and a surge of memories flooded his heart.

"Benjamin, dearest, had I known you were coming home, I would have prepared a grand dinner for you," Anne said as she placed some beans over the fire and wiped her hands on her apron. Her eyes then turned toward Jeanne, as if to indicate that her sister had no apparent purpose in the kitchen.

"It has not been easy, Benjamin." Anne said, addressing him with a sigh and a shake of her head, her tone and expression growing suddenly solemn. Jeanne became solemn too, as if knowing what Anne was about to say. The chatter and activity that filled the house seconds before was replaced with a silent melancholy that hung heavy in the air. "Life here has not been the same since you left Rennes last year." Anne's voice was strong though she blinked back tears.

Jeanne made no attempt to conceal the tear that streamed down her left cheek. Only the muffled sound of a sob could be heard along with the ticking of the grandfather clock.

"There, there, Jeanne, do not cry," Anne said, gently placing her arm around her sister's shoulder.

"Now you have made them cry," Paul said upon his entering the kitchen.

"Is it true, Benjamin, what Anne told me last night?" Jeanne asked.

He started, thinking that she had somehow learned of his missionary plans. "Is *what* true?"

"Is it true that God has a reason for our sufferings even if we cannot understand what it is?"

"Perchance it is better explained that we can find reason in everything that happens," he answered, relieved that his plan had not yet been discovered. Looking upon the kitchen's crucifix, he explained, "God does not abandon us in our suffering. He is with us even more so. Christ humbled himself to share in our human nature so that one day we humans might glory in His divine nature."

"Here, sit down," Anne said, taking Benjamin by the arm and leading him to a chair. "You must be exhausted from your ride."

"Please don't make a fuss over me."

"I'll get you some tea," Anne said as she hurried to the stove. "It is so good to see you, brother."

Jeanne wiped a tear from her eye.

He handed her his handkerchief. "Here." His eyes were fixed on the reddened coals in the fireplace; he began to realize how much he would miss his family. "Where is Mother?"

"In town," Paul said.

"She should arrive in time for dinner," Anne replied.

"Perhaps you were right," Benjamin said. "I am a bit tired. I think I shall retire to my room until dinner is ready. I apologize for being such poor company."

"But what about your tea?" Anne approached Benjamin with the cup on its saucer.

"Thank you. I'll take it with me." Anne handed him the cup and saucer.

He turned and went upstairs to his room.

Petit was awakened by the familiar voice of his mother.

"Benjamin." She appeared in the doorframe.

"Mother?" He was disoriented from the late afternoon nap; at first he thought it was morning.

"It is good to have you home, son."

The light from the setting sun streamed in the bedroom window as he heard the sound of plates and the clank of silverware downstairs.

"Dinner is ready."

His eyes adjusted to the light and he saw her matriarchal face surrounded by her gray-streaked black hair. He thought he would have an opportunity to speak to her alone, but she turned and walked out of the room.

They took their places at the dining room table, each standing behind his or her designated chair. "Benjamin, do the honor of saying grace for us this evening," his mother asked.

Benjamin looked around the room at his mother, brother,

and sisters and bowed his head. He began with the traditional meal prayer but added several petitions for his family and the soul of his father. He finished with the sign of the cross and everyone took their seats.

Paul launched into a monologue about the financial difficulties he had been having all year.

"Benjamin doesn't want to talk about money, Paul," Jeanne interrupted, dropping her fork at the side of her plate. "And quite honestly, neither do I."

"Why not? It is a serious matter! Why, if the truth be known, Mother was in town on related business just today. Of course, I could discuss the political unrest in—"

"Paul," Madame Petit stopped him. "Your brother has come to visit. Let's remain charitable. Dinner time is a time for gaiety and charity—at least it was at one time in this house." The girls looked down at their food; Paul and Benjamin had had similar conversations before.

Benjamin looked around their dining room table that seated six; only five places were occupied. The armchair at the head of the table stood silent and empty. His father's place. Looking around the table at his family, he decided that now was not the right time to declare his missionary intentions to them. He would wait until tomorrow, before he left for Paris.

That night, before he retired, he sat on the edge of his bed. "Lord, why am I unable to speak about this most important decision with my family? Surely Mother would understand, yet I find it difficult to even bring myself to speak with her. Why, Lord? For the first time in my life, am I unable to make a decision? What would You have me do?"

He waited in silence as if anticipating an audible reply. He observed his room and noticed that it was accumulating dust and cobwebs. He watched the flickering flame from his bedside candle waver and bounce, casting dancing shadows on the ceiling.

After he prayed Compline (night prayer) he couldn't sleep. He had every intention of changing clothes, getting into bed, and going to sleep—or at least trying to sleep—but how could he? This would be his last night at home. He glanced at the crucifix above his bed's headboard. If he was to become a missionary he would have to do what other missionaries had done before they departed on their journey: spend the night in a prayer vigil.

He decided to ride to Saint-Germaine Parish. Placing his neatly folded bedclothes back in the dresser drawer, he carried the candle out of the room into the hall, down the stairs, and to the back door. He lit the lantern hanging at the door and left the house, lantern in hand, and made his way to the livery stable. Through the trees, the moon was shining brightly and with it Venus, Jupiter, and Mars.

At the livery he found his caramel beauty, Bijou. "So," he whispered, "my friend, you are awake too? Well, since neither of us can sleep, let us go for a ride." Bijou nodded as if to agree. Benjamin secured her saddle and reins and walked her to the lane, careful not to make noise or else someone would likely hear him and try to prevent his leaving. When Bijou was at the road, Benjamin stepped into the stirrup and snapped the reins. The blue moonlight illuminated the way to the church enabling Bijou to achieve a steady gait.

When he arrived at the church he dismounted Bijou and tied her reins to one of the hitching posts. He walked to the church and entered the nave, where he removed his hat and dipped his hand in the holy water font, crossed himself, and genuflected. In the light of the flickering flames of votive candles in front of the statues of the Blessed Mother and Saint Joseph, Benjamin's shadow danced up and down the wall.

As he knelt at the altar rail in front of the sanctuary's crucifix, the words of Christ came to mind: *Whoever wishes to save his life must lose it.* "O Lord, is it your will that I go?" he prayed aloud. He had been strong in his decision for weeks, but now in the last hour, in the familiar territory of home and family, his resolve wavered. "Grant me the grace to not only know your will, O Lord, but to do it."

He walked to the front pew where his family had gathered many times before and knelt. He focused on the face of Christ while the sanctuary candle glowed red. "O Lord, must I die in order to live? Shall I go? O Lord, I am uncertain of my decision. Regardless of my choice, my life will never be the same. Grant me Thy grace to know the way." He choked back emotion as his words failed.

Regaining his voice, he said the prayer of Saint Ignatius of Loyola. "O Eternal Word, Only Begotten Son of God, teach me true generosity. Teach me to serve Thee as Thou deserve, to give without counting the cost, to fight heedless of wounds, to labor without seeking rest, to sacrifice myself without thought of any reward, save the knowledge that I am doing Thy will. Amen."

He stood, walked to the communion rail, pushed open the gate, entered the sanctuary, and knelt on the steps of the altar in silence. Realizing that this was to be a total oblation, he stretched out his arms and lay prostrate in cruciform in front of the tabernacle, placing himself completely at the Lord's service.

"Take, Lord, and receive all my liberty, my memory, my understanding, and my entire will. All I have and possess and call my own. Whatever I have or hold Thou hast given all to me. O Lord, I restore it all to Thee and surrender it wholly to be governed by Thy will. Grant me only Thy love and Thy grace, and I have wealth enough to ask for nothing more. I ask this through Christ our Lord."

Pausing, he inhaled deeply and exhaled the word *Amen*. With that breath he let go completely. A sense of peace like a warm bath on a cold autumn day came over him, feeling very much like the first time he ever met with Simon Bruté. Resting in the Lord's presence, he knew not only of what he must do, but he also knew that the Lord would be with him come what may. He felt he had the necessary courage to tell his mother, brother, and sisters.

With that epiphany, his eyelids became heavy with sleep.

Benjamin awoke to the sounds of the pastor of Saint-Germaine readying the chalice and paten for morning Mass. He explained his all-night vigil and the priest gave him his blessing and asked him to serve his Mass. Following Mass and prayers of thanksgiving, Benjamin stepped out of the church and paused on the steps to admire the sight of the sunrise. A fiery red mantle stretched over Rennes while the rising orb blazed through the quickly evaporating morning fog.

As he untied Bijou, he felt a certain thrill of excitement as he wondered what his future held in store. He rode to the church cemetery and stopped at the grave of his father. He said a *Pater*, an *Ave*, and a *Gloria*. A flight of sparrows filled the air as they dotted the red morning sky and sang their morning paean.

When he finally rode up the Petit's lane to the livery, his brother, Paul, was standing akimbo outside the carriage house. Benjamin's stomach fluttered with anxiety at Paul's presence.

"*Where*, in the name of God, have you been?" Paul cried out. "Mother is worried sick!"

"I was praying," Benjamin said as he neared Paul.

"All night?" He continued.

Benjamin dismounted Bijou and tied her to the fence. He removed his hat. Paul stepped up and wasted no time in confronting him. "Where were you praying all night?"

"At church."

"Why? What could require so much prayer? Are you well? The girls were worried sick that something happened to you."

"Yes, I'm fine. I was simply praying. I didn't mean for anyone to worry."

"What were you praying about?" Paul demanded.

Benjamin felt as if he was a defendant in a courtroom and Paul was the prosecutor cross-examining him.

"I must have fallen asleep in the sanctuary sometime during the night, but I did wake up with the first light." He attempted to be evasive about his vigil. "Did you see this morning's sunrise? It was absolutely astounding."

"Don't try any of your lawyer tricks on me. Answer my question. What would require you to spend the night in prayer?"

"I have been specifically praying for something . . ." Benjamin broke off, not wanting to say too much. He wanted his mother to be the first to know of his plans.

Paul stepped closer to his prodigal brother. "What's this unannounced visit of yours all about, Benjamin? You haven't been yourself since you arrived yesterday."

"I'm not sure what you mean." He feigned ignorance.

"You're keeping something from us! Why else would you spend a whole night in church?" Paul's voice grew more dissonant.

"I stayed for morning Mass and lit some candles for Father and all of you—" Benjamin avoided eye contact with Paul before he stopped mid-sentence. His mother stepped outside and quickly made her way to him.

"Benjamin, where have you been?"

"He says he spent the night praying in church," Paul replied for him.

"Is this true?" She crossed her arms.

"Yes, Mother."

"He won't tell me anything." Paul was now inches from Benjamin's face.

"I have been specifically praying for something," he answered in a monotone.

"Is it something serious? You are not ill, are you?" his mother asked with concern.

"Serious yes, but not in relation to my health, I pray," he replied, obviously only making his brother and mother more curious and apprehensive.

"What does that mean?" Paul retorted, his eyes wide.

"I face a great decision. When I return to Paris I must have an answer. I see that my family knows me all too well; I knew it would be difficult to keep it from you. I've been trying to find the courage to tell you."

"Tell us *what*, Benjamin?" his mother came closer.

"I am to become a missionary. I am one of several seminarians and priests from Europe who have been invited to become missionaries to America."

"America? You will decline, will you not?" his mother asked.

"I intend to accept the invitation. I am to meet the bishop of the Diocese of Vincennes tomorrow. I shall give him my answer then."

"You? A missionary?" Paul laughed and turned away.

"Vincennes?" Mother closed her eyes slowly.

"Vincennes is in Indiana—one of the states of the United States. At one time it was an outpost in New France."

"Is this the idea of that exiled Breton priest, Father Bruté?" Paul asked.

"He is not in exile and he is a bishop." Benjamin answered.

"You are sickly and have a frail constitution," his mother argued. "You'd never make it in the New World."

"If he even makes it there alive," Paul said.

"Benjamin, how long have you known you might make this decision?" his mother questioned him.

"For some time. I first learned of the possibility last spring. Prior to my journey home, our rector took us to dinner and arranged for us to meet with Bishop Bruté. I have already received permission from the bishop of Rennes—"

"And you are only now telling *us*?" his mother asked.

"I was waiting."

"Waiting? Waiting for what? Any longer and you would have written us of your departure from the deck of the ship," Paul said.

"You actually intend to leave?" his mother asked.

Benjamin paused, but before he could answer the question Paul spoke again.

"Do you realize what you will be getting into?" he exploded. "Shipwreck, fever, starvation! Why just last year—"

"Saint Paul endured all sorts of hardships, including shipwreck," Benjamin reminded him.

"Yes," Paul huffed, "and you are not a saint."

"Paul was the greatest missionary the Church has ever known," Benjamin reasoned.

"Yes, and Saint Paul was beheaded if I remember correctly."

"No one here is asking you to do this, Benjamin," his mother reentered the conversation. "You have already done more than many Catholics will ever do. You renounced a law career and abandoned the opportunity to have a family of your own. What more can be asked of a man?"

"I have done it all for the Lord, Mother."

"Is that eccentric Bishop Bruté pressuring you to join him?" His mother sighed.

"No one is pressuring me to do anything."

"What is with these bishops?" Mother asked aloud. "It seems to me they could be doing a whole lot more than sending our sons off to no man's land to live among unappreciative savages—who would just as soon scalp you as believe in Christ. I feared that I would lose you or Paul in war but never to the Church! And if the savages don't burn you at the stake or tomahawk you, then an anti-Catholic American mob will kill you."

"Did you not see the sunrise? Red sky in the morning, sailors take warning," Paul retorted. "So I say you are a fool."

"A fool for Christ," Benjamin replied.

"You must tell our sisters of this absurd idea."

"I thought you wanted to become a parish priest," his mother said.

Benjamin looked at her but said nothing.

She then asked him plainly, "Benjamin, will you ever return?"

"He'll never return, Mother," Paul said. "He's infatuated with this missionary dream. He has more regard for the Church than his own family."

Perhaps Paul was more of a realist than Benjamin cared to admit.

"What are you *thinking*?" Paul asked. "Who put this foolish idea into your head that you should abandon your loyalty to your family and become a missionary to the Americans? Are you unaware of the many shipwrecks during this time of year? The cyclone season has just begun. You'll be driftwood in two weeks' time. And if you somehow make it there alive, the white plague or the swamp fever will kill you. Countless lives have already been lost, families destroyed. We lost father five years ago. Are we to lose yet another member of our family? Your leaving would crush the girls.

"And why the so-called United States? From what I read, they are on the verge of political war over slavery. You know what kind of country it is. There is no room for Catholics. America is Protestant through and through. Imagine you as a priest there. If they are capable of attacking Catholic laborers and Irish immigrants, then how much more willing will they be to attack or even kill an immigrant, French-speaking priest? Are you prepared to endure the trials and tribulations that await you there?

"Well, whatever you decide, don't say I didn't warn you. Go ahead and board one of the coffin ships. You're only inviting disaster upon yourself."

Benjamin longed for the day when his brother could share his joy. Much of what Paul said was true and Benjamin knew that there would be hardships and difficulties and struggles—just the pioneer experience itself would be enough of a challenge. Yet the added burdens of a Catholic missionary weighed heavily upon his heart and mind. But no matter, his mind was fixed.

About that time, his sisters ran outside to greet him. He welcomed the diversion. "Benjamin, where have you been? We were all so worried," Anne called out as Jeanne darted around her.

"Benjamin, are you all right?" asked Jeanne as she ran to him for a reassuring hug.

"Yes, I am fine, ma petite Jeanne," Benjamin said, embracing her. "I was at church, praying."

"Benjamin, dear," said Anne with great relief as she smiled and clutched his left hand.

"Let's go inside, my dear sisters. I have something I must tell you."

"What is this all about, Benjamin?" Anne asked as they entered the house. Before he could get a word out, Paul answered.

"I'll tell you what it's all about," Paul said. "Saint Benjamin has decided to sail for the New World so he can get killed."

"What?" asked Anne.

Jeanne looked shocked as she clutched Benjamin's left hand in her right.

"I believe God is calling me to be a missionary in America." He was surprised at how easily the words came out of his mouth.

CHAPTER **5**

AU REVOIR

*On the subject of my brother's and mother's letters of oppo-
sition, Bishop Bruté thought it best to call upon my mother
in Rennes in an attempt to set her heart at ease. His efforts
were in vain. When he returned to Paris, three more letters
of protest had arrived; two from mother and one from Paul.
Yet despite all obstacles, the Lord will provide.*

Paul Petit vehemently protested Benjamin's decision to become
a missionary. Paul wrote Benjamin in Paris to inform him that
he had written letters of protest to the Bishop of Rennes, the rector of Saint-Sulpice in Paris, and Bishop Bruté.

Bishop Bruté stopped Petit after vespers at Saint-Sulpice the
next evening. "Benjamin, this morning I received two letters
from Rennes protesting your decision to become a missionary.
They are from a Madame Chauvin Petit and Monsieur Paul
Petit. They are terribly concerned for your weak chest and
lungs."

"Yes, as a child I suffered from asthma." Petit sighed, knowing that oftentimes one's relatives are the ones who understand
one's desires the least.

"Asthma? I suffered from asthma in my youth as well. It
weakens the lungs."

Petit nodded.

"I have written both your mother and brother stating my
belief that you have the necessary qualifications for the mis-

sions," Bruté said, returning to the subject of the letters. "You are zealous for the Lord and have the strength of character. I also believe that, with the help of God's grace, you would have the resolve to be courageous in the face of adversity and privation."

"Here is the letter I have begun to write to your mother." He revealed the letter and handed it to him. The two men paused in the shadow of a marble pillar as Petit unfolded the note and read.

Dear Madame Chauvin Petit,

I write you concerning your son Benjamin and his vocation to the priesthood. The will of God is an elusive reality. Your son's call to become a missionary is such that I believe it is impossible for me to withdraw my invitation. I came to France and Europe to seek help in securing seminarians and priests for the Diocese of Vincennes. It is the charity of the Apostles and the zeal of the missionaries that has converted the world. I assure you that there are in America souls awaiting the generosity of a French mother whom the Lord will know full well how to console in her loneliness.

Petit looked up from the letter.

"Do you think she will respond in a positive manner?" Bruté's eyes met Petit's.

"By the grace of God," Petit replied as he held out the letter to the bishop.

"All is grace, Saint Augustine reminds us." Bruté smiled as he took the letter from Petit's hand.

As the sacristan extinguished the candles of the high altar Bishop Bruté genuflected, dipped his hand in the holy water font, and exited the church leaving Petit alone.

27 MAY 1836

Benjamin Petit would soon be on his way to Le Havre harbor

in the company of the venerable Bishop Simon Bruté; seminarian Michael Evelyn Edgar Shawe, a distinguished Englishman of forty-five years who was a former British naval captain, decorated war hero, and veteran of the Battle of Waterloo, and a student at Saint-Sulpice; Reverend Stanislaus Buteaux, an Austrian priest and volunteer missionary in his late forties; and the Reverend Celestin de La Hailandière, also forty-five years of age, a native of Coumbourg, Brittany, and a lawyer himself before becoming a priest. Together they were to set sail for the United States. There were twenty missionaries in all, seminarians and priests.

They left Paris for Le Havre via Rennes. Petit took in the scenery of the familiar ride. Even though he had traveled that road countless times, this time was different. It would be his last time. The houses and villages with their flower gardens, flower pots, and flower boxes in full bloom all gave him a sense of consolation, but he knew all too well the disquietude in his heart and mind owing to his family's objection to his decision to leave Europe.

Fathers Celestin de La Hailandière, Stanislaus Buteaux, and Michael Shawe remained at the bishop's residence in Rennes while Bishop Bruté accompanied Benjamin Petit to visit his family in an attempt to allay their fears.

How does one explain the call? Paul Petit's religious fervor was one of dutifully fulfilling an obligation. Benjamin Petit's faith had come to mean something more. It was rooted in the person of Christ and His Church. The lives of the saints were a constant inspiration for him, especially the martyrs and saints who abandoned all their wealth and career in order to serve God: Saints Peter and Paul, Saint Boniface, Saint Francis of Assisi, Saint Ignatius of Loyola, Francis Xavier, Isaac Jogues, and Jean Brebeuf among others.

"I lost my brother to Bonaparte's war," Petit's mother told the bishop, "and every day I thanked God that my own sons were spared from the carnage of war. Yet now I have lost my brightest son to the Church." It was an awkward moment. Benjamin bade her adieu and promised to write. Paul embraced him, albeit reservedly; a sad farewell. Benjamin left Rennes in the company of the bishop. From there they took the stage to Le Havre.

Jesus' words were heavy on Benjamin's heart:

I have a baptism to receive. What anguish I feel till it is over! Do not suppose that I have come to spread peace. My mission is to spread, not peace, but division . . . to make a man's enemies those of his own household. Whoever loves mother or father, son or daughter, more than me is not worthy of me. He who will not take up his cross and come after me is not worthy of me. He who seeks only himself brings himself to ruin, whereas he who brings himself to nought for me discovers who he is.

CHAPTER 6

MEMORIES

Today I bade farewell to my family; I am to become a priest in the New World.

---◆-◇-◆-◇-◆---

On the morning of 29 May, the day after Corpus Christi Sunday, they departed Paris for Le Havre. It had been raining since vespers the evening before, and it had not stopped. Petit thought back on his final day in Paris at the great Church of Saint-Sulpice. The Mass remained vivid in his mind: sunlight illuminating the colors of the stained glass windows and marble pillars; hundreds of glowing candles covering the altars; pealing bells and choruses praising God; reverberations of the pipe organ converging with the sweet aroma of incense and thick clouds of smoke lifting high into the vaulted ceiling of the cathedral. It all filled his heart with gladness.

His Psalter was open to Psalms Forty-Two: *These memories I will recall as I pour out my soul, how I went in procession with the throng, leading the rejoicing crowd into the house of God; amid cries of gladness and songs of thanksgiving, the multitude full of joy.* All of these memories would serve as a radiant reminder to him of the day he had chosen to become a missionary to the New World.

Rennes soon disappeared from the horizon. Now, a day later, as they neared Le Havre, the past few days' memory all seemed a blur. Bouncing along roughly in the carriage, he glanced out the window at the deluge. The downpour had turned the French hillsides into muddy streams, flooding much of the valley as the trees bowed low to the ground, saturated by the torrents, contorted by wind gusts. Exhausted from lack of sleep, the unpleasant jolting ride, and a headache, Petit slumped in the carriage seat, allowing his forehead to rest against the window. As the skies wept their frigid mist, he wondered when he would ever arrive at Le Havre.

Visions of shipwreck and drowning at sea fed his imagination. He opened his breviary and his eyes focused on the Psalms again: "My soul is thirsting for God, the God of my life; when can I enter and see the face of God? Deep is calling on deep, in the roar of waters: Thy torrents and all Thy waves swept over me. Why are you cast down, my soul, why groan within me? Hope in God; I shall praise Him still, my savior and my God."

As he breathed on the glass, it fogged up. It was much too early for a cold autumn rain during the spring, but that was what the rain was like. His companions had been asleep for a while. He closed his eyes but couldn't sleep, not now, not on the eve of his leaving the Old World for the New. The memory of his leaving home, family, and the familiar surroundings of Rennes, along with his subsequent departure from Paris, weighed heavily upon his heart.

He knew his mother, brother, and sisters were mostly angry, shocked, and hurt for not finding out about his decision until a few short hours before his departure. He wished he could have prepared them more in advance and eased the grief that was setting in with them now. As for himself, he wished he could board the boat so he could begin grieving. Instead, he felt suspended between France and America in a state of Limbo. He had said his goodbyes, yet here he was, still in the Old World, not yet bound for the New, longing to see the waters of Le Havre, the gateway to the West.

He knew that he was, like his mother, brother, and sisters, in an emotional upheaval. Of course, all of the events of the past two weeks had happened so fast. The reality of leaving Europe altogether was numbing. It was happening too fast, and yet the carriage ride to the coast of Le Havre seemed much too slow. Of course, he and his companions were excited. He had expressed excitement and genuine zeal for this apostolic mission. This is what he had decided to do with his life. *I am to become a priest,* he said to himself. Unlike some of the other seminarians who left Europe with the thought of possibly returning to France if things did not work out, he had deliberately deeded his inheritance to his brother, Paul.

He shifted in his seat in an attempt to get more comfortable and closed his eyes again, remembering his farewell to his family in front of the Petit home. His mother and brother and sisters were lined up, more like mourners at a funeral rather than a group gathering to see their brother off to a new life in the New World.

The first face was that of his sister Anne. She took it like the strong and steadfast young woman that she was. "I truly believe that this is God's will for you," she said.

He thought she would have been angry; instead she was only sad that he had waited so long to reveal his plans. He should have told her what he was considering. "I am a coward, I fear."

"You're no coward!" Anne's words cheered his heart. "A coward would not make such a journey. You just keep everything to yourself, brother. You always have, but no matter. It is true we are to lose another member of the family, but at least this time it is not to death." She smiled and gripped his hands, her brow wrinkling with worry and grief. Returning the smile, he touched her cheek and embraced her.

His sister Jeanne was trying hard to be brave, but her sensitive nature made it difficult for her to restrain the tears which came in waves of great heaving sobs throughout the entire farewell. She told Benjamin not to worry about her. "I have a handkerchief this time," she said holding up the white linen. They both laughed but her laughter dissolved into a cry. She threw her arms around his shoulders and wept into his chest, leaving the front of his cassock damp. He held her until she finally let go and gave him one last smile amid her tears.

Paul appeared to have put away his anger. "If I have seemed a bit harsh, it is only because I am concerned for your welfare," he said as Benjamin neared him. "Godspeed, brother." Benjamin found himself enclosed in Paul's embrace.

"Adieu, Paul." It took all of Benjamin's strength not to weep.

"Please, don't leave us yet, Benjamin!" Jeanne's voice cracked while tears formed in her eyes.

"Ah, Jeanne." Benjamin coughed back emotion as his vision blurred.

"Promise to write," she said.

"I promise. Take good care of Bijou." He wiped away her tears and kissed her on the forehead and cheeks. Truly there was a great temptation for him to remain in France.

Finally his mother stepped forward to bid him adieu. She said nothing. He embraced her; she caressed his neck and the back of his head, running her fingers through his hair, as if he were once again her small child. She finally spoke, taking his hands into hers. "I feel as if I will never see you again."

Benjamin had no response. Only tears. After a long embrace, he stepped up in the carriage with the bishop and waved adieu for what might be the last time. The driver gave a clicking noise with the snap of his whip and the coach lurched forward.

His family was the last thing he saw in his mind's eye before a dreamless sleep overtook him.

●◦●◦●

When he awoke, his neck was stiff from sleeping upright with his head against the window of the carriage. He had no idea how long he'd been asleep. His companions were still sleeping, leaving him alone again with his thoughts, hopes, and aspirations of being a missionary—except for when they were interrupted by hard jolts that nearly knocked him out of his seat.

The bumping and swaying finally came to an end when they stopped for the night at Rouen in Normandy. Rouen was where Jeanne d'Arc had been burnt at the stake in the fifteenth century. Father de La Hailandiere had practiced law in Rouen prior to his entering the seminary. The future missionaries had accommodations at the seminary in Rouen.

The next morning when they awoke, they celebrated Mass and met their luggage at the port on the Seine. They carried their valises and other baggage to the wharf in a downpour; it soaked them through. Petit was happy to exchange a carriage for a boat up the River Seine to Le Havre.

Once aboard the boat, the rain-swollen river violently chopped at the vessel as it moved north through the mud-stained waters toward Le Havre harbor on the English Channel.

He prayed from his breviary: "O Lord, Thou dost not desire sacrifice and burnt offerings, but an obedient, open ear. Holocausts and sin-offerings Thou dost not require; instead, here am I; Thy commands for me are written in the Law. To do Thy will is my delight; my God, Thy law is in my heart!"

He looked up from the page, mouthing the words, "Here I am. Behold, I come to do Thy will."

His reverie was interrupted when the boatman tied the boat to the dock of the harbor. As he and his companions emerged from the cabin, they rejoiced to see that the rains had at last stopped. The dismal, overcast milk-pale clouds and the frost in the air made this spring morning seem like a wintry day.

Could the inclement weather of the past week be a portent of things to come? Petit quickly dismissed such a superstitious thought.

Have no fear, the Lord will provide, Bishop Bruté assured them.

The missionaries-to-be made their way to the docks, hauling their few worldly possessions down the quay.

"What irony," Bruté said. "We who have renounced worldly possessions, embracing poverty in exchange for heavenly treasure, are about to embark on our journey to the New World in an American sailing vessel named the *Merchantman*."

De La Hailandière spoke of Bishop Bruté with reverence. He was convinced of the man's sanctity. He shared stories of some pilgrims in Paris, who, upon seeing the bishop, attempted to tear his clothing so as to secure relics. Bruté firmly responded, "Would to God that we all be saints. Then all our garments would be relics." Another time when Bruté was a young priest, an elderly priest with a stomach tumor at Saint-Sulpice had asked Bruté for prayers. After receiving communion from Bruté, the priest was totally healed. Nevertheless, Bruté eschewed any comparison of his life to that of the saints.

There were those in the Church who considered Bruté eccentric and absent-minded, but Petit knew otherwise.

Bruté was a saint.

CHAPTER 7

DEPARTURE

May my sacrifice for the sake of the Kingdom of God bear fruit in eternity.

Petit looked through the crowd of people. Along the wharves there were suspicious characters who appeared to be eagerly awaiting the opportunity to steal a trunk full of clothing and jewelry or a valise containing assorted treasures bound for America. He eyed the men as he went to lift his trunk from the pier; his mind filled with dark imaginings, recalling the numerous criminal cases that he had both witnessed and argued in court. One of the men on the wharf looked familiar, perhaps from the courtroom.

Suddenly someone bumped into him from behind. He wheeled about to defend himself should it be a brigand with a dagger. It took him a moment to recognize the face of Michael Shawe.

Shawe laughed. "It's just me, my petit Frenchman."

"Shawe. Thank God, it's you."

"Were you expecting someone else?" Shawe asked.

"It's good to see you are prepared to do battle, Benjamin," came the voice of Bishop Bruté. "Although spiritual battle is preferred."

"Your Grace," Petit was embarrassed and had no idea the bishop was standing there.

"You have the constitution required of a missionary." The

bishop smiled and then turned to collect his conspicuous group, all dressed in black and huddled close together. Bruté's bright eyes darted quickly about as he counted each head aloud. When they were all accounted for he began the introductions and commended them for willingly renouncing everything in order to bring the Gospel message to the New World.

The *Merchantman* was an American sailing ship, 125 feet long and 25 feet wide, fully rigged with three masts and sails. As the missionaries boarded the vessel, the American sailors, vulgar and impolite, hoisted the anchors to the deck and unfurled the sails one after another. They swung from the masts barefooted, their feet like the paws of old, ragged hunting dogs. They clenched their pipes between the few remaining blackened, grimy teeth they had left in their heads and puffed out smoke as they ogled and smirked at the female passengers.

There was a musical troupe on the dock singing familiar French folk songs as a send-off to those who cared to listen. The melancholy wind carried the melody to sea. The canvas sails billowed out, swiftly speeding the boat away from the shore, as the seagulls flew overhead, crying out full-throated.

The sounds of the Old World soon faded into the noise of splashing water and scent of salty breeze. Petit wondered whether he would ever see Europe again. With his rosary beads in hand, he prayed for his brother and sisters, but especially for his mother, that she would come to understand both the dignity of the priesthood and the value and sacrifice of his becoming a missionary.

Soon Le Havre was no longer in sight, yet the gulls continued their flight alongside the boat; a few nestled in the ship's cordage. Pure ocean. Wave after wave after wave.

Many of the American seamen and sailors aboard the *Merchantman* were highly suspicious of black-robed Roman Catholic priests. Petit and his companions, missionaries clothed in religious garb, soutanes and birettas, attracted quite a lot of attention and only represented more of the same Romish passengers that some Americans had come to loathe.

As he was standing in line, an old ragged-looking seaman began going down the deck issuing clean dishes and utensils to the passengers. Each passenger would be expected to keep the utensils clean and use them for the entire month and a half journey.

"Here you are, priest," the ragged seaman said. "A knife, fork, spoon, a tin cup, and soup plate. Don't leave them out where they can be stolen or lost. You won't get any more." Petit hardly understood the man's English.

"What did he say?" Petit asked Shawe.

"These are the only utensils that will be issued to you for the entire journey."

"Are you sure he said it like that?" Petit looked askance.

"No, of course not." Shawe clicked his teeth, rolled his eyes, and sighed aloud. "The Americans are intent upon destroying the King's English."

The rough codger motioned for the next person to step forward.

"Hey, mates," the vulgar old sea dog hollered through a broken-toothed smile. "I think these priests think we ought to show them more respect." Another seaman on the deck laughed raucously, though they were more discreet about stifling their laughter.

Petit noticed that a few of the passengers were amused at the confrontation. "Here's your respect, priest!" The sea dog spat at Shawe's feet, leaving a trail of laughter along with spittle as he moved onto the next person without so much as a second glance. Shawe's jaw locked and had he had his naval sword he may have drawn it at the show of such disrespect.

The bishop stepped from behind and gripped Shawe's shoulder, helping him regain his composure. "Remember, Michael, you are in the Lord's army now. All of you take note," he nearly whispered, "our Blessed Lord was mocked and spat upon." Bruté reached for his handkerchief and knelt to wipe the spittle from Shawe's shoe. He quoted the scripture, "When Christ was insulted, He returned no insult; when He suffered, He did not threaten."

Many of the other passengers moved away from the group of religious after the incident. Catholicism had been attacked and the missionaries hadn't even left Europe.

"Gentlemen," Bruté spoke, motioning for his flock to move in closer. He waited until he had everyone's attention, then he spoke, not with hesitation, but boldly and loudly for all those around to hear. "You must be prepared to brave the elements of a sea of prejudice. What just happened to Monsieur Shawe is not uncommon. You must become accustomed to such treatment; otherwise you will be unable to endure life in the New World. You must not become discouraged by the insults of others. I have told you before, America is a cauldron of Old World hatreds alive in the New. I implore each and every one of you to pray for God's strength. I have a gnawing feeling that we may be baptized, immersed as it were, as Catholic apostles."

He led them in a prayer before their group dispersed and retired to their bunks in the hold for the night.

Down below, Petit observed the small wooden shelf that was to serve as his bed for the next month or so. From the stern to the bow along both port and starboard sides, bunks lined the hull. The bunks were nothing more than double-tiered shelves measuring two by six feet with rugged canvas drapes hung in front of each sleeping compartment to provide for some degree of privacy. Petit shared one of the compartments with Father Celestin de La Hailandière for the voyage.

The next morning Petit awoke to a bright blue sky streaked with wisps of white clouds. He stood on the deck admiring the beauty of the still sea and sky. The Psalms were in his heart: *Let the heavens and the earth sing praise, the sea and whatever swims through their waters.* He squinted and it seemed the blue of the sky melted into the deep blue of the ocean until there was only vast blueness as far as the eye could see. *O Lord, where can I hide from Thy Spirit? From Thy presence where can I flee? If I ascend to the heavens or descend to the netherworld, Thou art there. If I fly with the wings of dawn and alight beyond the sea, even there Thy hand shall guide me, Thy right hand hold me fast.*

The late summer sun revealed itself. Petit closed his eyes and looked toward the sun, letting the warmth of it immerse him. *The sun comes forth like a bridegroom from his chamber...there is nothing concealed from its burning heat.*

Its dizzying, almost intoxicating, effect warmed him through-out. The experience of complete stillness and solitude, only the sound of the water lapping against the boat and the seagulls screeching their song overhead, caused Petit to give a sigh of total wonder. *Let the sea and what fills it resound. Look at the sea, great and wide! It teems with countless beings, living things both great and small. In His hands are the depths of the sea.*

"Beautiful day, is it not?" the voice of Celestin de La Hailandière startled him from his prayer.

"Celestin! Why yes, it is a most remarkable day. Forgive me, I did not see you."

"No, it is you who should forgive me. In the midst of God's creation, such beauty does inspire prayer." De la Hailandière turned his attention to the sea. They silently observed it together.

"Sometimes it doesn't seem a reality that we are on our way to the New World." Petit smiled.

"Yes, a New World it is indeed," came the familiar voice of Rev. Shawe. He joined them looking out to sea.

"Rev. Shawe."

"Benjamin."

"I hope you do not misconstrue what I say," Shawe said, "but it seems that when the bishop speaks to us of the New World he speaks only of hardships."

"And you think he should offer more encouragement to a group of young priests who are already filled with much fear and apprehension? Is that it?" Celestin asked him.

"Well, yes." Shawe said puffing on his pipe.

"I believe he is merely trying to prepare us," Celestin speculated. "The bishop does not wish for any of us to have illusions about life in the New World."

"Yes, I believe you are correct." The words were those of the toothless Bishop Bruté.

The three missionaries-to-be turned and knelt in his presence.

"Gentlemen," he signaled for them to rise. "Please. Unless I prepare you for what you will encounter, then you may become disillusioned later." It seemed Bruté appeared from nowhere.

The three men walked with him atop the deck as the breeze whipped their black cassocks like the sails of the *Merchantman*.

"Allow me to explain," Bruté paused for a moment, producing his pectoral cross from inside his cassock. "These Americans are a restless lot." He grasped the cross at the end of the chain with his right hand and rubbed it between his thumb and fingers. "The new found freedoms of the independence movement have spread everywhere. The Americans have no roots. They can be violent and greedy. Commerce and land is everything. Unfortunately a lot of these free thinkers are anti-Catholic as well. Then there are the atheists who have completely rejected all Old World values, good or bad. Instead of freedom of religion, they desire freedom from religion."

Bruté ambled silently, his head bowed ever so slightly, his lips in a serene smile, and his hands folded as if in prayer. He stopped and looked up. "Did not our Lord say, 'Blessed are those who are persecuted for the sake of righteousness. The birds have nests, the foxes have lairs, but the Son of Man has nowhere to lay his head'? You will find that the American way of life with its ideals of freedom and independence sometimes conflicts with the teachings of our Church.

"The common opinion of a Protestant minority in America is that the pope in Rome is preparing to carve out new Papal States in the New World in order to compensate for his loss of political power in Italy. Conspiracy theories of papal plots to overthrow the U.S. government abound. Such are the fears of the Native American population. Of course, these natives are not the indigenous copper-skinned peoples of North America.

"To the American mind, the *natives* are those Americans who can claim their ancestry among the first wave of immigrants to the shores of the United States. The nativists desire that America should be first and foremost for Americans. They believe that immigrants should not receive the same treatment as American-born Americans. Immigrants such as yourselves will be looked down upon as foreign contaminants to the American experiment in freedom and democracy. Some will claim that our presence in America is solely to interfere with their democratic principles or to topple the Republic altogether."

Petit and the others listened with great thought and concern to the bishop's words. The four stood atop the deck near the bow of the ship, basking in the sun and gentle ocean breeze.

"The Irish Catholics are just one group in particular that is viewed with increasing suspicion," Bruté continued. "Alcohol and religion are two factors weighing heavily against the Irish being welcomed to the United States. I understand that there are hopes of one day restricting an immigrant's right to vote by requiring a twenty-one-year residency before U.S. citizenship can be granted to an immigrant.

"And one must not forget the slavery issue. Whether we are speaking of the southern Negroes who work the cotton fields or the northern immigrant factory workers who are paid a mere pittance and live in ghettoes, the industrialization of the west raises new moral questions. Their southern economy is inseparable from slavery, what they call their *peculiar institution*, a deceptive euphemism, and the northern economy relies upon cheap immigrant labor, which treats the worker as a means to an end, and pays the immigrant in liquor.

"There are those leaders of business whose only goal is a free market with no tariffs or taxes, just profit by any means necessary. The grave danger in this economic freedom is that some of the profiteers gain control of the market and exercise tyranny over the poor. The power of a few manufacturing entrepreneurs can control the worker. Either way, African slaves or Irishmen enslaved to whiskey, economic slavery is tolerated in America. *Pecunia regina mundi* (money rules the world).

"From Boston and New York to Philadelphia and Cincinnati, and west and south to St. Louis and New Orleans, immigrants are suspect of election tampering. Catholic clergy have been accused of scandals and accosted. Churches have been torched, and Catholic and Protestant clashes have broken out in the streets of some cities. At least one book supposedly detailing the abuses one woman received at the hands of a priest has been circulating in America.[1]

"One of the main points of contention deals with the public school question of whether Catholic children should be required to read the Protestant King James version of the Bible and whether public funds should be allotted for the establishment of Catholic schools. As it is, the Protestants require Catholic students to read the Protestant version of the Bible.

"Some Catholic lawyers argue that it is a violation of their First Amendment rights, which states that Congress shall establish no state religion," Bruté explained. "Yet Protestant beliefs are taught in the government-sponsored schools."

"Perhaps Father de La Hailandière and I, as civil attorneys, might be able to offer our services to the situation," Petit eagerly suggested.

"I wouldn't be so quick to enter into American politics," Bruté cautioned, "or else you might find yourself at odds with Rome like our dear Feli de Lamennais."

Just then a French female passenger approached the bishop and expressed a desire to go to confession.

The bishop placed his hand on Petit's shoulder. "You all have many virtues—courage, strength of character, fortitude, a sense of justice. But never forget, the most important virtue is love. Without merciful love, the love Saint Paul spoke of in his letter to the Corinthians, we are nothing. Remember this and you will not only be compassionate priests, but saints." With that Bruté departed with the woman to hear her confession.

"Benjamin, why are you silent?" Shawe inquired of Petit.

---

1 In 1836, Maria Monk authored a book Awful Disclosures of Maria Monk, or The Hidden Secrets of a Nun's Life in a Convent Exposed. The abuse was alleged to have taken place in Montreal, Canada, at the Hotel Dieu Nunnery. In it all priests are held suspect of lechery. It, and other books like it, fueled much anti-Catholicism during the 1830s and on into the 1850s.

"If we had all the answers to life's questions, Father, we wouldn't need faith," Petit said.

"There you go again, Benjamin," said Father de La Hailandière.

With that their conversation turned to more trivial matters as they made their way to dinner in the hold below.

After dinner, Petit went up to get some fresh air. It was evening, the temperature had dropped, and a glimmer of the Aurora borealis streaked across the dark July sky. An array of starlight accompanied by the crescent moon silently proclaimed the grandeur of the heavens. "*Sanctus, Sanctus, Sanctus,*" he prayed in a whisper.

When I behold the heavens, the work of Thy hands, the moon and the stars which Thou arranged, what is man that Thou keep him in mind, mortal man that Thy heart goes out for him in care? (Ps. 8:4-5, Vulgate).

The heavens proclaim the glory of God and the firmament shows forth the work of His hands. No word, no voice, no sound is heard, yet their wisdom reaches to the utmost bounds of the world (Ps. 19:2, 4-5).

Petit prayed that his decision to give up home, mother, brother, sisters, children, and land for the sake of the kingdom might be fruitful for the Church.

The first month at sea was bearable—except for the stench of the latrines, which was wretched.

ATLANTIC CROSSING

*The only thing separating us from death was the ship's
warped and seasoned hull; the vessel moaned aloud as if it
were about to spew us into the sea.*

The next few weeks were rough sailing. Even though it was early
for the Atlantic storm season, the *Merchantman* was tossed to
and fro in one long storm. The ship bobbed in the ocean like a
piece of driftwood. The sailors and ship's crew told the passengers this was relatively smooth sailing. Petit and the others feared
what havoc rough waters might bring.

The filthy conditions and dark living quarters gave mice, rats,
lice, and fleas ample breeding ground. Many of the emigrants
refused to clean the decks or wipe their tables. Some of them,
mostly men, rather than use the few latrines that were available,
relieved themselves when and wherever they thought was most
commodious. Petit quickly learned that his brother had not
been exaggerating about the conditions on the high seas.

The cruiser plunged through the dark mist and raging sea,
wreathing and rocking. On the deck above, the sails whipped in
the wind while the salty sea splashed high into the air, across the
sides of the boat, and up onto the deck, granting the illusion that
the trip was being made shorter.

In the lower deck, long wooden tables with benches fixed to
the floor were spaced between the starboard and port rows of the
sleeping bunks. One of the ship's crew would ring a bell to alert

the passengers that the meal was about to be served. The missioners were repelled by the lack of manners on the part of the sailors and many of their fellow travelers who ate without napkins upon their laps and used their fingers to scoop and spoon their food into their mouths. The American sailors were especially obnoxious in their ribald language and gestures; even the French and Germans on board understood what was meant without an interpreter.

Petit closed his eyes and found himself back in the great Church of Saint-Sulpice. The Gregorian chants of the *schola cantorum* wafted to the arched ceilings and bathed him in an ocean of music. He longed for the sonorous harmony of the great pipe organ of the Gothic cathedrals and the melodies of the monastic chants he had heard in France, such as on his pilgrimage to Chartres.

Suddenly the crest of a wave engulfed the ship and a surge of water pounded the hull. The rain and sea furiously flooded the ship, swamping the craft so much that one could barely see the top of the masts. The wind swept sheets of cold, salty mist making it nearly impossible to breathe. Menacing black and gray clouds, fierce bolts of lightning, and deafening thunderclaps terrified the passengers. Some of the sailors seemed to be enjoying the storm and remained on the deck as if daring Neptune to swallow them alive.

The sailors clung tightly to the slippery railings, grabbing for ropes or rigging, hanging on despite being submerged in the foamy sea. Some of the seasoned travelers said that the storm was a hurricane. The seamen struggled to keep the sails and gearing in position, but their efforts were useless against the blasting gale and fierce tides, which all but submerged the ship. Sounds of the wood creaking and the sails ripping in the squall echoed on board.

While the missioners were earnestly praying, fearful that it might be their last hour, the mariners were swearing at one another. Some of the men were angry at the methods of navigation used by the captain. A fight ensued and turned to a bloody melee. Rumors circulated the ship later that two of the inexperienced sailors had fallen overboard in the midst of the mayhem. Out of fear, none of the passengers questioned the sailors whether it was true, and if it was, no one asked whether it was an accident or murder. No one wanted to walk the plank and meet the same fate. Bishop Bruté dismissed the story as rumor.

The incredible energy of the raging Atlantic Ocean, with its walls of waves was a sight to behold. Petit and Shawe climbed up the steps and stood out on the deck. The mist and foam took Petit's breath away as he imagined himself the reluctant prophet Jonah about to be swallowed up by a monster of the deep. Another series of tall waves battered the sails and masts and splashed against him nearly washing him off into the abyss of ocean. He was stunned by the icy waters.

The violence of the ensuing storm tipped the boat at forty-five degree angles as the wild blue threatened to plunge the ship into the depths. At that, Shawe the former seaman appeared, grasping Petit, squeezing him back down into the hold. The desire to remain atop and experience the majestic display of God's omnipotence and His creation was tempting, but the gravity of the situation gave way to sound reason as Petit acquiesced to the former sea captain and obediently returned with the others below.

The sailors cleared the deck and began battening down the hatches. This meant that no air could circulate in the ship. The stench within the passengers' hold and the odors from the livestock in the cargo hold were hardly bearable, not to mention the smoke from those who were cooking aboard. Those who were seasick tended to remain on the top deck despite the inclement weather and waves, but once the seamen battened down, those who were sick further sullied and polluted an already foul and unsanitary living space. ·

The seminarians and priests, along with the bishop, clutched their rosaries in the flickering candlelight. Over the sounds of swelling waves and gusting gales, the groaning, moaning and creaking of the wooden craft imbued the men—indeed all aboard—with the greatest of fears that the ship would, at any moment, rip open like an old wineskin.

Bishop Bruté's voice rose above that of the gale; he was praying the Psalms from his breviary: "The Lord raises a storm on the sea, makes lightning, brings forth the winds, and the depths are moved with terror. The clouds pour down rain, Thy flashes light up the world, Thy arrows shoot to and fro, the skies send forth their voice, Thy thunder rolls round the sky. The earth moves and trembles, for Thou summons the gale, tossing the waves of the sea up to heaven and back down into the deep; the souls of Thy servants melt away in their distress."

Minute by minute and hour by hour, throughout the duration of that hellacious storm, none of the missionaries slept for fear the very next creak, squeak, moan, or groan of the vessel might be its last. The wooden hull could only endure so much strain before one of the seams was to open up, sinking the ship to the bottom of the cold, black sea. The only difference between life and death was a thin shell of wood planks nailed together. If the hull were to give way, then all on board were dead men: no more to be remembered, buried in a common grave on the bottom of the North Atlantic's ocean floor.

Petit now understood clearly the phrase *coffin ship*. With the reality of death so close, what was said of the sea is true: the sea unites more than it separates. If Petit or any of his companions were to ever make it safely to America, they would always remember that they nearly died together.

Never before had the words of Saint Benedict ever been so

clear: *mortem cotidie ante oculos suspectam habere* (keep death ever before your eyes). As the skiff rolled about on the waters, beds, possessions, anything and everything soared from side to side, up and down the boat from bow to stern, starboard to port—plates, candles, luggage, men, women, and children alike. There were brief moments, instantaneous, nearly silent pauses where the boat would heel and lift up, unrestrained, seemingly coming completely up out of the water only to plunge back down hard into the sea, jarring all on board. The storm swept the boat in circles, causing much illness aboard. The name of God had been invoked for days—and not always in prayer. Yet the Catholics aboard called upon the God of sea and storm, and they also invoked the protection of the Blessed Mother.

"O Mary, Star of the Sea, *morituri te salutamus!*" Bishop Bruté lost his balance and nearly dropped his candlestick as he prayed. "*Ave, Maria, gratia plena, Dominus tecum. Benedicta tu in mulieribus, et benedictus fructus ventris tui, Jesu.*"

"*Sancta Maria*," Petit began with the others in one voice, "*Mater Dei, ora pro nobis peccatoribus, nunc, et in hora mortis nostrae. Amen.*"

Bruté continued to pray aloud from the Psalms. "Out of the depths I call to Thee, O Lord. The waters engulf us, the torrent overwhelms us, and seething waters threaten to drown us!"

Petit silently prayed the words of the Gospel: *Lord, save us, we are perishing!*

The bishop then granted general absolution to all Catholics on board. That was only done in extreme emergency when those in need of confession were in danger of death. The privilege of receiving the sacrament under such circumstance did nothing to allay their fears.

The storm pounded on till morning. It was Sunday and all the Catholics had been fasting since the night before in anticipation of receiving the Eucharist. That morning the bishop prepared to celebrate Mass in spite of the raging storm.

"My dear children," Bruté said as he looked at each of the missionaries and the few other Catholic souls, "this storm is a ruse of the devil. Fear not; we shall not perish. In the days of the apostles, Saint Paul celebrated the sacred mysteries at sea during a storm."

He looked at his charges and saw the fear on their faces. "Oh, ye of little faith. This voyage will not result in the loss of lives." Bruté said confidently over the sound of the waves and wind.

Petit tried to ignore the cries of the sailors and other passengers.

Before long the wind and waves were pounding the ship so violently that water began to seep into the hold. "Fear not. I trust in God that all shall be well," the bishop smiled a wide, toothless grin as his cloudy, hazel eyes revealed a metaphysical depth. He opened a small valise containing the assorted materials necessary for Mass. He placed a white cloth over the end of one of the tables and carefully placed a prayer book upon the makeshift altar. Next he poured a small amount of wine into a silver chalice and placed some small pieces of the flat unleavened bread upon a smaller silver paten. He held the chalice, which would have otherwise easily rolled off of the altar had he not.

As Bruté got to the part of the Mass where he was to consecrate the elements of bread and wine, transforming them into the Eucharistic body and blood of the Lord, a loud ripping noise resounded in the hull. More deafening sounds followed. The boat sounded as if it were being axed apart or beaten into pieces. At this, Bruté unflinchingly took the bread, gave thanks to God in front of them all, elevated the host above his head for all to behold and prayed the words, "*Hoc est meum corpum*" (This is my body, which will be broken for you).

A loud cracking and splintering sound followed by a crash and thunderous vibration rocked the ship. Petit, expecting to hear the mighty roar of waves and bracing for a wall of water to explode upon the worshipers, made the sign of the cross, blessing himself for what might have been the last time this side of eternity.

The ship's hull miraculously held, surviving the gale and sustaining the rupturing force of crashing waves. Later that day the storm began to subside. It seemed the word *miracle* was on everyone's lips, Catholic, Protestant, and heathen alike. When the tempest finally ceased, the sailors of the badly beaten vessel ascended from the hold to inspect the damage. Michael Shawe and the bishop were two of the first from their group to emerge from the floating prison.

As Petit ascended the stairs, he beheld a rainbow over the calm sea, arching from horizon to horizon; the Covenant Promise made to Noah had been renewed for his Church. There were assorted fish scattered across the deck's surface and the sails were torn; one of the masts had snapped, splintered, and crashed through a portion of the deck. Even after the boat had ceased rocking and reeling, many of the passengers were still suffering from sea sickness and all that that entails. Some couldn't even get out of their bunks, so nauseated were they from all the ship's movement.

Some of the passengers were also ill with ship fever or typhus. Bishop Bruté, a skilled physician himself prior to his entering the seminary, tended to some of those who were ill. The symptoms of the dreaded ship fever: a dark red rash, sweating, delirium, bloody hemorrhages, and the cough of consumption were often the sentence of death aboard the sailing vessel.

The sick and dying received little or no care, neither medicine nor spiritual consolation, and the dead were thrown overboard and buried at sea without any of the rites of their Church. Fortunate for the Catholics aboard, Mass had been offered and the sacraments were available, especially Extreme Unction. Some of the Protestants who either were dying or whose loved ones were dying refused the consolations of the Catholic priests on board—they would rather die than be prayed over by a Catholic priest. The missionaries watched in vain as the sailors threw the dead overboard without as much as a prayer.

In the hold, gallons and gallons of water were stored for the passengers. A sentry kept watch over the metal water containers to make sure no one took more than their allotted share or used it for any purpose other than drinking. By the sixth week out, some people were even begging the guard to let them bathe in it. Yet for the trip, each passenger was only allotted sixty gallons of water, one hundred pounds of salted provisions, and one hundred pounds of bread. The weekly allowance was four pounds of bread, one pound of beef, one pound of pork, a half pound of potatoes, one pint of peas, five gallons of water, one ounce of tea, and two ounces of coffee.

Due to the storm lengthening this particular trip, the food had to be rationed. The biscuits and vegetables already had not fared too well in the hold. The wooden barrels in which they were stored had been infested with worms, rats, and mold. Much of the meat had also become rotten. Scurvy affected some of the passengers due to a lack of fresh fruit and vegetables, and others contracted typhus from the tainted drinking water. Some of the sailors mixed in rum with the water to keep it drinkable. The irony of it all was the fact that they were surrounded by water but the risk of the passengers dying of thirst was very real.

It was common knowledge that some of the poorer passengers and stowaways would eat rats if they were desperate. Some considered them to be very good. One wealthy French woman in first class had brought her dog on the voyage. The rumor aboard ship was that in the middle of the night some of the stowaways hiding in the baggage hold took her dog from its cage, killed it, and cooked it. The story passed through the ship for the remainder of the trip. By the end of the journey, the rumors had evolved into the tale that the ship's cuisine consisted of stowaway rats and travelers' favorite pets. Her dog was never found.

CHAPTER 9
NEW WORLD

After being at sea for more than a month and a half, the men, women, and children, were huddled together in the darkness, their beds teeming with all abomination, filth, excrement, urine and vomit, spawning disease and death. I prayed for landfall.

Petit's fellow Breton attorney Father Celestin de La Hailandière was somber and didn't seem to be himself. Petit had noticed changes in Celestin since they had left Rennes. It seemed that the odyssey had even aged him.

On the afternoon that land had been sighted, Celestin was on the top deck with Petit. Celestin asked Petit, "What do you make of the younger seminarians, Benjamin?"

"What are you referring to?"

"What kind of men are they?"

"Faithful, yet adventuresome," Petit answered.

"Doctrinally adventuresome?" de La Hailandière asked.

"No, I mean they are full of zeal and hope for the Church in America and the world."

"These younger men have no traces of Liberalism or the sophistries of that republican apostate, Lammenais, do they?"

"They are loyal sons of the Church." Petit wondered why the priest was asking him such questions.

"Even this *distinguished* Englishman, Michael Edgar Evelyn Shawe? What kind of a man is he?"

"He is a man of great moderation, very English." Petit was taken aback at Father de La Hailandière's questions and felt as if he was on the witness stand. "He has a firm grasp of finding a balance between rigid orthodoxy and extreme liberalism."

"Orthodoxy is not rigid. It is orthodox. Remember that, Benjamin. Rules must be maintained. As a lawyer you should be one of the first to recognize the need for law."

"The law was meant to serve man's needs. The Sabbath was made for man, not man for the Sabbath." Petit perhaps spoke without thinking.

"I know the scripture, Monsieur Petit." De La Hailandière turned away.

"Pardon me, Père," Petit nodded respectfully, anxious that he had offended the priest.

The two men were both lawyers, but de La Hailandière had no use for the philosophy or thoughts of the Liberal Catholics. The foremost thinker of Liberal Catholicism was the French priest, Felicité de Lamennais. He was known simply as Lamennais. He was a friend of Bishop Bruté and had been for thirty years. Over the course of time, Lamennais had come to embrace the republican ideals that were gaining acceptance and influence in Europe. In light of the French Revolution and its aftermath, Lamennais called upon the pope and the Church to accept religious freedom, freedom of the press, freedom of conscience, and freedom of education. He reasoned that the Catholics in America enjoyed the liberty of them all, so why couldn't all Catholics?

Lamennais believed that only a strong papacy could guarantee the Church's future. He opposed the restoration of the French Monarchy, and believed the Church could no longer afford to be intimately identified with the royal French government. He was also an Ultramontane, believing that the Church should be independent and look to Rome for unity under the leadership of a strong papacy.

Lamennais wrote that the Church must not place her hope in the privileges bestowed upon it by civil government. He even argued that the church should renounce its legitimately acquired rights if the exercise of those rights compromised the Church's witness or mission. He had seen enough corrupt churchmen—in exchange for power and prestige—allowing members of the royal government to dictate the Church policy.

As it was, the leadership of the French church insisted upon retaining its pre-Revolution privileged status and failed to renounce its union with the throne. As a result when the monarchy was ultimately deposed, the Church suffered; not only was it rendered powerless, but, in large part, it was becoming irrelevant in the eyes of many.

In 1834, the same year his friend Bruté was named bishop, Lamennais was condemned by the Church for his progressive ideas; the pope excommunicated him and declared him an apostate.

The lines of demarcation were clear: Father Celestin de La Hailandière had no use for Lamennais. Petit, on the other hand, knew that much of what Lamennais advocated was already in place in the United States. Privately, Petit believed that the Vatican was hasty in its condemnation of his ideas, but he would never openly share that with his superiors, particularly Father de La Hailandière.

Bishop Bruté, before he had been named bishop in 1834, had even urged Lamennais to become a missionary to the New World. Lamennais ultimately rejected the idea fearing the decision might be interpreted as escapist on his part. He was determined to force the issues of Liberal Catholicism in Europe and on his own terms.

Bishop Bruté was rather enigmatic himself. As a European priest he could not advocate liberty of conscience or freedom of the press, but as a bishop in America he could preach and teach freely in a religiously pluralistic society and write freely for both the Catholic and secular press. The dichotomy between the Catholic Church in the Old World and the New World was undeniable. Yet the two worldviews could not coexist indefinitely.

So far Petit had avoided arguing with de La Hailandière about the Menaissian Movement, as Lamennais' Liberal Catholicism was called, but Michael Shawe had not. Both the bishop and Shawe believed that liberty of the press allowed for the dissemination of all ideas, true and false, good and bad, but it was a necessary evil for the exchange of ideas if the truth was to prevail.

The liberal view held that if the Church was called to be prophetic, it must raise its voice against injustice in the world. *Thy kingdom come, thy will be done on earth as it is in heaven.* The church must also be free from governmental control. This included dependence upon the state for its existence. The Church must cut itself free from civil governments and partisanship. Lamennais believed the Church should focus its energies on the rebirth of its faith in Christ and the evangelization of the Gospel message. His was not a call for a retreat from politics but rather for a Catholic initiative to secure truth, justice, and charity in society and the world that transcends partisan and political ideologies.

De La Hailandière turned back to Petit, smiled, and changed the subject of the conversation to the pleasant weather and the fact that they were nearly to America.

CHAPTER 10

BLACKROBES

21 JULY 1836

*We, the members of our motley band of missionaries,
emerged into the crowded streets of New York, our identities
now hidden. I felt as if I was one of the early Christians
with nothing to set me apart from the swarming mass of
humanity except the Word of God burning in my heart.
Within a week's time we would be traveling to
Philadelphia, and then on to Emmittsburg, Maryland,
before making our way west to Vincennes, Indiana.*

The *Merchantman* arrived in New York harbor a month and three weeks since their departure from France. After surviving the indignities of sea travel, Petit stepped on American soil for the first time. As he carried his trunk up the dock, he saw many of the workers along the wharf eyeing him and his companions suspiciously. They had been forewarned not to accept any assistance, especially from the overly friendly and solicitous, for they were the ones most likely to carry off the luggage and valises of the unsuspecting. Many bewildered, travel-weary immigrants found themselves empty-handed when they arrived at the customs office with the explanation that the kind gentlemen who had helped them off the boat had absconded with all their worldly possessions.

Fatigued from inadequate sleep for over a month, Petit

walked through this American city like a disoriented sheep being led by an ever-vigilant shepherd. Bishop Bruté seemed to be the only one holding up well under these trying circumstances. When the Americans saw the contingency of blackrobes, as they were called, they glared at them as if the blackrobed gentlemen were threatening to abduct American women and children. The customs officer sent them on their way cautioning them to be on guard against brigands and ruffians. Walking amid his new world, Petit saw men wearing swords and carrying daggers, pistols, and rifles. The male citizenry was arrayed in various types of clothing: everything from leather shirts and animal hides to Old World cravats and frock coats. Petit strained to pick out any familiar English words in the midst of the strange dialect. Every walk of life seemed to be in this one place, as if foreshadowing the Kingdom of God.

Petit and the others were taken to one of the principal Catholic Churches in New York City. It was dedicated to St. Patrick and was a modest chapel of stone. The Irish pastor welcomed them and arranged for all of the men to find lodgings at various inns and taverns in the city. The bishop spent the night at the rectory while Father de La Hailandière and Petit were shown to their quarters at the Washington Hotel. They both collapsed in their beds. The sheets were fresh and clean. Petit said a prayer of thanksgiving for this simple blessing before falling asleep. It was the first decent night's rest he'd had since leaving Europe.

The next morning they attended Mass for the first time in America. The church's exterior was simple and its interior unfinished—much like the Americans they had encountered so far. Afterwards they were invited to breakfast by the pastor. He made it quite clear that Catholic clergy and religious, especially missionaries, should avoid wearing clerical garb in public. There were certain Americans who were only looking for an excuse to deport all foreigners, especially Catholics. A recent wave of violence had been waged against Catholic immigrants; the immigrants were being blamed for the nation's economic woes.

The kindly pastor sent his housekeeper out that morning to purchase enough civilian clothes for all of the men. Bishop Bruté seemed unscathed by the priest's revelations, and looking at his serene and unmoved face, Petit knew Bishop Bruté was neither afraid nor surprised.

So it began. All of those things that the would-be missionaries were warned about were coming to pass. Petit remembered the respect that a black soutane and biretta inspired in the Bretons. Now he was being told to hide his identity and deny his tradition. The words of Isaiah rang true: "He was spurned and avoided by men, a man of suffering, accustomed to infirmity, one of those from whom men hide their faces, spurned, and we held him in no esteem."

Petit put on a pair of gray pantaloons, which bagged in the seat and in the knees, and saw how ridiculous he looked. He hadn't realized until this moment how much he enjoyed the admiration that clerical garb brought him. This cloak of humility fit poorly. "Lord, what a proud and arrogant man you prove me to be," Petit prayed aloud. "Help me to bear this indignity."

He refused to look in the full-length mirror, which stood in the corner of the room, not wishing to make his cross any heavier than it already was.

CHAPTER II

PASSAGE WEST

AUGUST 1836

Bruté was welcomed from Philadelphia to Emmitsburg like a long lost son returning from a forgotten war. From the way the people clamored to see and hear him. I was reminded of some of the accounts of Saint Paul in the Acts of the Apostles. The Americans—Catholic and Protestant alike—revere this man.

Since leaving Pittsburg I have been traveling with my fellow missionaries, the distinguished Englishman, Michael Edgar Evelyn Shawe, and the Austrian priest, Father Stanislaus Buteaux. I derive great benefit from their presence. Perhaps I will come to love this adopted land as much as my beloved Brittany. Time shall reveal all things.

From Emmitsburg they traveled to Pittsburgh in the company of the bishop. At Pittsburgh, the bishop and most of the others prepared to leave for Vincennes, Indiana, aboard stagecoaches. Petit and his two traveling companions, Buteaux and Shawe, were to board a steamboat on the Ohio River. They were given the task of securing all the baggage and luggage to Vincennes. Spying a holy medal around the neck of one of the Irish ticket agents, they confided to the man their identities and mission. He granted them passage aboard the *Clarksville*. They were to disembark at Evansville, but from there they would be on their own to travel the sixty miles north by stage to the diocesan seat of Vincennes.

The main cabin of the steamboat was fifty feet or so and lined with benches. The same benches converted into berths by night, and upper berths were unchained from the wall and lowered to provide for a second tier; canvas curtains separated the berths. Shawe and Petit shared a makeshift compartment. The first night it was difficult sleeping due to the party atmosphere on the upper deck; being tossed from the upper berth after the boat hit a sandbar didn't help either. The following morning Petit was awakened by a deckhand armed with a hand bell. The stranger pulled the curtain open without warning; it was a good thing Petit and Shawe were clothed!

Petit soon forgot about Vincennes; his immediate concern was surviving the steamboat trip on the Ohio River.

Bishop Bruté was quite correct in his assessment of the American lifestyle. The chief concern seemed to be for self, pleasure, and the rewards of worldly gain. One got the impression that Americans viewed others as either stumbling blocks or stepping stones—or both. They were an aggressive lot, rude and boisterous, without much cheer—unless induced by alcohol or the presence of women.

Yet the United States is truly a New World. Petit could not help but marvel at the American landscape, the beauty of God's creation. The spectacle of nature at play upon the river filled him with the most wondrous awe. The Ohio River's waters were incredibly pure; one could see to the bottom of the channel. Large, hundred-pound fish inhabited the virgin waters of this river called La Belle Riviere. *Beautiful River* in the savage tongue is rendered *Oyo*; the Americans spelled it *Ohio*. The waterfowl and wildlife along the riverbanks was astounding. By day, tortoises and various species of birds sunned themselves upon rocks and logs, and by night, frogs and insects sang their nightly praise. Flocks of geese flew in formation overhead, while the skies occasionally blackened as swarms of passenger pigeons swept across the face of the sun, casting a great shifting shadow upon the earth. Particularly beautiful were the ivory-billed woodpeckers and the loons.

After five days aboard the boat, Petit was weary. He sat in an uncomfortable and worn chair on the top deck of the steamboat to write a letter to his family in Rennes. The relentless sun warmed him. He longed for a light rain, or even the hint of a breeze, anything that felt remotely like a Breton August. He wiped the back of his neck with his handkerchief then quickly placed the piece of linen over his mouth and nose just in time to catch a sneeze. His nose and throat had been irritated since his arrival in America. The fear that he may have contracted typhus aboard the *Merchantman* seized him. Be it real or imagined, the possibility was real.

How embarrassed Petit had been on the third day of their Ohio River voyage. A charlatan selling his wares on board the steamboat claimed to have a remedy for typhus. He almost subscribed to the gimmick until he discovered that the extraordinary elixir was simply whiskey in a medicine bottle.

He placed his handkerchief in his breast pocket and forced his attention back on the letter. He thought back on all he had seen the past several days aboard the steamboat. Nearly a week aboard the vessel left him world-weary of the affairs of men.

The New World's newness was wearing off, and the frontier was becoming more and more settled as people moved farther west, establishing towns and cities.

The environment aboard the boat was coarse: cursing, drinking, and gambling; it seemingly confirmed everything his brother, Paul, had warned him about.

Some of the French passengers told the missionaries how they'd been aboard other steamboats when one captain had challenged another captain to a race. During a recent race, one of the boat's boilers exploded killing several passengers. Petit and Shawe believed it was stories like these that seemed to confirm the restlessness in the American heart.

Petit wondered if the heat and humidity of July was making him as disagreeable as the Americans. He could hear Paul say, *"Of course. It's just as I told you it would be. Don't say I didn't warn you."*

He didn't finish the letter to his family.

As the boat passed by Kentucky, Petit became aware of a great commotion on the shore. A crowd of people gathered at the side of the boat to witness a spectacle along the riverbank. He worked his way through the crowd and saw a large African man being roughly manhandled by two white men. They shoved him down into the dirt of the muddy shoreline, chained his feet together in shackles, and cuffed his hands. The man was crying and didn't struggle to free himself, but rather he wept like a child despairing of ever seeing his mother again. There was no fight in him as he lay helpless in the dirt. The men kicked him and violently screamed at him. His moans of anguish rose above the men's angry shouts of "nigger."

Petit had heard this contemptuous term *nigger* used frequently to refer to the Negro slaves. It was a term—like much of the American tongue—that he had never heard until boarding the *Merchantman* and arriving in the New World. The sound of that harsh epithet had become as offensive as God's name used in vain.

Michael Shawe and Father Buteaux joined him on the deck

and observed the hideous display of American injustice: the apprehension of a runaway slave.

A Frenchman from New Orleans told the missionaries that the practice of kidnapping freed blacks and returning them to slave states was big business along the river. Even some dishonest constables and sheriffs would turn a blind eye to this injustice if they could achieve their price.

Many of the Americans seemed used to this sort of thing because they carried on as if nothing was happening. Were they so used to seeing people chained up like wild animals and placed on auction blocks that it no longer shocked them? The terrible sight of that man crying like a child, his face in the dirt, and his hands and feet bound made Petit want to defend him. But how? The slave had no recourse to justice under American law. All Petit could do to help was pray. Yet somehow that didn't seem like enough.

What must it be like to be chained? Why did these Americans detest anyone who was different from them? Fear?

Petit could hide his Catholicism behind civilian clothes. He could keep his mouth closed and conceal his French tongue. But this man could not conceal the color of his skin. Petit observed some of the Negro slaves aboard the boat, many of them had made their way over to the railing to witness the incident. They were unmoved, as if there was no use in protesting such treatment.

Some of the slaves on board were made to keep the boiler fired. There were wood yards stationed along the river for fuel stops. The slaves would disembark and chop wood and then load it on the boat. Men and women chained and shackled was a terrible contradiction in the American Republic: The Land of the Free.

CHAPTER 12

INDIANA

25 AUGUST 1836

*After nearly a week on the Ohio River, we landed today
at Evansville, Indiana, a town in the southernmost region
of the Diocese of Vincennes. We learned that it is a town
of about fifteen hundred people, mostly Protestant. There
is neither a Catholic Church nor a priest here.*

Once the boat sounded its whistle at the Evansville riverfront
they debarked. Four men unloading barrels and crates from a
flatboat on the wharf approached them. One of the men spoke
German to Father Buteaux. The man explained that the few
Catholics in Evansville had been expecting their arrival. They
were to be taken to the Mansion House Hotel. It was owned by
a fine Bavarian Catholic immigrant gentleman named Francis
Xavier Linck; he was one of the first Catholics to settle in
Evansville. He also operated a sawmill on the riverfront.

Petit was glad he was finally in what seemed friendlier territory. Father Buteaux explained why they were traveling incognito.
They learned that Bishop Bruté had returned to Vincennes and
sent word that if anyone was to meet three Europeans—an
Englishman, a Frenchman, and an Austrian who looked out of
place—they were to be taken to the Mansion House Hotel at
once. The bishop had made all the necessary arrangements for
their accommodations. Mr. Linck assured them it was his singu-

lar privilege and pleasure to bestow hospitality on three travel-weary missionaries of God.

The way the Catholics of Evansville—all fifteen of them—fawned over the missioners, one might have thought they were three of the Lord's original apostles. When their baggage was brought from the ship's hold, the Evansville men wheeled it up on a cart toward Main Street. Petit's valise was wet; he carried it up the wharf. The three men made their way up the riverbank along Water Street, walking through the dusty, horse-dung-covered dirt street and swarms of buzzing flies, careful where they stepped. At least First Street had a plank sidewalk and was flanked by clapboard houses. They soon converged upon the Mansion House Hotel at the intersection of Locust Street.

Petit listened as Shawe and Buteaux told the tale of their experience of surviving the hurricane, seasickness, and bigotry aboard the *Merchantman* and enduring the indignities of the *Clarksville* steamboat.

Shawe resented the fact that he and his companions were discouraged from wearing their clerical garb.

"You will soon see that a lot of things in America are different, gentlemen," Mr. Linck said. "Let us praise God for your safe arrival!" He looked at Buteaux, "Father, will you offer Mass tomorrow?"

Buteaux assured him he would.

Petit retired to his upstairs room and collapsed in one of the feather beds. He slept until he was awakened by a bell the next morning.

Father Buteaux celebrated the sacred mysteries in the hotel parlor. After breakfast, Father Buteaux inquired whether there were plans to build a church in Evansville. Mr. Linck answered,

"We are in mission territory. This is not Paris, Vienna, or London."

They all chuckled.

The missioners boarded the stage in front of the Mansion House Hotel. The coach arrived headed by four horses. The drivers were hard on the poor beasts as the animals neighed and snorted.

"French horsemen would never treat their worst animal in such a ghastly way," Petit remarked as the driver used the whip mercilessly upon the horses, lashing them as he shouted and spat. Petit flinched with each snap of the lash upon the horses, thinking of his beloved Bijou.

"*Les incompetent,*" Shawe replied, "No English gentleman would ever treat his enemy's horse in such a manner."

Vincennes was two days by stage from Evansville. On the road to Vincennes, the missionaries took note of men wearing homespun clothing and coon skin caps and toting axes and Kentucky long rifles. There were several stops along the way where the horses were swapped for fresh ones but each time the drivers treated the fresh ones just as badly.

When they arrived in Vincennes the three missionaries realized that the bishop was not exaggerating its mission status. The streets were unpaved, speckled with dung, and swarming with flies. Cows, pigs, goats, dogs, and cats roamed freely; the cathedral Church of Saint Francis Xavier looked more like a barn than a church. Petit had expected to see at least a cross atop a spire. There was neither a cross nor a spire.

"Bishop Bruté assured us that conditions were primitive," Shawe said as he leaned toward the carriage's window.

"Gentlemen, welcome to the life of a missionary," Father Buteaux said with a wry smile.

Petit imagined what his mother might say upon seeing the conditions.

CHAPTER 13

VINCENNES

NOVEMBER 1836

The Vincennes cathedral is unfinished to say the least and our seminary dormitory here is a long, narrow room the width of a hallway with narrow straw-covered planks serving as beds—radically different from the church and opulent halls of Saint-Sulpice in Paris. Despite the adjustment to poverty and American seminary life, there is much to be learned and I am still about the challenging task of learning English at the hands of Michael Shawe. In turn, I am teaching Latin to younger seminarians. Adapting to the English language and the American culture consumes time and energy that could be better spent on theology. This is a great frustration. My continued study of Saint Thomas requires much patience and time.

One consolation here in Vincennes is the fact that we clerics may wear our cassocks and birettas in public without fear of anti-Catholic backlash. The American intolerance for Roman Catholics is not as disproportionate in the French enclave of Vincennes.

--◆-○-●-○-◆--

In their time together, the bishop had been educating the men concerning the culture in which they now found themselves. The Americans referred to native or aboriginal peoples of Indiana as the savages. Universally they had come to be known as the American Indians. The Jesuit missionaries, the *robes noir* (blackrobes), had first spread the message of Christ among the native peoples in the seventeenth century. Isaac Jogues, called Ondessonk, and Jean Brebeuf and their companions were martyred by the Mohawk. The Jesuit Marquette and the French explorer La Salle had also traversed parts of Indiana.

Sieur de Vincennes brought a small band of soldiers and a contingent of Piankeshaws from the Vermillion River. They established the post that bears his name. The French and Indian fur trade was interrupted when the British, in an attempt to control the fur trade, enlisted the help of the natives against the French traders and pioneers in what came to be called the French and Indian War. In 1736, a band of Chickasaw warriors captured Vincennes and a French Jesuit, Father Senat, and burnt them at stake. Later when the American colonists were at odds with Britain, the French were convinced to side with the American cause.

Pierre Gibault of Quebec, Canada, a missionary priest assigned to the Illinois country at Kaskaskia, later made his way to Vincennes. He assisted the Virginia General George Rogers Clark in his conquest of the British who held Vincennes and all of the territory that came to be known as the Northwest Territory.

The northern forests of the Vincennes Diocese were the home to several tribes of Indiana Indians. The Shawnee and the Miami either removed from the state by 1835 or else they had assimilated to the American way of life. The one tribe that remained was the Potawatomi. There were many bands of the Potawatomi in America, but the majority of them were located in southern Michigan and northern Indiana.

Some of the Americans pitied the natives as "the poor Indians," and believed that in the best interest of the natives they should be removed from the American territories and placed on reservations—all done with governmental funds. Unfortunately, this was a vocal minority that was prejudiced against the red men; they advocated their removal as soon as possible.

Many of the original French residents and their descendants had intermarried with the Indians and regarded the Indians as their neighbors. They did not advocate removal. However, with the influx of American settlers and Irish immigrants, the French influence was dying away even in Vincennes.

The Potawatomi people were held in contempt simply because they were Indians. Black Hawk's War of 1832 has poisoned the minds of many Americans to regard every Indian as an enemy to the Republic. And even though the Potawatomi were not involved in that war, some of their number had taken part in the Battle of Fallen Timbers, the Battle of Tippecanoe, and the Fort Dearborn Massacre, to name a few. In war, many atrocities were committed on both sides.

A popular notion among white Americans was the idea that they alone were the true natives of their country, not the indigenous peoples, such as the Miami, Potawatomi, Cherokee, or any other tribe. Another reason that some of the Protestants in America disliked the Indians so much was due to the fact that so many of the Indians, if they did convert to Christianity, preferred Roman Catholicism.

Bishop Bruté has assigned the Belgian missionary, Father DeSeille, to the Potawatomi reserve in northern Indiana. Indiana: The Land of the Indian. For how much longer would it be the land of the Indian? The American settlers continued to migrate westward, encroaching upon Indian Territory.

Petit could not imagine the grief and anguish the natives would feel if the Indian removal policy was enforced in the northern territory of Indiana. Too many tribes have been forced off their ancestral homelands like an unwanted herd. The mention of homeland reminded him of his own sacrifice. He had yet to receive any letters from his mother or siblings. Would their letters even reach him in the wilds of Indiana?

As for the anti-Catholic sentiment, Petit had been warned, but no amount of preparation could quite prepare him for the actual experience. He and his companions now recognized that being a religious in Europe and America are two totally different things. At least in Europe one knew what to expect from the old prejudices. Catholicism in America was increasingly suspect of a malicious conspiracy of great magnitude. Thanks to a free press, these theories were disseminated throughout the states. On the other hand, through the Catholic and Democratic presses, the truth was also in print.

Christ's Church was accused of grievous intentions, the Bishop explained, because the Church is made up of erring human beings who often desire their own will more than God's. How hard it is to choose God's will over one's own. There is great fear of what would happen if one did.

The bishop prayed that his seminarians and priests would trust in the Lord when fear crept into their minds again and again, like a silent unseen slithering serpent. Would the Christians of this country ever welcome the stranger? Had they not forgotten that they were once strangers in this land? How long must one live in the States before being accepted?

The winter in Indiana was as extreme in its temperature as it was in its snow. A great warmth cheered Petit's heart on 16 December when he received minor orders and two days later on 18 December when he was ordained a subdeacon.

In January 1837, Bishop Bruté named Father Celestin de La Hailandière his vicar general. In that capacity as the deputy to the bishop, he assumed certain administrative responsibilities over the diocese. De La Hailandière had assured everyone that he was no great missionary to the wilderness like the peerless Bruté, and he knew that he would never match the holiness of the patriot priest Pierre Gibault or the refugees of the French Revolution and the Reign of Terror, Jean Rivét and Bishop Flaget.

Celestin de La Hailandière grew up in Coumbourg, Brittany. As a boy, the repercussions of the Revolution were still ravaging France. His father gave sanctuary to a refugee priest who lived with his family for several years before Napoleon lifted the ban on the priesthood. This priest instructed him in the faith and educated him in the classics. When Celestin was nineteen he began his study of law and at the age of twenty-two he was admitted to the bar. He practiced law for two years, but one Sunday at Mass, a visiting missionary priest inspired him to become a priest.

His father and mother were both opposed to his abandoning a legal career for priestly studies, so in 1822 he accepted the position of judge at the Civil Tribunal of Redon. Nonetheless, later that year, he abandoned his legal career and entered the seminary at Rennes. He finished his studies in Paris and was ordained to the priesthood at Saint-Sulpice. In 1836, Bishop Bruté invited de La Hailandière to become a missionary to America. He accepted.

Now Bishop Bruté was to travel south to New Orleans and east to Washington City in the spring. In his absence, he planned to leave the administrative tasks to de La Hailandière. The question among the seminarians and priests was whether de La Hailandière would take it upon himself to address the anomalies concerning the Indian mission in northern Indiana.

When Petit attended vespers, the resounding harmonies of the Gregorian plainchant and the sweet smell of incense were solace for a troubled soul. Afterwards he joined Michael Shawe in silently marking the Stations of the Cross in the cathedral nave. They genuflected to the high altar's tabernacle and departed together. In the warm February air, they stood on the front steps of the cathedral church and observed the Wabash River cresting well out of its banks.

Shawe's appearance was flawless, his soutane perfectly pressed smooth, the fringed sash neatly at his side despite the breeze, biretta perfectly balanced atop his head with its tassel fluffed, and the cuffs of his snowy white shirt protruding from the sleeves of his soutane, with the golden cufflinks glistening in the sun.

"Unseasonably warm weather, Benjamin."

Petit lowered his head in a slight, but profound bow. "Yes, it is."

Shawe grimaced, lifting his eyebrows and flaring his nostrils in a most uninviting stare. Though Petit's greeting was brief, it was still enough for the Englishman to take note of the flawed English pronunciation. His face relaxed into its usual friendly freshness and slowly turned into a smile. "Have you been taking English lessons from one of the Irish canal workers?"

"No."

"It is my better judgment that English uttered by a Frenchman does not need an Irish lilt."

Petit laughed.

"This weather is inappropriate for February," Shawe complained. "It's far too warm."

They descended the steps and walked beside the remains of old Fort Sackville and stopped at the site where the original church dedicated to Saint Francis Xavier had once stood. "It's hard to believe that it was here in a log church," Shawe pointed to the ground, "that the British commander, Governor Hamilton, surrendered to George Rogers Clark, and with his capture, all of the Northwest Territory was handed over to the government of the United States, relinquishing it from British rule. Ohio, Indiana, Illinois, Michigan, and Wisconsin all in exchange for the return of a British general," Shawe smiled.

"It couldn't have ever happened had it not been for the patriot missionary priest, Pére Pierre Gibault," he added, "who convinced the French inhabitants here to side with the Americans when Clark's volunteers stormed the garrison."

Neither of them spoke as they followed the row of trees, which marked the path to the cemetery. Their cassocks and the sashes about their waists flapped in the breezy air as they walked through the midst of the graves, passing by the various metal crosses and tombstones of all who sleep in Christ. They paused when they came upon the grave of the pioneer priest, Jean Francois Rivét.

"Father Rivét escaped the terror of the Revolution and Reign of Terror," Shawe explained, reflecting upon the many stories of the selfless devotion of this beloved pastor of souls that they had heard during the short time they had been in Vincennes. He and Bishop Flagét came to America together. President Washington commissioned Rivét to open a public school here, making him the first headmaster of Jefferson Academy. For the seven years Rivét headed the school, he was never compensated financially by the government even though Congress appropriated him two hundred dollars a year. After his death the school closed briefly but later reopened as Vincennes Academy.

Shawe and Petit walked along the bank of the Wabash, observing a colony of great blue heron before retiring to the seminary for dinner and evening benediction. In the late afternoon sun, the northern sky in front of the cathedral was darkened with a flock of passenger pigeons, *Ectopistes migratorius*. Millions of the birds descended to the forest on the opposite side of the Wabash.

A warm wind from the southwest began to blow violently and a storm began to rage.

The storm became so wicked that the day became as night, taking everyone by surprise. The rains came with lightning, thunder, large hailstones, and strong winds. Approaching from across the river at an incredible speed was a rotating funnel-shaped cloud coming down from the thunderhead. Touching the earth, the whirlwind stirred up the ground and the white column of cloud turned black as it rotated with dirt and debris. Bishop Bruté, watching from the open doors of the cathedral, was determined that no cyclone would ever destroy the Catholic Church or Catholic homes again as it had in 1826. He prayed for the safety of the citizens of his see city.

At the height of the storm, the whirlwind lowered out of the dark clouds and bore down on the cathedral. Heedless of peril, Bishop Bruté left the security of the sanctuary, braving lightning and hail, and went to the riverbank. He stood on the hill between the old fort and the ferry dock, and extending his hands as Moses of old, begged God's mercy to spare the city from the devastating tornado. At once the twister ascended into the clouds and the storm ceased.

He then knelt in the mud and prayed that tornadoes would never again strike the city.

The tornado followed a path just above Church Street. Some farmers south of town observing the storm said they had never seen anything like it. As soon as the cloud cleared the city, the twister dropped down again and blew apart a couple of barns, killed some cows and chickens, and cut a swath through the forest.

On 12 March, the bishop ordained Michael Edgar Evelyn

Shawe a priest; on 25 March, the bishop ordained Reverend Anthony Deydier.

Deydier had accompanied the young Father Bruté to America in 1810. Deydier was ordained deacon a couple of years after arriving in America and taught at Mt. Saint Mary's Seminary for four years before leaving the seminary for New York. Deydier was an accomplished musician and taught music for twenty years in Albany, New York. In 1836, Father Deydier left New York and enrolled in Bruté's seminary at Vincennes. Now that he was ordained, he was appointed first resident pastor of Evansville, Indiana.

Bishop Bruté left Vincennes for Baltimore on 27 March where the bishops of the United States were gathering for a council. He has left his vicar general, Father de La Hailandière, in charge of the diocese.

In April, the Hackaliah Bailey Circus came to Vincennes. Posters and handbills advertising the coming spectacle had been distributed and the playbills littered storefront windows and trees throughout town. Father Michael Shawe and subdeacon Benjamin Petit witnessed its arrival.

Two boats loaded with circus animals, entertainers, tents, and equipment landed at the foot of Main Street on Water Street. Animal trainers, clowns, acrobats, and the entire entourage of wagons and carts paraded up Main past Adam Gimbel's Department Store and Main Street Tavern and the various shops and hotels. Covered wagons gaudily decorated with mirrors and large colorful paintings of elephants, acrobats, and clowns filled the street. A brightly costumed band performed marching music while the tramp clowns performed tricks and acrobats tumbled in the street providing laughter and entertainment for the citizens. Ferocious lions and tigers roared behind bars in rolling cages while chimpanzee monkeys and show horses followed. The three elephants and two camels spooked many of the children and adults who had never seen such exotic creatures.

The theatrical troupe paraded their way down Water Street leaving trails of elephant dung. Commerce came to a halt as nearly everyone in town came to see the extravaganza of such a promenade. The roustabouts busily set up the large canvas tents in an open field near the old Vincennes fort, Fort Sackville.

One of the clowns went around town dressed in his checkered coat, striped pants, and long, pointed shoes curled up at the toes. He wore a pointed hood with bells at the top and ass's ears protruding from under it. The members of the circus troupe stayed at several Main Street taverns.

Father Shawe convinced Petit to go to the circus during one of its performances. It was hard to concentrate on the show because three performances occurred simultaneously as the circus band played constantly. In one ring, lions and tigers were forced to jump through burning hoops of fire. In another ring, scantily-clad women balanced themselves atop elephants or dangled in the elephants' trunks. In the third ring, a trained bear jumped rope for its trainer. Outside the three center rings, chimpanzees rode atop ponies as a clown towered high above the crowd walking on stilts. Other clowns juggled, told jokes, or played musical instruments. High overhead, acrobats risked their lives by dancing on a rope all for a few moments of applause.

As Shawe and Petit watched the ropes above, their attention turned to two clowns chasing each other with pails of water. The two drenched each other and quickly dipped their pails in a large water barrel. Then one of the clowns came towards Shawe and Petit, rearing back as if to splash the crowd. Petit called out to

Father Shawe in order to warn him. He and the others seated nearby were doused in a shower of hundreds of tiny bits of paper. Petit laughed as the two prepared to depart the big tent.

But as they left the tent they were accosted by one of the circus talkers in an attempt to lure them into his small tent called the sideshow.

"Come on over, gentlemen! See a sight you'll never forget! This is the greatest freak show in America! We've got dwarves and the Jumbo Lady!"

It was a bizarre scene. The sign read "Watch the Jumbo Lady eat." There were several people in line to enter the tent. Even though the two men didn't venture in, the flaps of the tent were open wide enough for them to behold hucksters shoving food into the mouth of a poor, corpulent woman while two dwarves were made to dance around her.

Petit avoided the crass-talking hawker peddling in human exploitation. It was beyond his comprehension how anyone could put human beings on display like specimens in a laboratory for all to gawk upon and abuse—all for a pathetic display of entertainment. Despite all appearances, Petit knew the poor creatures were still created *imago Dei* (in the image of God).

The sight triggered a memory of the runaway slave on the banks of the Ohio. How could a people so blatantly disregard a segment of the population, considering them as less than human? Were Petit not a praying man—and a subdeacon— there were times when he feared his anger would render him capable of doing violence.

When the circus finally left, the hubbub in town was that one of the circus monkeys had either gotten loose or was "borrowed" and wound up on a barstool at one of the Vincennes taverns and ordered a glass of grog. The monkey's keeper rescued the frightened creature from some of the rowdies before they could get the creature completely pixilated.

CHAPTER 14

PROTO-SACERDOS

*I met the first priest ever ordained in the United States:
Father Stephen Theodore Badin. Concern for justice is
of the utmost importance to him. The issues of slavery,
Indian Removal, and capital punishment are hotly
debated here in America.*

—◆◇◆◇◆—

Petit learned that Father Stephen Theodore Badin was en route
to Vincennes for a visit while Bishop Bruté was in Baltimore.

Badin was called America's *proto-sacerdos*, since he was the
first priest ordained by Archbishop Carroll of Baltimore. Father
Celestin de La Hailandière believed Badin was under the
influence of Liberalism and Liberal Catholicism inspired by the
republican-minded apostate priest, Feli Lamennais, and tainted
with his own brand of *Theologiae Americana*. Badin permitted
the use of French, English, and Potawatomi vernacular in the
liturgy instead of the canonically required Latin. He also
employed the use of a female interpreter in the celebration of the
sacraments.

In 1828, he began traveling through Ohio, Michigan,
Indiana, and Illinois. It was during that time that he began his
mission to the Indians, living with different tribes but his heart
was with the Potawatomi Nation. He was beloved by the
Potawatomi tribe and was given the Indian name *Maketakônia*
(blackrobe). Badin hoped his new mission at the south bend of
the St. Joseph River could support a school for all races and

denominations. He argued with the federal officers and land commissioners over the Indian removal policy.

Badin was now nearly seventy years old.

One April afternoon, as Petit was studying in the seminary, he heard a horse whinny and a strong, but raspy, aging voice echoed from the porch. The bent figure of a white-haired man in a tattered cassock appeared in the open doorway. The priest was short and chubby. He had an aquiline nose and gray eyes. He was bald except for white hair just above the ears and around the back of his head. His nose and cheeks were streaked with bright red veins. He smoked a pipe and walked with a limp, assisted with a walking stick in his left hand. His right hand and arm were stiff as if resulting from a stroke. He periodically held his right arm with his left.

"*Bonjour, Pére,*" Petit said. "Good day, Father."

"Is Benjamin Petit here?"

"I am he."

"I am Father Badin." He puckered his lips and a smoke ring rose from his pipe's bowl.

"Reverend Father Stephen Theodore Badin?"

"Yes, but you don't have to address me as you would a bishop." He focused his eyes on Petit. "I'm a missionary. Look at me. I've worn this cassock everywhere."

The faded black garment was frayed at the hem.

"No one's ever given me any trouble. You just have to have faith in God. Our Lady will look out for you."

"*Dominus vobiscum,*" Badin limped towards Petit, favoring his left leg.

"*Et cum spiritu tuo,*" Petit replied as the two embraced cheek to cheek. "Welcome to Vincennes."

"The pleasure is mine." Badin gently pushed himself away from Petit, regaining his slouched position. "But I should welcome you. I first visited Vincennes well before you were even born." A twitch of pain streaked across the old man's face as he leaned on the back of a chair.

"Father Badin, please have a seat."

"Merci beaucoup." Badin collapsed in one of the wooden chairs.

Petit nodded, pondering the man's words. "In all humility, I hope to give glory and honor to God in my exercise of the priestly ministry."

Badin winked and nodded from behind a puff of tobacco smoke.

"Father Badin, did you arrive by boat or stage?"

"Neither. I rode from Bardstown." He removed the pipe from his mouth.

Petit couldn't help but look at the old man incredulously. Bardstown was at least 160 miles from Vincennes.

"Now don't go looking at me like I'm too old to be riding. I was riding a horse long before the United States had a Constitution and even before your parents were married."

"You have my utmost respect, Father Badin," Petit bowed slightly to this patriarch of the Church in America.

"When I arrived today I passed by execution square on the courthouse lawn. I see that your gallows tree is still yielding the fruit of human blood. May I ask how effective the noose has been in reducing crime?"

"I don't believe killing is a solution," Petit answered, "if that's what you're asking. The specter of the inquisition still stalks the Church, especially here among Protestants. Prior to entering the seminary I practiced law."

"Before I left Bardstown, there was a murder," Badin began. "A young farmer killed another man in a fight over a barmaid at Talbot's Tavern. At his trial, he was found guilty and condemned to death. I spent the night in jail with him before he was put to death. He wasn't pious by any means, and he wasn't

Catholic, so I couldn't hear his confession, but when the hangman came for him in the morning, he began to express remorse over his mortal sin as I accompanied him to the gallows.

"When the hangman placed the rope around his neck, he asked God to forgive him. Those were his last words. I went down and stood at the foot of the platform, holding his mother and praying with her as the trap door was sprung.

"The whole affair illustrates the uselessness of killing a murderer. The Lord Jesus said, did he not, 'Forgive as I have forgiven you. If you do not forgive others their offenses committed against you, I will not forgive you your offenses against me'? No man, by killing another, can restore the deceased to life, nor bring about any happiness in this world or the next; only an injustice and an assault upon the law of charity is done by adding sorrow to sorrow and tears upon tears."

The old priest straightened up in his chair, put his pipe back in his mouth, and continued to preach. "Did not Christ himself say, 'Let him who is without sin cast the first stone'? Saint Paul wrote, 'All have sinned and fallen short of the glory of God.' Why, even the newborn is stained with Adam's sin. Have we forgotten that Christ came to call the sinner, even the most wretched? Wasn't the death of Christ in the shedding of his blood not sufficient for the soul of a murderer? If not, then we are guilty of placing conditions on God's unconditional love!

"I saw firsthand where the guillotine leads a nation. I barely escaped France with my life at the height of the Revolution. Be it the hangman's noose, a sword, a firing squad, or the triangular blade of the guillotine, killing a man for killing a man defies logic. Does hanging a man—in the name of God—provide solace in the face of injustice or does it merely provide the masses with an amusement?"

He didn't give Petit time to answer.

"Never mind the hangman. Did you know that the guillotine

was designed as a humane way to kill criminals? Dr. Guillotine rued the day the murderous device was ever named after him. After he died, his family changed their family name."

Petit had known half a dozen aged priests in Europe who, in their old age would ramble and preach at will such as Badin was, and he longed for the day when he could speak out such as this septuagenarian. Badin's passion for souls was so intense that even though the man was slumped of shoulders and unkempt, his exterior was of a blessed ruggedness exhibiting a wisdom achieved by scholarship tempered by years of pastoral experience with sinful humanity. He discerned a radiant holiness upon the face of the *proto-sacerdos.*

"The Catholic author, Victor Hugo, is leading the reform movement to abolish the death penalty in France. Happily, there are also Americans reading his work, *Le dernier jour d'un condamné* (The Last Day of a Condemned Man), but the majority of them are Quakers, Utopians, and Transcendentalists.

"In Michigan, I witnessed the power of love when the family of the victim forgave the murderer. The story continues to change people's hearts. Now there is a state senator in Michigan who wants to abolish the death penalty in his state, requiring capital offenders to be sentenced to life imprisonment rather than death. The Louisiana legislature is also considering a similar bill." He held his pipe with his left hand but kept it in his mouth.

"Oh, that towering gibbet with its throttling rope or sharpened scarlet blade is a monstrous sight. If the revolutions in France or America had been honest, they would have left everything of the *ancien régime* behind, including the scaffold. To call for the abolishment of the death penalty should be natural for a Christian. How many Protestants condemn Catholics with the word *Inquisition?* Therefore, we ought to lead the way by dispatching the executioner—metaphorically, of course.

"Whether the blade falls in France or the noose swings in America, every death only quickens the desire for more blood. People today are obsessed with letting blood, as if bleeding the human race will improve it. The only time bleeding a man ever wrought justice was when Christ mounted the gibbet of the cross!

"In 1831, the executioner at Albi dropped the blade five times and the poor sinner was still alive with a severed neck. Those in the crowd called for pity but a gendarme wrestled the man to the ground and decapitated him with his sword. Now if that's justice, I long not to live.

"Victor Hugo predicts that one day criminals 'that were once scourged with anger shall be bathed with love. The cross shall replace the gallows.' Beautiful thought, is it not? Unfortunately, we're not likely to see the end of the death penalty anytime soon in America as long as a man's crime and his last breath are exploited by editors to peddle newspapers.

"Now as for slavery . . . ." With that, Badin went on at length, enumerating upon the evils of that *peculiar institution*.

Badin remained at Vincennes for several days. One day Petit saw Fathers de La Hailandière and Badin, both in their cassocks and birettas, walking down Church Street accompanied by a distinguished gentleman in black top hat and dark green coat. Surprisingly, Badin was wearing a new, clean cassock and his boots were greased to a shine. The dapper man carried a walking stick and wore white gloves, a cravat tie, and a cutaway suit perfectly pressed and unmarred by the heat. Petit reckoned that he was a statesman. Walking along the boardwalks and into the dusty street, the man carefully watched his step so as to avoid tainting his polished button shoes with horse-apples and tobacco spittle.

"Gentlemen, this is Governor Wallace of Indianapolis," de La Hailandière introduced him to the men.

"This is an honor, Governor," one of the priests said.

"The honor is mine, gentlemen." The governor bowed slightly and removed his felt opera hat.

"This heat is ghastly," the governor exclaimed, "but then again it could be raining, so I suppose we should count our blessings. I don't know Father, perhaps the rain would be more of a blessing than this infernal heat. It might actually cool things off a bit." The governor wiped sweat from his brow with a fine linen handkerchief that bore his initials.

"Not necessarily, Governor. The summer rains of southern Indiana only tend to intensify the humidity," Father Badin chuckled.

The governor replaced his hat and then removed his gold watch, which was secured to an Albert chain stretching from one of his overcoat's buttonholes. "It's only nine o'clock in the morning and already so abominable."

The men laughed, all except for Father Badin.

"You don't know how *hot* hot is," Badin interrupted, rolling his eyes. "You ought to try living on a Kansan or Nebraskan prairie with the Indians where there's hardly a tree to provide for shade in the scorching heat."

Petit looked at the governor, uneasy that Badin would introduce the controversial treatment of the American Indians to the governor.

The governor smiled slightly as if to humor the old man. "I hope my esteemed Reverend Fathers won't think it too informal of me if I dispense with my hat, coat, and gloves—at least until the ceremony." He draped his coat over his left arm and tugged at his cravat with his right hand, loosening it just enough, leaving it slightly awry.

Petit wished he could peel off a layer of his clothing. Indeed, he had rarely been hotter in his life. He, too, employed a handkerchief to catch the drops of sweat that dangled at the tip of his nose and trickled down his forehead and temples. He had been fasting from food and water since midnight in anticipation of the morning Mass. His mouth was dry and he felt light-headed and weak. The long black cassock soaked in the sunlight, inviting the heat. At least he didn't wear the hair shirt, a penitential garment made of the coarsest horse hair worn under the shirt.

Father Badin did. He felt that the sacrificial nature of a hair shirt would bring him closer to God, unite him more intimately to the cross, and enable him to share in the sufferings of Christ. He felt modern comforts made one complacent, and adopting the hair shirt was an effort to mortify himself and drive worldly thoughts and temptations away. The constant scratching against his skin reminded him of his humanity and his lowliness, a perpetual act of humility. He had already adopted a Spartan diet, believing that even milk and eggs were a luxury for the wealthy. No worldly pleasure should ever displace the experience of penitential suffering, he believed, offering it up to God, especially for the suffering souls in purgatory. Prayer and penance were the marks of a good priest.

"It's good to know it's usually this hot here," the governor sighed, plunking down in one of the wicker chairs on the seminary porch. "At least I won't be blamed for the weather. That's about the only thing I won't be blamed for. Everyone's looking to the government for far too much. Then the abolitionists and state's rights adherents all want attention."

"Perhaps Jefferson was right, Governor" said Badin as he dropped into a chair next to him. "I once met Jefferson in Baltimore. He worried that slavery would divide the nation and dissolve the union. He said that he trembled knowing that God's justice would not sleep forever," Badin boldly stated, pointing his finger heavenward. "How can we ever justify the buying and selling of human beings like they're nothing more than cattle or cotton?"

The governor reached in his coat pocket and pulled out a pipe, a leather pouch of tobacco, and a small box of wooden matches. He filled up the bowl and worked to light it. After puffing a couple of times, he resumed his thoughts. "I too have a growing concern over the spread of slavery. The southerners naively think that as long as the number of slave states and free states remain equal, then things will be just fine. They want the government to annex Texas, but if it does, they want it to be a slave state. Some of the abolitionists have been eagerly courting President Van Buren. The Democrats won't take a stand on it and the Whigs are divided over it. The whole thing's a wild boar if you ask me."

"A wild boar, yes. Governor, Congress does have the right to prohibit or allow slavery," Badin cleared his throat, but his voice was still as raspy, "but there's a higher law, a law higher than our Constitution. It states that all people are created in the image of God! You may also recall that our Holy Father has renewed the Church's condemnation of the slave trade."

"Yes, yes, very well." He puffed out smoke from his mouth, puckering and smacking his lips. "But then again, there are those who think that the Negro is generally happy, well cared for, and secure, far better off than some of the poor or unemployed Irish Catholics dwelling in shanties or being paid in gills of whiskey."

"You're listening to the wrong people," Badin quipped with an edge of laughter in his throat.

"In the South there is a debate among Catholics whether the pope has actually condemned the institution of slavery or only the slave trade," the governor said.

"There have always been those who strain for gnats of ambiguity to justify their immorality," Badin said, folding his arms. "Democrats or Whigs, slavery is wrong."

Petit and the others stood still, not sure where the exchange of wits would lead.

"Then to whom should we listen?" He looked to Badin with sincerity.

"God would be my first choice." Badin spoke softly, winking at Petit and de La Hailandière.

"Yes, well, God's kept himself rather silent if you ask me."

"I find his word to be quite clear. Or have you politicians simply not heard his voice in the rising cries of a people oppressed?"

The governor looked stunned as he puffed on the end of his pipe, leaning back against the weaving of the chair causing it to squeak.

"Do you agree with your party's decision to oppose any efforts to abolish or interfere with slavery?"

"I don't want to argue with you, sir." The governor removed his pipe and raised his eyebrows. "I don't know what to think." He stuck the pipe back in his mouth. "What about all the fear-mongering the Whigs have whipped up concerning the influx of Catholic immigrants? They say a vote for the Democratic ticket will destroy the Union."

Badin kept the conversation going. "I was in Vincennes when the Whig leader, William Henry Harrison, signed the treaty with Tecumseh."

Harrison's mansion still stood in Vincennes and the tales of the unfortunate war with the Indians were common knowledge.

"Don't bother giving me the details," Governor Wallace huffed. "Besides, the Whigs don't even have a party platform!" Wallace was winded and red in the face as smoke escaped his lips. "Harrison broke treaties with the Indians and forced them into exile."

"As President Jackson's Indian Removal policy will do despite the Supreme Court's ruling?"

Governor Wallace jerked his head in Badin's direction, as if he had suddenly been slapped.

"Yes, I know all too well how politics works," Badin sighed. "The Indians are our flock. Let us pray they remain." Touching his throat as if to hold back emotion, Badin continued, "Many of them would rather die than be pushed out to a western prairie."

Petit sensed that Badin would probably say more. Former President Andrew Jackson had signed into law the Indian Removal Act, but the new president, Martin Van Buren, would be the one to enforce the actual expulsion. Wallace looked away and repositioned his pipe. Upon examining it he saw that it had gone out and he nervously fidgeted with it for a while then stuck the pipe back in his pocket.

Wallace sighed noisily and pursed his lips. "Believe me, Reverend, there are nights I lie awake in the silence of my chamber and mull over how we as a nation treat the Indian and the Negro." He pulled his pipe out again from his pocket and struck a matchstick, working to light the tobacco. As it began to smoke, he puffed a couple of times and continued, "Of course, America is a good *Christian* nation."

"With all due respect, Governor," Badin sighed, "Americans have much to learn concerning the Gospel."

"Where's your patriotism, man?"

"In heaven there are no countries, only peoples of every nation, race, tongue *and tribe* gathered around the throne of Grace. Patriotism of the American extreme is a sin against the Mystical Body of Christ. The true country of the Christian is heaven."

"I realize some people are still sore over the Indian Removal Act, and are closely following the Cherokee case, but where else than in America would a government offer to pay a people to leave their land, cover their travel expenses, and then give them a year's worth of wages? They ought to be grateful. Look at all the land we're ready to give them!" Thick smoke encircled his face.

"Yes, and look at the land we've taken from them! Why, by the time your government is finished pushing them west, they'll fall in the Pacific Ocean!" Badin furiously straightened up, standing over the governor. His audacity surprised Petit.

"My government? Aren't you an American as well?" Wallace coughed, nervously shifted in the creaky chair, and scooted away from Badin.

"This is *Indiana*, the land of the Indian. So where are they? Except for the few Potawatomi in the north, the rest are languishing in a western prairie. I'd like to prevent my brother and sister Potawatomi from dying in a Kansan prairie. I lived among their people for years. They're good people, the most civilized of tribes—more polite and more devout than many Americans. Let us pray the Potawatomi are never declared fugitives on their own land, forced off at gunpoint by your troops, or made to walk seven hundred miles into a sea of grass."

Wallace was agitated and wiped sweat from his forehead.

"As a statesman," Badin continued, "you should know that the pillar of true prosperity in a nation is its respect for human dignity. Did you ever stop to consider that the American economy failed after the current administration began removing the Indians? Was it a coincidence or is it a sign from God?

"Remember that your own ancestors were compelled to leave their homeland, driven from their homes in the Old World, and persecuted to the point of becoming aliens on their own soil. Now America is guilty of driving its native population, the original possessors of this land, into an unknown land. The American colonists were at one time defenseless, persecuted, and the victims of aggression, yet now they have become the aggressor and persecutor of another people. Many Americans think they are the people of Israel and the west is the Promised Land. Mark my word, it will only be a matter of time before your government takes the so-called Indian Territory away from them as well.

"Reverend, this *is* a Christian nation."

"So much for all that talk of a Christian nation. Rubbish! Only a fool would think that on Judgment Day America won't have to answer for her atrocities."

"Are you quite finished?" Wallace was on the edge of his chair.

"I was just getting started," Badin said as de La Hailandière moved towards him, as if to restrain him.

"I thought you were going to vote for me?"

"I might."

"I thought Catholics were Democrats?"

"I am a Catholic, first and last. Perhaps all Democrats should become Catholic."

Governor Wallace looked at Badin, and then turned to Father de La Hailandière. "Father de La Hailandière, I did not come here for this. If I want criticism I'll walk over to the Gazette's office." The governor turned away, tugged on his pocket watch, and opened its face. He put the watch away and then pulled out a book from his inside coat pocket.

Petit read the spine: *The Hunchback of Notre Dame* by Victor Hugo. The English author Charles Dickens and the French author Victor Hugo were popular with the Catholic Utopians and Liberal Catholics. However, the Church discouraged Catholics from reading their works because both authors had been influenced by Rousseau, Voltaire, Liberalism, Republican ideals, and Jeffersonian Democracy. In the Church's mind, reading such books was a precarious walk along a narrow ridge of orthodoxy between heterodoxy and heresy.

Hugo's book in its original French was entitled *Notre Dame de Paris*. He had also written *Le dernier jour d'un condamné*, his polemic urging the abolishment of the death penalty.

Petit had read both books while he was a law student.

"Governor, have you ever read Monsieur Hugo's other work, *The Last Day of a Condemned Prisoner*?" Badin asked.

"I've never heard of it," Wallace replied.

"Well, then, would you care to entertain my thoughts on the death penalty?" Badin addressed the governor.

"Not particularly, sir. I've heard enough of your thoughts for one day." The governor stood, tapped his pipe against his shoe, knocked the tobacco out, and appeared quite anxious before settling back down in his chair and opening the book.

"*That's what he thinks,*" Badin laughed aloud, saying to himself. "*I was just getting started. If he stays for Mass, he still has to listen to my sermon.*"

Over the next few days, Father de La Hailandière seemed to grow tired of Badin. Badin, for his part, never tired of telling stories detailing his time among the Potawatomi in northern Indiana and southern Michigan.

Between 1 April and 15 May, de La Hailandière was the administrator of the diocese. Father Shawe and Benjamin Petit, remained with Badin and de La Hailandière. De La Hailandière wanted Bishop Bruté to enforce uniform observance of the Roman ritual, requiring that the sacraments be only celebrated in Latin and not the vernacular of the local people. After the precedent set by Father Badin, and permitted by Bishops Carroll and Bruté, Father DeSeille was celebrating the sacraments in the

Potawatomi tongue and allowing female translators to say the parts of the Mass aloud while he was praying.

Badin explained his mission to Father de La Hailandière. "I lived at St. Mary of the Lake or Notre Dame du Lac in the midst of the Indian missions. What is happening to the people is a tragedy. No words can describe the evil that the American government is preparing to do against the Indian nations. Many of the Indians were told they could keep a small acreage in their native land, and they placed their religious hope in the Catholic Church to protect them from further deception because many of the Protestants abandoned their missionary efforts among them, claiming the Indians were incorrigible heathens."

Badin explained that Father DeSeille had replaced him as the blackrobe at Chief Menominee's village. DeSeille was Flemish, born in 1800 in Ghent, Belgium. Ordained a priest in 1821, he volunteered for the American missions in 1832 and emigrated then. He was assigned to the Diocese of Detroit, Michigan, and was soon sent to the mission at St. Joseph River.

For his part, Father Badin had long taken up the cause for the American Indian. He ministered to the Potawatomi in northern Indiana—along with the half-French-Canadian, half-Indian woman Angelique Campeau. Mademoiselle Campeau lived with the Potawatomi Indians for years as a lay-Catholic missionary. She was well-educated and read Latin serving as an interpreter for the Indians during catechism. During Mass she translated the Latin into the Potawatomi tongue, and when the Indians came for confessions, she knelt and mediated the translation between the Indian penitents and Fathers Badin and DeSeille.

"Bishop Bruté allowed this?" de La Hailandière asked.

"Yes," Badin replied.

"When the U.S. bishops met in Baltimore the issue of the celebration of the sacraments in the vernacular came to the floor. The practice was clearly condemned."

"Are you willing to deprive the native peoples of the sacraments simply because they are celebrated in the natives' own language?" Badin argued.

"The Council of Trent reaffirmed that the language of the Church is Latin, and Canon Law is clear—" De La Hailandière was cut off.

"I am quite familiar with the readings of the Canons!" Badin said as he stamped his cane.

De La Hailandière put his left hand to his forehead and pinched the bridge of his nose, pushing his thumb and first two fingers over his eyebrows. "You didn't allow me to finish my thought."

"We have always taught that we must present the Gospel to the unbelievers on a level that they can understand," Badin argued.

"There is more to the story."

"Oh, yes. God forbid that the natives actually hear the Gospel in their own language!" Badin shot a glance at both Petit and Shawe who were silently standing by. "The Jesuits were expelled from China because the pope insisted that the missionaries could only pray in Latin! Is God illiterate? The early church prayed in Greek. Certainly the Almighty can understand Potawatomi! The ancient Romans knew Latin, not these aboriginal people. I'm not saying we can't teach them some Latin, but must we shut them out from the kingdom of God?"

Petit pondered Badin's words. Badin's argument called into question the authority of all bishops and the authority of the entire Church. Petit was uncomfortable at the tone Badin took with the Monseigneur, yet he couldn't simply walk away.

De La Hailandière said, "Father Badin, I could suspend your

priestly faculties for translating the Latin of the Mass into Potawatomi. As for the woman, Mlle. Campeau, I will forbid her from teaching catechism class and translating the Latin into Potawatomi."

Petit looked at Shawe; neither men said anything.

"Have you gone mad, Monseigneur?" Badin asked. "The woman has taught the Potawatomi for years! She is part Indian herself. Bishop Bruté approved her ministry."

"Allowing a woman to translate the words of absolution and to say the Canon of the Mass is heretical!"

Badin tried to reason with de La Hailandière that the regulations against women in France might not be appropriate in America owing to the missionary status of the Church here, but the Monseigneur only shouted at him, lecturing about the need to strictly enforce the liturgical rubrics.

"The early Jesuit missionaries used the vernacular in the liturgy—"

De La Hailandière raised his right hand and waved Badin off, wanting to hear none of it.

Badin continued, "We ought not oppose the practices of Catholics in America unless the customs oppose Catholic doctrine, violate the Commandments, or contradict the teaching of the Gospel." Badin looked at Petit and winked.

De La Hailandière declared, "You are going to end up like the apostate Lammenais."

"When I was ministering in Michigan, there were three religious sisters who served as my interpreters at the missions there. I celebrated the sacraments here in Vincennes when Indiana was still the Northwest Territory. You've visited the Utopians at *Colonie de Freres* of *Sainte Marie* in Illinois? I thought you understood their whole purpose for coming to America."

"Religious liberty," de La Hailandière answered.

"Ah, yes, but what does that entail?" Badin asked.

"To plant the faith of our Fathers here and foster a devotion to Our Blessed Lady."

"But what about democracy? The Church is to assimilate faith with the new political movements." Badin again introduced an unorthodox thought: "I might remind you that your bishop, Simon Bruté, is a friend of the Liberal Catholic, Lamennais—"

"And even after pleading with him to curb his rhetoric and renounce his radical ideas, Lamennais would not submit to the pope and is an excommunicate and apostate."

"Are freedom of the press and freedom of conscience so radical?"

De La Hailandière didn't answer, likely realizing that anything he would say would agitate Badin even worse. He glanced at Petit.

"Bruté has rejected an aristocratic image of the Church," Badin said. "That's why he came to America. He understands the American Catholic's political goals and social aims."

"Father Badin, no matter what political changes we effect here on earth, they will be nothing compared to the paradise of the Kingdom of Heaven."

"That doesn't mean we can't at least try to render this world a more just society."

"I agree wholeheartedly and I pray for it daily, *adveniat regnum tuum; fiat voluntas tua, sicut in caelo, et in terra*—" (Thy Kingdom come, thy will be done on earth as it is in heaven), a petition included in the Lord's Prayer.

"I know the *Pater Noster*." Badin rolled his eyes as he leaned on his cane.

De La Hailandière looked at Shawe and Petit.

"We are *poor banished children of Eve, heavy with sighs, mourn-*

ing and weeping in this vale of tears, our land of exile, but must we simply accept our fate as it is?" Badin plead.

Petit observed the river's edge where ten to twelve great blue heron with their sharp, pointed bills and flapping wings lifted from the Wabash. The four-foot tall wading birds' legs limply slung below as their long folded necks rose above their flapping wings stretched out in a seven-foot span.

"Sometimes when I see the forest animals and birds and all the natural beauty of America I think this must have been what Eden was like," de La Hailandière said, turning to the other men.

"Tell that to the southern slaves under the whip or the Indians dying of a white man's disease," Badin quipped, "or the Irish dipsomaniacs."

"Now I'm the utopian liberal and you're the Jansenist." De La Hailandière smiled as if to ease the friction.

"Have any of you ever read *Notre Dame de Paris*?" Badin asked them. The English translation was entitled *The Hunchback of Notre Dame*.

"Hugo isn't on a priest's reading list," de La Hailandière replied. "His work was placed on the *Index*."

"One can learn much from fiction, gentlemen." Badin tried to draw Petit and Shawe into the conversation. "Fiction often speaks more loudly than theology manuals."

"Hugo was influenced by Rousseau!" de La Hailandière said.

"Saint Augustine was influenced by the Manichees and Saint Thomas was roundly condemned as an Aristotelian."

"Yes," de La Hailandière countered with a smile, "but Henry VIII was named Defender of the Faith before he became a heretic."

"And Jeanne d'Arc was burnt at the stake by Church authorities, and Thomas More died at the hands of the King of the State that he so loved," Badin sighed and shook his head.

"I am banishing you from the diocese," de La Hailandière said loudly.

"What?"

"You heard me. You are banished from Vincennes—the entire diocese!" de La Hailandière thundered.

Petit was quite uncomfortable witnessing this exchange.

"Why? Because the Gospel is being preached? Isn't that rather extreme for America's *proto-sacerdos*? I've been dispensing with Latin ever since Bishop Carroll, the *proto-episcopos*—first bishop—of America, gave me permission to use the vernacular when and where I deemed it necessary."

De La Hailandière's face was turning red as he glared at Badin. Shawe touched Petit on the arm as if to indicate he was leaving.

"I am going to petition the Holy Father and the Sacred Congregation of Rites securing permission for the use of the vernacular in America," Badin said.

"I do not appreciate your brand of theology. I should have the bishop excommunicate you."

"For what?"

"Besides your disregard for Church law, you also have had no right to get involved in the present political debate over the death penalty. A priest's place is in the sanctuary, not the legislature!"

At that, Badin began to argue with de La Hailandière trying to convince him why the Church should oppose the death penalty.

"Should we leave?" Petit whispered to Father Shawe.

"Not yet," Shawe whispered back.

"Why kill a man to show that it's wrong to kill a man?" Badin asked them all. "How can you teach mercy and compassion if you're killing the man? Christ said, 'love your enemies,' not *execute* your enemies. Bishop Bruté risked his life during the Reign of Terror taking communion to prisoners awaiting execution."

"Father Badin, you are a loose cannon in my diocese."

"*Your* diocese?"

"*Non compos mentis.* You are an eccentric, feather-headed old man. You embarrassed me in front of the governor."

Badin reminded the vicar general that he would continue to criticize the American treatment of the Negro and the Indian and call for the abolishment of the death penalty. Badin then reminded him that there were "enslaved Catholics in chains and dead Catholics swinging from the hangman's noose. The Utopians at Sainte Marie, Illinois, are abolitionists of *both* slavery and the death penalty."

"Father Badin, I must ask you to leave," de La Hailandière repeated himself. "You are banished from the diocese and if you do not leave, I will be forced to excommunicate you. Your ideas contradict the Tradition of the Church. I would be interested in knowing which books and writings have polluted your mind so the Church could place them on the *Index Librorum Prohibitorum*, forbidding others from dabbling in their heresy."

"I have had it with you, Father de La Hailandière," Badin snapped. "Your leanings are with the *ancien régime,* and as a lawyer, the gallows' snare and scaffold's scarlet blade are part and parcel of your legal training in the old school of the aristocracy."

"This has nothing to do with me!"

"What if Catholicism was declared unconstitutional? There are precedents, you know. Suppose you were arrested and imprisoned or condemned to death?"

"I don't think that—"

"Don't be so sure." Badin turned away.

"Your lack of prudence in allowing a woman to dispense with Latin in favor of an inferior tongue is astounding," de La Hailandière said.

Petit knew the canonical prohibitions, but he felt for Badin all the same.

"What can I say? Hearing confessions is one of the most important pastoral duties of a priest."

"Don't you think I know that?"

"Must we passively accept everything as God's will? Do you think it is God's will that the Negro is a slave? Is it God's will that the Cherokee nation is about to be forcibly removed from their ancestral homelands? How long will it be before the Potawatomi are removed at gunpoint?"

"I have no easy answers, Father. As missionaries, we're here to change people's hearts, not to engage in political arguments."

"But don't you realize that we must challenge political thinking in order to change hearts?"

"The Church's teaching is clear and the Church—" de La Hailandière began

". . . is slow to embrace change," Badin replied.

There was silence between them. All that could be heard was the water lapping up against the shore while a couple of herons hovered above soaring on motionless wings.

Shawe pulled Petit aside and nodded indicating that now was the time to leave Badin and Monseigneur de La Hailandière to themselves.

Benjamin Petit knew that the issues of Liberal Catholics were complex, but de La Hailandière was almost desperate to cling to the medieval heritage of the Church in an age of upheaval and change, believing, as did many faithful Catholics, that Liberalism attacked all that was holy.

Father Badin left that afternoon.

CHAPTER 15

THE INDIAN REMOVAL ACT

MAY 20

Many Americans pity the Indians as poor, uneducated savages and believe that Indian removal is the best solution since it is believed that the two cultures—American and Indian—cannot coexist. Therefore, the Indians are to be removed west of the Mississippi River and relocated in what the U.S. government calls Indian Territory.

The Indiana legislature—speaking for many citizens of Indiana—believes the Indian presence is a hindrance to progress, public works, projects, and the growth of the white population. The state officials and land speculators want the land. Indian agents are quick to point out that since the Indians don't farm their land like the Americans, the valuable land is actually going to waste. There is a national sentiment that the notion of Indian rights is anti-American.

Some of the northern states are advocates of Indian rights, and some of their same spokesmen are advocates for the abolition of slavery. Supporters of the Indians believe that the Indian nations are sovereign nations within the United States. Some of the senators and representatives argue that it is morally wrong to displace the native peoples. Some legislators are seeking to prick the conscience of the nation, and they have even warned of divine retribution if Indian removal is enforced.

Bishop Bruté returned from the Third Provincial Council of Baltimore early in May. He was ill with a serious cough. He took ill on his way east when he rode atop a stage in the cold and rain. He returned to Indiana via Evansville. While there he spent a day with the Lincks and recognized a need for a priest in the southern Indiana region since more German and Irish Catholics are immigrating to the Indiana diocese. Bishop Bruté sent the newly ordained Father Antony Deydier to Evansville as its first pastor.

The bishop also received word that the Indian agent had expelled Father DeSeille from the Indian villages of Chickakos on the Tippecanoe and Menominee's village on the Yellow River. DeSeille had been accused of interfering with the U.S. government's plans to remove the Indians. The elderly catechist and interpreter Angelique Campeau was also ordered away. DeSeille had written to say that he was on his way to Detroit to obtain permission from the Office of Indian Affairs to live with the Indians as before. Indian Affairs were under the president's direct control, though the Secretary of War carried out the duties toward the Indians.

The U.S. government was clearly pressing forth with their plans to remove the Potawatomi from Indiana. American agents were being assigned to enforce the Indian removal. Bulletins appeared in newspapers pitching the call for able-bodied men to help effect the Indians' removal once it commenced.

When Andrew Jackson had been elected to the presidency his solution to the "Indian problem," as it was called, was to have the Indians move westward. He introduced legislation into Congress called The Indian Removal Act. The Cherokee Nation's case went to the U.S. Supreme Court; the Court had decided the *Cherokee Question* in the natives' favor: the Cherokee could remain.

If the Cherokees could remain in Georgia, then why couldn't the Potawatomi remain in Indiana? The Cherokee had been granted permission to remain in Georgia and function as an independent government and people within the state of Georgia. However, other American leaders realize that if the law was governed by exceptions to the rule, then the exceptions would be the rule.

The Indian Removal Act did not give the U.S. permission to remove the tribes by force. The *Cherokee Question* reverberated through the country and its decision was foremost in his mind; whatever happens with the Cherokee will be the precedent for dealing with all other tribes. In his heart he feared that all the native peoples may one day be forcibly removed from their territories by the U.S. government. He prayed he was wrong.

The adherents of Indian rights maintained that treaties were contracts between independent communities. The United States had made treaties with Indian tribes for decades, and if the Indian tribes or nations were not independent sovereign nations, then how could the United States have ever negotiated treaties? Indian rights advocates pointed out that Indian communities had been called nations since the discovery of America in the fifteenth century.

Many of the Protestant missionaries held that President Jackson was correct in his assertion that the Indians were not sovereign. They believed it is wise to remove the Indians from the States since they had no rights to the land they occupied.

"These treaties are nothing more than official bribes paid for by the U.S. government," Father Badin has declared. "The goal of the Indian agent is to 'enroll' as many Indians as possible for removal west; band by band, village by village, the agents are dividing and conquering our people."

On the eastern shore of Lake Maxinkuckee was the village of Chiefs Neeswaugee and Quashqua, two Indian brothers.

When their people were required to leave Indiana they submitted peacefully. Chief Neeswaugee gave a speech that was translated and appeared in the Vincennes newspaper.

My white brethren, I have called you here to bid you farewell. My band and I start at sunrise tomorrow morning to remove to an unknown country the government of the United States has provided for us west of the Missouri river. I have sold my lands to the government and we agreed to leave within two years. That time is about to expire and according to the agreement we have made, we must leave you and the scenes near and dear to all of us. The government has treated us fairly, and it is our duty to live up to that contact by doing as we agreed and so we must go. The white settlers here have been good and kind to us; in leaving them it seems like severing the ties of our own kindred and friends. We go away and may never return, but wherever we may be—wherever our lot in life may be cast, we shall always remember you with sincere respect and esteem.

Their ponies burdened down with their packs, the natives marched in single file through the wilderness, following the ancient trails of their ancestors. They were decorated in a bright array of cloth, feathers, and red and black body paint. Their shields of dried buffalo hide covered in deer skin, decoratively painted with symbols and designs as were their tribal blankets robed across their breasts and draped over their shoulders. Their bows hung upon their backs with quivers, full of sharpened arrows, while some balanced rifles over their shoulders.

Not a few tears were shed by all.

CHAPTER 16

INDIAN MISSION TRIP

1 JUNE 1837

*Father Shawe and I argue for Indian rights, as do other
Catholics—clergy and laity alike—though Bishop Bruté has
advised us to stay clear of political arguments. The bishop is
concerned that there might be a backlash against Catholics,
thereby renewing a wave of anti-Catholic persecution; in
the worst scenario, it might render Catholicism illegal in
America. Perhaps these are unfounded fears, but the bishop,
who experienced the French Revolution and its subsequent
Reign of Terror where Catholics—priests and laity—were
often executed simply because they were Catholic, did not
wish to take any chances by giving the enemies of
Catholicism any evidence of what some Americans might
regard as anti-Republicanism.*

Monseigneur Celestin de La Hailandière had asked Petit to
attend the bishop on his mission trip to the northern part of the
diocese. On 29 May, he accompanied the ailing Bishop Bruté to
Logansport. The bishop didn't feel up to the trip, but he
believed that if he didn't make his presence known, the missions
would suffer. Immigrants from Ireland, Germany, France,
Alsace, and Lorraine were digging the Wabash-Erie Canal. At
Logansport there was a large Irish population; the parish is made
up of a large number of the canal workers.

When they arrived in Logansport a letter from Father
DeSeille was awaiting the bishop. DeSeille was now at South

Bend. His request to return to the Indian reserve was denied by Secretary Lewis Cass of the Office of Indian Affairs, a branch within the Department of War.

The fifty-year-old Indiana senator, General John Tipton, a Tippecanoe Battle veteran and resident of Logansport, met the bishop with accusations that Father DeSeille had violated U.S. law.

"Your priest DeSeille has incited the savages to disobey the order to enroll and remove west," Senator Tipton argued.

The bishop mumbled something back in broken English as Senator Tipton, still in his saddle atop his steed, stared down at Bruté and Petit. Tipton was a six-foot, broad-shouldered man, with a full head of sandy brown hair. Buried deep within sunken sockets in his chiseled face were two gray eyes. His stare was intimidating.

"I've been an Indian fighter all my life," he declared. Tipton described how he was born in Tennessee. "When I was only seven years old, my father was killed by Cherokee. My mother and I then moved to Indiana." Tipton was the Indian agent prior to his being elected U.S. senator.

"I don't know why you Frenchmen are wasting your time with these savages. I fought against them here back in '11. All the land at the Tippecanoe battleground site I bought with my own money. I've donated it to the state so a memorial can be erected so that no one will ever forget what the savages did to my people. My best friend, Spier Spencer, died there. And I've never forgiven the Indians for killing my father either. I've sworn to avenge both their deaths and all other American deaths."

"Senator, not all Indians are collectively responsible for the death of your father and friend," Petit interjected.

"Frock, you'd feel differently if your father or friend was

killed by Indians." Tipton then cautioned both of them to obey the law with regard to what they would say to the Indians.

Bruté turned to Petit and spoke in French.

"And if you're going to live in *America*," Tipton said, "then you'd best learn to speak like an American."

"And what native Indian tongue might that be?" Bruté said in nearly perfect English.

"*English.*" Tipton spat.

Petit witnessed the last of the Potawatomi tribe gathered in Indiana in their regal splendor, living out of their dome-shaped lodges and wigwams made of sticks, straw, and mud overlaid in bark and animal pelts and fleece. The natives were hospitable and happy. Their swarthy skin was not quite red and they bore some resemblance to Asians.

The Potawatomi were part of the Algonquin tribes and were related to the Ojibways, Chippewas, and Ottawas. The Potawatomi word for their tribe was *Neshnabek*.

Traveling further north, Petit and the bishop made their way to the remaining Indian lands. Five miles southwest of Plymouth there were three lakes. North of the middle lake was Menominee's village.

Chief Menominee was very religious and was recognized as a prophet among his people. He and his band were devout Catholic Christians and many were baptized by Father Badin. Chief Menominee was a large man, over six feet tall, with large hands, a stern look, creased facial features, and penetrating brown eyes. He was forty-eight years old, had white hoary-frosted hair, red copper skin, and two feathers in his braided hair. He wore leather leggings decorated with ribbons, a fine silk shirt, and a ceremonial red and black blanket was draped over his left shoulder.

Menominee required his people to abstain from liquor and other vices and led his people in morning and evening prayers. He remembered the blackrobes from many years before and had passed the traditions down to his people. He taught that each man will one day reckon an accounting of his behavior to the Great Spirit and that the human spirit lives on after death and is immortal.

The village was located on the north bank of the middle twin lake and some of the wigwams were large permanent wooden structures, almost cabin-like. The wigwams' dome-thatched roofs were made of plant stalks, reeds, bark, and hides placed over bent branches to form the arch.

The Indian men wore buckskin loincloths, leggings, and shirts while their women wore leather shirts and fringed leather skirts. Their moccasins, shirts, leggings, and skirts were made of beaver, deer, bear, buckskin, and buffalo hides. Uncured animal skin—rawhide—with all the fur scraped off was used for drum heads, shields, and robes.

Many of the natives wore fine clothing *a la Indian style*, in the words of the Americans. A number of them dressed in cloth—reds, blues, and whites. They wore frilled and ruffled shirts but instead of tucking them in, they left them out, secured at the waist with a sash or belt. Some of the Indians mixed stylish European and American clothes with native wear. It was not uncommon to see some of the men wearing fine shirts, ties or cravats, and frock coats with fringed and ribboned leather leggings and beaded moccasins. Some men went barechested but wore frock coats with cravats or kerchiefs about their necks and sashes about their waist.

Most of the men wore red or white silk turbans decorated with one or two feathers. The turbans were often long on the ends, and the ends fell from the head and were draped over the shoulders, either in back or in front. Some of the native men even wore top hats, but this was more uncommon. The men wore silk sashes of many colors, especially reds, yellows, and blues, about their waist or draped diagonally across their chests, from one shoulder across the breast.

The Indian style was unpredictable and yet just as fashionable as the Americans' styles. Men often wore their hair long and pulled back with a kerchief. Animal fat was used to grease their locks. Their pendants, rings, bracelets, and earrings of silver and copper bore the French influence. The women wore a mix of traditional deerskin, blue calico dresses, and leather moccasins. They often wore red and black blankets as mantles.

Both men and women wore jewelry, face paints, and tattoos. They used porcupine quills to pierce their flesh and introduce raspberry and blackberry juice under the flesh to make the tattoos. The men either braided their hair at the front, decorating it with turkey feathers, or else they wore turbans with one or two feathers.

The men and women also wore earrings and jewelry of polished shells called wampum beads, ribbons, silver ornaments, animal bone, bear claws, and deer hooves around their necks. Some of the women wore elaborate dresses that were covered with jewelry and silver ornaments. Tattoos were common for both the men and the women. Some of the natives wore face paintings of black and red as well. The baptized would wear red scarves around their necks; perhaps to symbolize the blood of Christ.

SUMMER 1837

The men hunted while the women farmed, sewed, and cooked. The women grew corn, squash, beans, and tomatoes. Corn, squash, and beans were called the three sisters; three sister soup is a favorite dish of the Indians. Only the men were allowed to grow and cut tobacco. It was considered sacred by the Indians.

Indian babies, affectionately called papooses, were carried in a baby carrier called a cradleboard. The baby was placed in the cradleboard and then strapped to the mother's back. Babies were blanketed in soft rabbit skin and buckskins. Children up to a year were carried in the cradleboards.

The native peoples' existence seemed a natural monasticism—without the vows of celibacy—a communal life, poverty of spirit and obedience to one another. However, Potawatomi marriages were often polygamous; this posed an impediment to the reception of the sacraments.

They believed in God—and the existence of evil—and their lifestyle reflected that belief. The religious sense of the Potawatomi was profound. Badin and DeSeille and Petit believed—as did the Jesuit missionaries before them—that the Indians had a natural religious sense of the sacramental. Their faith taught them that they could hear the voice of the Great Spirit in the wind and stream, and the glory of the Creator was revealed in every leaf, flower, and stone.

The Indians regarded the Protestant missionaries' preaching about the total depravity of Man to be both arid and incompatible with their understanding of human nature. Some of the Potawatomi believed that the Americans were depraved in their lust for land and money.

The Indians preferred Catholic missionaries who believed that the Indians and their culture could coexist with the American culture. Unfortunately, the majority of Americans did not concur with this opinion.

The Catholic missionaries' task was to render the life of the savage holy and not necessarily to require him to abandon his lifestyle as he incorporated the teaching of Christ and the Church into Indian culture.

"The Indians are our best congregation," Bishop Bruté said on many occasions. "Father Jean François Rivét desired to educate the Indians—that is the Catholic approach. The American approach is to contain the Indians—and then remove them. As a result, the natives have turned away from American civilization, not because they are barbaric or uncivilized, but because 'civilized' Americans have turned the Indians' culture away."

Bishop Bruté and Petit arrived in South Bend to meet with Father DeSeille. At South Bend, the Catholic couple Alexis Coquillard and his wife, offered their home for the Sunday mass. Besides the Irish population, Bishop Bruté and Petit visited a settlement of German Catholics. The number of German-speaking immigrants to Indiana was increasing just as a large number of Alsatians had made their way to the Picquet settlement in southern Illinois at Sainte Marie, forty miles from Vincennes.

When the bishop and Petit met Father DeSeille, the two were surprised to find Father Badin with him. DeSeille was dejected. The bishop tried to lift his spirits. Badin was there to meet with Bishop Bruté; Badin wanted to sell the land of *St. Mary du Lac* (St. Mary of the Lake) to the bishop.

Badin informed Bishop Bruté that Monseigneur de La Hailandière had banished him from the diocese, but Badin had remained when he learned of Father DeSeille's difficulty with the American agents.

"Your Grace, if you wish for me to depart," Badin said, "just say the word."

"I will not hear of it. You may remain." Bruté shook his head. "I am the bishop."

One of the seminary professors in Vincennes had said, "The American government claims these people have no rights, but they were here long before any of us. You can only oppress a band of people for so long before bringing about a revolution.

"History teaches us that you can't subjugate a segment of the populace for years and then be surprised when they rise up in anger and rebellion. If the Negro were ever to win his freedom and unite with the Indians, America might find itself at war from within."

Petit had initially pondered those words and now recalled them as he considered the implications as he attempted to make sense of his adopted land of America.

Petit was eager to rejoin the Indians; he could not believe such piety could exist. "Their exemplary life!" Bruté had exclaimed. "We thought them barbarous with neither law nor religion, but they have a natural piety."

However, bigoted Indian agents and traders gave the Indians liquor and under the influence of alcohol, the natives signed many documents that forfeited their lands.

Col. A.C. Pepper, Superintendent of Indian Emigration in Indiana and Illinois at Logansport, had accused Father DeSeille of trying to prevent the removal of the Potawatomi.

"Col. Pepper maintains that you have been a troublemaker," Bishop Bruté said to DeSeille.

"I did not encourage the Indians to resist the removal. I can assure you it is their sentiment. Besides, the government has ceased paying the $280 per year for the Indian missions."

"Col. Pepper claims that you and Chief Menominee petitioned him seeking permission to establish a school on Yellow River at Menominee's reserve."

"Yes, I desired to build, but Col. Pepper denied us permission because he claims it betrayed the Indians' plans to remain in Indiana. However, immediately afterwards the colonel then sent me three hundred dollars. Was this a bribe to keep me quiet and acquiesce to their removal?"

Bruté, biting his lip, did not answer.

Later that day the assistant Indian agent at Logansport, Lewis Sands, in the company of Col. Pepper visited the Indian country. Sands was adamant that Father DeSeille had influenced the Potawatomi to believe that their lands were their own and that they could remain. He took the bishop to task. "Unless this priest is removed, the Indians will not remove! He has told the Indians that the Yellow River Reserve's treaty with the U.S. government was fraudulent."

The argument among the agents, the bishop, and Father DeSeille heightened. DeSeille's American citizenship was now in question. They regarded him as a foreign agitator. He was told he might be deported. Pepper was the one who had made DeSeille leave Indian Territory. DeSeille was now forbidden from communicating in any way with the Potawatomi people.

"I encouraged assimilation by teaching them how to farm," DeSeille said. "I made no point in openly opposing Indian removal. I simply defended their right to retain their ancestral lands."

"Clearly you could see how that encouraged the Indians to disregard American demands," Pepper retorted. His facial features were distinct: he had a slightly crooked nose as if it had once been broken and almost feline gray-green eyes.

"I know you are behind most of the Indian protests," Col. Pepper said.

"My business with the Indians is chiefly about spiritual concerns," DeSeille answered.

Pepper didn't believe him. As before, DeSeille invited Pepper to any of his church services as evidence that he was not encouraging rebellion, but Pepper wasn't convinced.

Col. Pepper had held a council two years earlier in August 1836 with Chief Menominee and three other chiefs who shared the land, Black Wolf, Pepinwah, and Rattlesnake. At this time, these other chiefs had been deceived with bribery and liquor and signed the treaty with Pepper. They were to receive a dollar per acre in May of 1838.

Chief Menominee refused to sign Pepper's treaty. (Menominee still held the Tippecanoe Treaty of 1832 and refused to sell his lands.) Now two years had passed and Menominee remained adamant. He was not leaving his homeland. He had never signed any treaty transferring his interest in the property—twenty-two sections of land (14,080 acres).

Yet Pepper cautioned Menominee that his pleas were futile; it was no longer a matter of *if* but only *when* the Indian removal would occur.

Pepper said he was prepared to charge Father DeSeille with obstruction of justice. He had already ordered DeSeille off the Indian lands and forced the interpreter Angelique Campeau to leave as well. DeSeille had entertained the thought of retreating north to just the other side of the Indiana border in Michigan where he could stay at the Indian village of Pokagon. Pokagon's band was going to remain.

When Father Badin joined Bruté, Petit, and the agents, Col. Pepper said to Badin, "I wish I didn't have to deal with you Catholic missionaries, especially you, old man. I thought you was gone for good. You're worse than DeSeille. You're the one who started this mission in the first place."

Col. Pepper turned to Chief Menominee, "The president in Washington City has heard your complaints about the white settlers who have taken your lands. He has made arrangements for you and all your red children to be removed from the evils that surround you."

"The Great Spirit gave us these lands and my bones will be laid next to my ancestors," Menominee stood and adjusted his blanket on his shoulder. "You talk to me as if I were a child. My people and I are no fools. The only concern of your government is to remove us so that it can sell the lands. Let it be known that the land is neither yours nor mine; the land belongs to us all. A man can no more sell the land than he can sell the sky above or the air we breathe."

"These treaties are nothing more than official bribes paid for by the U.S. government," Badin interrupted, speaking to the agents. "Concerning the treaty with the Indians, I hope that it will be respected with the principles of eternal justice, and by honorable means quite distinct from tricks and deceit, unworthy of a great, rich, and powerful nation, such as you have the honor to represent. Although I was born a Frenchman, I am happy in telling you that I have American feelings and that I have breathed more air in my adopted land than in my native country, having landed at Philadelphia in March 1792, so I may boast of being an American citizen.

"Finally, let it be remembered that the Independence of the United States has been procured, in a great measure, by the military, naval, pecuniary, and diplomatic assistance of two Catholic nations and Catholic heroes. You must admit that an impartial government as yours has witnessed our peaceable, patriotic, and constantly loyal conduct and devotedness of the Catholic clergy and of the Sisters of Charity amidst the terrors of the cholera. Do not be deceived by the imprudent and pernicious effusions of the press or certain Protestant pulpits.

"Look at my poor body. My arm dangles uselessly and my legs barely shuffle me along here and there. Soon I will perish and join my fathers. My body will sleep in the good earth and I hope to be saved by the just Judge of all men. I have taken an oath of allegiance to the Constitution and government of the United States. I was an American in feeling and conviction long before I became a naturalized citizen of this Republic. I would now die with a devotion next to that which I owe my God for the country of my choice. But for America to remain great, her citizens must fulfill the commands: 'love thy neighbor,' and 'do good to them that hate you, bless them that curse you and pray for them that persecute and calumniate you.'"

Bruté was hunched over his horse and he struggled to inhale every breath as they made their way to Chief Menominee's village. Petit was concerned the bishop would not survive the trip back to Vincennes.

Chief Menominee explained how the year before he and Chiefs Black Wolf (Mackatawamah) and Rattlesnake rode to Washington to meet with federal officials concerning their lands. The government officials promised them they could remain where they were as long as they owned the land.

Bruté was obviously stymied as to how to deal with the U.S. government's Indian policy and plans for the Indian removal. He was reluctant to allow his priests to get involved in the legal quandary. As a lawyer, Petit wanted to get involved, but the bishop made it clear that his only duty was to speak for the Church. In some ways, Petit felt that the bishop's effort at keeping the peace between the Church and the U.S. government compromised justice. He believed it might constitute a sin of omission. If so, it was an act of injustice. Father DeSeille felt the same as Petit did, but neither would challenge their bishop.

The bishop and his priests believed that the mission to the Indians was effectively at an end. America had moved west. And the Americans were preparing to move the Indians further west.

South of Lake Michigan and north of the Wabash River was Potawatomi territory. Nearly two thousand Potawatomi lived there. Pokagon's village was near the Lake of St. Mary's just inside Michigan territory near Niles. Chief Pokagon vowed he and his people would never leave and said, "I would rather die than agree to their treaties."

Badin had sought to secure property near the natives. He bought a house and converted it into a chapel. He then purchased fifty acres two miles from the chapel near the village. He had long desired to establish a school and orphanage for the Indians near South Bend. At St. Mary's of the Lake, Bishop Bruté surveyed the land and prayed that one day a great Catholic institution named *Notre Dame* would educate young minds there.

Leopold and Elizabeth Pokagon were Potawatomi converts to Catholicism. They cared for the chapel and summoned their people to prayer every morning and evening. Angelique Campeau served as an interpreter for the missionaries, even when the priest heard the natives' confessions. Badin had said of her: "I know of no priest more pious or more zealous for souls than she. She instructs the Indians in the religion and eloquently expresses herself on all that which concerns the faith, the customs, the ceremonies, and the discipline of the Church. Again, I do not know of a priest more industrious, more persistent, more patient, more learned, more genuinely pious than she is in all of this country."

Petit met Mlle. Campeau at Pokagon's village.

Wabenem (White Dog), another Potawatomi prophet, said to Badin, "Father, you speak the truth. When I listen to you I am reminded of the presence of God. You are a servant of the Lord of Life and you have given His message to us."

The natives were patient and long-suffering in light of the abuses they had received at the hands of the white American settlers.

Badin said, "Would to God that American gentlemen abide by the Master's words as readily as the Indians obey the urgings of the Great Spirit. How can they claim America as a Christian nation while it continually breaks the promises of its treaties?"

The evening pow-wows around the campfire were mostly an opportunity to parley with one another and share stories and conversation. However, given the presence of the chief black-robe, one of the evening pow-wows around the campfire filled the forest with chanting, dancing, brass bells, rattling gourds, and the vital drums. The gourds were filled with beans or deer hooves. The drumbeat represented the heartbeat of the people.

Multiple drummers sat around one large, wood-framed deer hide drum. Each drummer had a drumstick with a head of feather-stuffed leather. The drumbeat was also employed to invite the Great Manitou (spirit) to join in the festivities associated with the pow-wow. For the Catholic Potawatomi, Jesus Christ was considered to be the greatest Manitou. The drumming was accompanied by singing. One of the elders played a reed flute.

Tobacco pipes and tomahawk pipes were common. Tobacco was sacred to the Indians. The first puffs were offered to the Great Spirit. The pipes were beaded, feathered, and ribboned. Fathers Badin and DeSeille and Bishop Bruté were treated as chiefs and were offered the pipe. In turn Petit was likewise invited to share in the ritual.

The men wore pes-mo-kins (shirts) with broad ruffles, leather leggings with wings of ribbons, sashes about their waists, frock coats, and turbans topped with feathers. The romantic image of the half-naked savage was nearly nonexistent.

The women often donned multiple bead necklaces and large silver earrings. They wore red and black blanket mantles decorated with ribbons and silver ornaments; many of the garments went down to their feet.

"The dance! The dance!" the Indians cried aloud. The evening was cool and they gathered under the moonlight. The keg drum was pounded upon rhythmically by several Indians while a fire was built in the midst of them. The Indians moved back away from the fire and formed themselves into a circle around the fire.

Some spread blankets on the ground and reclined or sat; others seated themselves on logs or tree stumps. Many of the men savored their tobacco from their tomahawk pipes.

Wee-saw, one of the chiefs, was called upon to dance, but could not unless he received a dollar. He danced around the fire to the beat of the drum and the song of Indian chant. As he did so, he intoned a song in their aboriginal tongue and encouraged others to join in the dance. More and more of them joined in until there were nearly fifty moving at a kind of dog trot. The chant and the drumbeat became louder at times and then the chant was hushed to nearly a whisper and the drum was merely tapped. Then the beat increased in intensity as did the vocal chant.

After a while, some of the Che-mok ko mon (white, pale faces) who were dressed *a la Indian* joined in the dance but their naivete was a cause for much laughter to both the Indians and the whites.

Then the dance changed. Each Indian man began hopping on one leg, alternating left to right, while quickly striking the foot against the ground three times in rhythm with the beat of the music. They would dance backwards, join hands with those they faced, swing each other around with whooping and yelling, and the dance would end with the Indians dancing two abreast.

Then the women who had been standing around the circle until now joined in the dance. But they merely shuffled along, barely lifting their moccasins from the ground as the hem of their mantles brushed the grass.

The natural beauty of the earth was overwhelming for Petit. The trees wept with gentle rain, and cool breezes moved through the lush green of the trees and the sweet smell of wildflowers. Petit delighted in the virginal beauty of the forests and rivers of the

New World. The splendor of the earth, the birds of the air, the animals of the forests, the trees of the woods, the sky and clouds, and the sun and moon and stars revealed the glory of God. What blessings he found there alone.

The late summer whine of the cicadae, almost a deafening high-pitched drone, rising and falling in the sultry heat served as a mantra in the humid, evening haze. The evening sight included thousands of fireflies engaged in their annual mating ritual and the sound of the katydids' repetitious three-note strain in chorus with the songs of crickets and frogs. Unfortunately, there were also mosquitoes. Very large mosquitoes.

A morning or evening walk along the river revealed cranes, ducks, geese, and other waterfowl. The trees were teeming with passenger pigeons, owls, red-headed woodpeckers, blue birds, and red and yellow finches. A literal orchestra of at least two dozen different types of birds, sparrows, swallows, and swifts composed a symphony of their own. It was a considerable pleasure when a migrating flock of northern loons landed on the lake to fish and rest for the night. The loons' mournful nighttime wail of lament and haunting yodeling laughter echoed over the water and through the woods.

The flight of the passenger pigeon was a visual wonder and an exhilarating hurricane roar of wings. The throng of millions of these blue and green pigeons darkened the sky and spanned in line many miles as they eclipsed the sun in the early morning or evening, sometimes taking hours to pass overhead. The male bird stood over a foot tall. They have a long, pointed tail, a slate-blue head, red eyes, a short, black beak, red feet, and wine-colored breast feathers with a green-purplish tint. The females were smaller and more subdued in coloration. Pigeons made a loud, harsh call similar to that of a thrush but they also emitted various soft coos. The oak forests were so thick with these birds that they were considered an endless source of meat and feathers.

The townsfolk and professional pigeon hunters would beat the bushes and trees at night knocking these sleeping birds from their roosts and collecting them in sacks to sell. They were in such abundance that, due to the sheer numbers, many people had grown tired of eating them. The birds fed off the nuts of the numerous beech trees, the acorns of the white oaks, and the berries and insects of the bushes that nestled the creek.

The wild turkeys were hundreds strong. Gobbling aloft, their pinions beat furiously as they foraged for their daily victuals in the woods while the hawk hovered overhead searching for carrion on the forest floor. The bald eagle with its ten- to fifteen-foot wingspan was a noble sight. The majestic bird fished by soaring down on the river's surface and reaching its talons in the water, snatching up its catch, regaining its altitude, and flying to its nest high in the trees. Along with the birds was the airy display of multitudes of diverse species of butterflies, May beetles, June bugs, bumblebees and wasps. The biting mosquitoes and wood ticks were the least impressive of all.

Locust trees blossomed with clusters of fragrant white flowers and the fruit of the tree resembled a locust on its leaves. The yellow poplar trees grew straight and tall and were a favorite for constructing buildings. The pillars in the cathedral at Vincennes were made from poplar timbers.

Though the residents of Vincennes and other towns had cleared most of the forest upon settling the town, the outlying forests of Indiana still reigned supreme. The poplar and sycamores were from ten to fifteen feet in diameter and 150 feet high; some of the trunks had a circumference of fifty feet. The oak and walnut trees were just as large standing at least two hundred feet high, nearly seventy feet to the first limbs. Cherry trees with trunks four feet wide flourished, as did groves of the mulberry and the chestnut. Wild strawberries, raspberries, and blackberries were a delectable treat from the woods.

The virgin timbers were home to a myriad of God's creatures, especially bear, elk, deer, wolves, foxes, panthers, bobcats, opossums, squirrels, chipmunks, and badgers. The bear and the panthers were the least desirable creatures to encounter in the woods.

Robins called all creation forth to worship just prior to dawn every morning with their carols ostensibly marking the canonical hours of prime and lauds. The cock's crow gave rise to a chorus of thrushes, mockingbirds, goldfinches, woodpeckers, cardinals, sparrows, crows, and jays. Waterfowl on brooding wings soared above the river, diving and making their catch only to rise again above the trees in an arc. In its many phases the moon brightly shone over the dark blue western sky, as ravens flew, calling out one to the other. The purple martins, barn swallows, and quails chirped as the red-winged blackbirds lingered at the edge of the corn rows, whistling, while killdeers made a fuss flitting about and running around on the ground. The dove's coo rounded out the morning.

Along the banks of the Wabash River in the morning, Petit beheld the fog gently hovering over the water's surface like incense. The trees were silhouettes against the rising sun. Piercing rays of light glimmered off the dew-dampened grass and thrust through the leaves of the trees while the eastern sky became a golden sheet. The shafts of sun streamed through the wispy, vaporous fingers of melting cloud bearing them away in the heat of the morning orb.

By the time the vesper sparrow had begun its chant, the refulgent evening sunlight glimmered on the water. The glorious color of sunset purple, blue, and red was followed by the song of cricket and cicadae, croak of toads and frogs, and the hoot and hiss of owls. The glowing evening sky apocalyptically perished into a scarlet purple, revealing a canopy of countless star lights. The heavens spoke ever so loudly to his heart.

Petit was sad to leave the northern reserves; he wanted very much to remain with the Potawatomi people. His love for Saints Isaac Jogues and Jean de Brebeuf made him want to become a blackrobe. "Stay with us," one of Menominee's tribesmen had said. He was a young Indian named Nanweshmah. His full name was Abram Nanweshmah Burnett. He looked to be about the same age as Petit.

The pungent smell of the campfires, the aroma of cooking food and tanning animal hides filled Petit's mind and heart with satisfaction knowing that he was fulfilling his hope of ministering in the footsteps of the renowned blackrobes of old.

Petit returned to Vincennes with Bruté, but his heart remained with the Indian people.

CHAPTER 17

ORDINATION

OCTOBER 1837

Oh, how I long to leave Vincennes and return north to the Potawatomi Indian reserve.

Bishop Bruté ordained Benjamin Petit to the diaconate on 24 September 1837. The bishop defended his decision to Petit by explaining that he may ordain him a priest sooner than expected. Two weeks later a black, sealed letter arrived from Mlle. Campeau conveying somber news that rendered Bruté's decision prescient: Father Louis DeSeille was dead.

Father DeSeille had died 26 September; news of this unexpected death reached Vincennes on 6 October 1937. It seemed that when DeSeille finally returned to his cabin at St. Mary of the Lake he took ill and died.

This is without doubt one of the severest tests of missionaries. But, since they expose themselves to the danger only for their love of God, He, being so good, does not abandon them without comfort and support to death. And, if He deprives them of a priest's presence, assuredly it is to embellish their crown of virtues with a final sacrifice. Indeed, I think He accords this favor only to those who are His sainted friends.

Many of the Indians said Father DeSeille's premature death was due to a broken heart so overcome with sadness at the inevitability of their removal. Other Indians were suspicious of the priest's death; perhaps one of Col. Pepper's agents had poisoned him. Col. Pepper had threatened DeSeille with arrest and deportation. Many of the people questioned how such a robust thirty-seven-year-old could suddenly drop dead.

Petit's thoughts and prayers were with the Potawatomi people. But who would minister to their needs now that DeSeille was gone? Mlle. Campeau begged the bishop for another missionary with half the zeal of Father DeSeille. Petit wanted to leave for the northern missions at once, but what could he do? Alas, he was not a priest.

At Father DeSeille's Requiem Mass, the bishop nearly wept as he eulogized the Belgian missionary. "So devoted a priest! So beloved! His death is hard to accept. For seven years he ministered to the Potawatomi people. Who will take his place? Everyday the Catholic Indians are daily being displaced by white settlers. Who will defend them against such injustices?"

The bishop's penetrating gaze met Petit's eyes. "Whom shall I send?" It was as if the words of the prophet Isaiah were planted in Petit's heart and became his own. "*Here I am, Lord. Send me.*"

Petit believed Bishop Bruté favored him. Petit was the same age the bishop was when he first contemplated abandoning his medical studies in favor of the priesthood. The bishop had suggested that he might dispense with Petit's two remaining years of theological studies and ordain him for the missionary field.

The bishop let it be known that the Potawatomi people would not be successful in having the removal law repealed. However faulty or dishonest, whatever may have been the law's origin, even if the fault lay in the documents upon which the law was based, we were admonished to refrain from meddling in what is not in our line of duties. "Allow your bishop this singular privilege," he told them.

It would seem just to allow the Indians to remain among the

citizens of Indiana. Petit found most of the flock of Potawatomi to be loving, reverent, decent, law-abiding, faithful to their spouses, and exemplary Christians. The white settlers among them held a similar opinion of them. The bishop, appalled at the fact that the government believed that the use of force to remove the Indians was a viable option, had resolved to entrust the matter to the Lord. Meanwhile, his health continued to deteriorate. Petit could not but think that his bishop's righteous indignation at the government's decision to remove all Indians has contributed to his poor health.

The sins of a few Indians were being held against the entire race of red men. The crimes of a few Iroquois should not be held against all Algonquin tribes; the Battle of Tippecanoe or the Fort Dearborn Massacre should not forever taint the memory of the Potawatomi nor should they be charged with complicity in the aggression of the Black Hawk and the Sauks. Nonetheless many Americans, both western settlers and eastern legislators, were of the opinion that all Indians were savage and a threat to the American way of life. The horrors of the French Revolution and Reign of Terror were not learned in America. The tragedy of holding all Indians accountable for the sins of a few Indians made as much sense as arresting and executing all aristocrats simply because they were aristocrats.

Such is the face of prejudice. One race of men—the one in power—holds another race or all other races as inferior. The saddest aspect of it all is that many Americans have never known the Indians they had set out to remove, preferring instead to fear the unknown, basing their opinion of the Indian on hearsay and campfire tales of past Indian raids. Yet from the Indians' perspective they were merely defending their ancestral homeland. Which is worse: defending one's homeland or driving a people from their homeland?

9 OCTOBER

"Benjamin, I must speak with you," Bishop Bruté said, grasping Petit's left arm and walking with him momentarily after Morning Prayer and Mass.

"Yes, Bishop."

"It concerns the untimely death of Monsieur DeSeille. The Potawatomi people have no priest. They have written me lamenting the fact. Here is the letter." He held it up for him to see.

"Were I ordained, my Lord, I would volunteer at once."

"Are you in earnest, my son?" he stopped walking.

"Oui," Petit said as he turned toward him. "Father Bernard Schaeffer is familiar with the territory."

"You bring me to the point right readily." He paused, looking intently at Petit. "I have also received word that Father Schaeffer died of cholera in Chicago on the second of this month."

Petit's stomach moiled; he and Schaeffer had endured the Atlantic voyage together. Schaeffer was barely thirty. Petit and the Bishop had just visited him at South Bend.

Bruté cleared his throat, regaining Petit's attention. "Your crazy Bishop Bruté now has the idea of ordaining you a priest."

Petit wasn't sure whether it was a crazy idea or if he had fallen out of favor with him. "My ordination?"

"Oui."

"But there are more capable men than I. Father Mueller is at Fort Wayne—

"Yes, and he will remain there."

"Father Claude François is at Logansport."

"Oui, but neither men are my choice for South Bend and Twin Lakes."

Bruté put his right hand to his forehead and chuckled. "Our beloved vicar general, Monseigneur de La Hailandière believes I am spoiling you as if you were my youngest son."

Petit said nothing as he studied the red buttons on Bruté's purple cassock that went from his collar to the hem. His matching purple mozzetta, a short hooded cape, covered his shoulders, and just under the mozzetta, his unadorned silver pectoral cross was pinned to the front button. Bruté adjusted his magenta zucchetto skullcap atop his sparse gray hair.

"Benjamin," Bruté paused and glanced down at the signet ring on his left hand. "I want to ordain you to the priesthood within the month."

"Your Grace, I need more time."

"I realize this. Please know that if I could give you more time I would."

"But what of Canon Law? I have three remaining years of study. I am not even a deacon yet. I must serve as a deacon before priestly ordination."

"Canon Law was meant to serve the Church, not hinder evangelization. Reverend Shawe, our Canon lawyer, will deal with the anomaly. The Potawatomi need a priest! How much longer they will be in our diocese is unknown."

Bruté took Petit's right hand in his. "The Potawatomi need you, my son. You are mature beyond your years. You have also acclimated to the customs of the American way of life and have become proficient in the English language, but most of all you are familiar with the ways of the Indians. Your time with Father DeSeille during the spring and summer of this year was invaluable. Even Chief Menominee asked when the quacking Blackrobe Petit will return. Did you not learn the Potawatomi tongue while you stayed at Menominee's village?"

"Yes, your grace, but hardly enough to become their pastor. I will need a translator."

"The Lord will provide. You are my choice as Father DeSeille's successor. Please allow me this one indiscretion. You will learn the language well enough. Most importantly, you love the Potawatomi people. Don't forget I was with you several days to observe your labor among the tribe. You are already a Potawatomi and soon you will be nothing but a Potawatomi. None of my priests has ever learned their tongue as readily as you have. You have the heart and soul of an Indian."

"I am hesitant to agree, Bishop," Petit said, "owing to my need for further theological studies to fully understand Church teaching. Yet in the present state of affairs, I should not object to my ordination if you judge it expedient."

"You must become a priest." Bruté was firm.

"Your Grace." Petit knelt and reverenced the bishop's ring.

"Then it is decided. I shall ordain you and send you north to minister to the Indians at Pokagon's village at the south bend of St. Joseph River and Menominee's village at Twin Lakes on the Yellow River Reserve."

Petit reached for his rosary and quietly told an *Ave*. His heart was already with the Indians. He prayed he could spend his life on the missions.

14 OCTOBER 1837

Three weeks before, Petit had been ordained a deacon. Now, a fortnight later, he was about to be ordained a priest. He approached Bishop Bruté. Reverend Shawe stood to the bishop's left holding his pastoral crozier, the symbol of the bishop's authority over his flock, and Monseigneur de La Hailandière, the vicar general, the deputy to the bishop, stood to Bruté's right.

Petit carried his priestly vestments on his left arm and carried a lit candle in his right. He knelt on the altar steps before the bishop's chair while Monseigneur de La Hailandière, read aloud to the bishop. "Most Reverend Father, our Holy Mother, the Catholic Church, asks that you ordain this deacon to the burden of the Priesthood."

"Do you know him to be worthy?" the bishop asked.

"So far as human frailty permits us to know, I both know and attest that he is worthy of this office," replied de La Hailandière.

"*Deo Gratias*" (Thanks be to God). Bruté paused, looking at Petit with a sweet tenderness which put him at ease. "With the help of Almighty God, we choose to raise this deacon to the Order of Priest. If anyone has anything against him, let him, for God and for God's sake, come forth and speak; but let him be mindful of his own condition."

An obligatory pause followed. The silence was displaced by the bishop's voice. "Blessed are the feet of them that preach the Gospel of peace, of them that bring glad tidings of good things! Have your feet shod with the examples of the saints, in the preparation of the Gospel of peace. May the Lord grant you His grace."

"Amen."

"My dearly beloved son," Bruté continued, "you are about to be consecrated to the office of the priesthood. Endeavor to receive it worthily and fulfill it in a praiseworthy manner. Offer sacrifice, bless, preach, and baptize. Let your doctrine be a spiritual medicine for God's people and may the sanctity of your life be the delight of Christ's Church; that by preaching and example, you may edify the family of God."

At that, Petit was directed to prostrate himself before the high altar as the choirmaster intoned the Litany of the Saints. Lying prostrate during this portion of the ceremony, he experienced the same total and complete surrender to the will of God that he had experienced less than a year earlier while lying on the floor of Sainte-Germaine's Church in Rennes the night he made the decision to come to America.

Afterwards, Monseigneur de La Hailandière assisted him to his feet, and Petit knelt before the bishop again. In striking silence, Petit felt the hands of Bishop Bruté cover his head as he prayed quietly. A warm sensation exuded from the top of his skull to his extremities as the bishop prayed: "Receive the Holy Ghost, for strength to resist the devil and his temptations."

The other priests in the sanctuary processed around, laying their hands on Petit's head in like fashion: de La Hailandière, Shawe, Buteaux, and others. Afterwards, the bishop handed the Book of the Gospels to him. "Receive the Gospel: Believe what you read, teach what you believe, and imitate what you teach."

Bruté then dressed him in his sacerdotal vestments. The bishop then sat again while the ancient hymn to the Holy Spirit, the *Veni Creator Spiritu*, resounded.

An attendant carried a small wooden box with three round tin containers of holy oils to the bishop. The bishop opened one of the tins of oil and dipped his thumb in it. He then held Petit's hands and smeared the oil on his palms. "Consecrate and sanctify these hands, O Lord, by this unction and our blessing." He made the sign of the cross over them. "That whatsoever they bless, may be blessed, and whatever they consecrate, may be consecrated and sanctified in the name of our Lord Jesus Christ."

Bishop Bruté then clasped Petit's hands and bound them together with a linen cloth. The bishop, holding Petit's hands in his, leaned towards him. "Do you promise reverence and obedience to me and my successors?"

"I do, with the help of God."

"The peace of our Lord be ever with you."

Petit stood at the bishop's signal and he then embraced him in the kiss of peace.

The bishop then spoke to him about the nature of the priesthood. "Believe that in bringing souls to Christ apostolic works alone cannot suffice; without personal holiness and a life of prayer, a priest is powerless to confer holiness upon any member of his flock. The priest, as *alter Christus* (another Christ), must willingly become a victim like his Lord, immolated for the glory of God and the salvation of souls. If a man seeks to share in

Christ's priesthood, then he must be prepared to share in his victimhood, placing himself on the altar as an oblation in union with Christ the Savior. All Christian believers are called to be ambassadors of Christ, but the priest is called to be so in a unique way for he gives of himself completely to Christ and the Church."

Whatever else the bishop may have said was lost to Petit; the idea of being a victim for Christ remained with him.

The bishop had Petit kneel before him one final time as the bishop imposed his hands on Petit's head. "In accord with Canon Law and by the apostolic powers granted me as a successor of the apostles, I bestow upon you the power of the keys given by our Lord to Saint Peter. Receive the Holy Ghost: whose sins you shall forgive, they are forgiven them; and whose sins you shall hold bound, they are held bound."

Petit glanced up at the altar and saw the painting of Saint Francis Xavier, the patron saint of missionaries.

His priestly mission had begun.

The next morning, Petit awoke at dawn and walked along the banks of the Wabash River pondering God's will for his life. He returned to the cathedral and prepared to celebrate his first Mass. He carried the veiled chalice and paten from the sacristy into the sanctuary of the cathedral and genuflected at the foot of the altar where he prayed. The stained glass windows of the cathedral's east walls were brilliant with the morning sun. He ascended the steps of the main altar and meditated upon the crucifix above the tabernacle as he prepared to celebrate the sacred mysteries.

Kyrie, eléison. Christe, eléison. Kyrie, eléison (Lord, have mercy. Christ, have mercy). *Sanctus, Sanctus, Sanctus* (Holy, Holy, Holy).

He lifted the paten with the host and after kneeling in homage, he raised the chalice of wine. He knelt again. He remembered his mother and brother and sisters and his entire family at the *memento*, the parts of the Eucharistic Canon where the priest calls to mind the living, and he called to mind his father at the commemoration of the dead.

After receiving communion and the concluding rites of Mass, he knelt on one of the sanctuary prie-dieus to offer his prayer of thanksgiving.

By mid-morning he began packing his belongings to make the journey north to take up his missionary responsibilities to the Potawatomi people of northern Indiana.

"May the Lord be with me," he prayed.

CHAPTER 18

MISSION

15 OCTOBER 1837

My prayers have been answered. By God's abundant and undeserved grace, the bishop has ordained me for ministry to the Potawatomi Indians. Although unworthy of the dignity, I am now a priest. My hands have been consecrated to God. The Lord has chosen a weak instrument to further His Kingdom. My voice now renders the Word of God flesh! How my lips trembled this morning at my first Mass when I commended my mother and family to God! And so shall I again tomorrow and the day after and every day of my life until the last!

I packed my tent and belongings and put them on Pierre, Father DeSeille's horse. The bishop gave Pierre to me as an ordination gift; however, he is an old horse.

My mission territory is over 200 miles north of the city of Vincennes, and I am going to a people that I hardly know. But it is God who is sending me to them; therefore, I will trust that all shall be well. I am nothing compared to the glory of God. Yet how well Saint Paul said it: "God loves to accomplish great things by using that which is nothing; he takes those the world considers nothing and makes them something."

I have always considered myself a fortunate son. I realize that I shall be all alone in the wilderness. The closest priest nearly one hundred miles away. Yet the Lord shall be my strength; His right hand shall hold me fast.

I must say that the dominant feeling in me is a profound joy under the burden of my new obligations. I feel so light at heart, so happy, so content, that I am wholly overwhelmed by it. To go from Mass to Mass and then on to heaven.

When I think that in two days I shall start from here all alone, I know that I am not alone for I go forward in the company of God who reposes on my breast night and day in the Eucharistic Presence, carrying on my horse my Mass kit: missal, paten, chalice, and the other essentials, the very instruments of the great Sacrifice, stopping from time to time in the depths of the forest and making the obscure hut of a remote Catholic the Palace of the King of Glory!

Ah, then I abandon myself willingly and, I must say, at this time that is so important in my life, I have not yet felt anything painful! All has been the sweet rapture of God's will, who Himself ordains and executes through His grace. Ah, with what delight I put my trust in Him! I have asked for prayers, for now is the time.

Although my future as a missionary in the middle of the Indiana wilderness is so uncertain—and there is no guarantee that I will not meet the same fate as my predecessor—I am overwhelmed with a sense of joy and urgency in spreading the Gospel message and administering the sacraments to the native peoples.

I am to bestow sacraments (graces ratified in heaven) among people whom I do not know, but to whom God sends me! I tremble at the thought of my nothingness. Therefore, I go to console a tribe of Indians who are without a Father.

I had always longed for a mission among the Potawatomi people and it is I whom the Potawatomi will henceforth call their beloved Father Maketakônia, robe noir—Father Blackrobe.

When Father Benjamin Petit arrived at Menominee's Yellow River Reserve, the natives surrounded him as he rode in on his horse. He dismounted and waded into the crowd of Indians to greet them as their pastor. He engaged in the handshake ceremony and listened attentively, attempting to learn their names and as many of the Potawatomi words as possible. Nanweshmah, the Indian man about the same age as Petit, spoke English and some French and served as Petit's interpreter. Thereupon Benjamin Petit was hailed as Maketakônia: Father Blackrobe.

"We were orphans, and as we were in darkness, you appeared among us like a great light and now we live," one of the influential young chiefs named I-o-wah said. He wore a red silk turban with a gold star sewed on the front and a single turkey feather.

The greatest spectacle in the community was the pow-wow and dance. Petit had partaken of one of their tribal dances before when he had first visited northern Indiana with the bishop. The evening was cool and under the starlight they gathered around the fire to a festival of chanting, dancing, ringing brass bells, rattling bean-filled gourds, clacking deer hooves and bear claws, and of course, the vital drums. The drumbeat was employed to invite the Great Manitou (Spirit) to join in the festivities associated with the pow-wow.

Chief Menominee emphasized that the drum represented the heartbeat of the nation and the people themselves. The drummers encircled the large drum; it was a deer hide stretched over the top of a hollowed out tree. The sound of the drum echoed through the woods and across the lake.

Menominee handed Father Petit a feather-stuffed leather drumstick and invited him to be one of the drummers at their dance. Petit sat on a buffalo-hide-covered log bench between Nanweshmah and Menominee. Furs, bear skins, buffalo hides, and blankets were spread on haystacks, logs, and the ground for everyone to sit or recline on while the great bonfire blazed in the center of the circle.

Nanweshmah, Abram Burnett, was well-educated and multi-lingual. He spoke French and English besides his native Potawatomi. He also knew some of the Ottawa tongue as well as some Shawnee, Cherokee, and Chocktaw from his days at the Chocktaw Academy in Kentucky.

Some of the young braves began to sing. One of the elders intoned a playful melody on his wood flute.

The head men ceremoniously presented Petit with a pistol for self-protection in the woods along his journeys. He refused it at first, but then he understood that it may be needed for self-defense. They also gave him a ceremonial calumet tobacco pipe. It was decorated with feathers, wampum, and ribbons. The men wore bear claws and deer hooves around their necks, and Nanweshmah presented Petit with a deer-hoof necklace. The women presented him with a blue, green, red, and white multi-colored blanket draped with ribbons, ornaments, and wampum.

Before retiring for the night, each Indian—man, woman, and child—came forward to Petit, ardently shook his hand, and bowed their head for a blessing. He obliged by then tracing the sign of the cross with his hand over their heads.

At daybreak the cool, dewy morning air was filled with the gamey smell of venison smoking over a hundred fires. The smoke hovered over the cabins, wigwams, and tepees, while shafts of brilliant sunlight pierced the wood smoke. Petit took in the natural beauty of the Indiana wilderness: the sweet smell of vegetation, trees, and wildflowers. The Indians bathed in the lake and encouraged Petit to do the same. He loved to swim and took advantage of the pure waters of northern Indiana. The cool, refreshing feeling of the water was a blessing untold. The bright sun, blue sky, white clouds, green forest, and fresh air were nearly sacraments themselves: to feel the warmth of the sun and the cool wind, hear the rustle of the leaves on the trees, and breathe deeply the air. Particularly pleasing to Petit was the splendor of the lake. The Indians teased Petit and said he liked the water as much as the ducks. He wasn't for sure, but he believed they had given him the Indian name *Chichipé* (duck).

He was taken with the chorus of birds, but of them all, the loons with their haunting cry and yodeling laugh and the ivory–billed woodpeckers' flute-like tooting. The whip–poor–will kept him awake sometimes with its nighttime call of "whip–poor–will," uttered over and over again hundreds of time.

Petit watched the women pounding corn into meal and corn-meal batter. The batter was shaped into cakes and baked or fried in a pan or over a griddle to make cornbread or hoe cakes, also called cornpone. Some of the Indians actually taught the white settlers how to make hoe cakes by baking them on the blades of their hoes. The women also farmed: hoeing, digging, planting, weeding, and looking after the plants. Likewise they kept the home fires burning, cooked the meals, and cared for the infants and children.

Some of the women not only shared in domestic duties, but also shared the same husband. The practice of polygamy was a matter of practicality, ensuring that all children and women would be cared for. Often two sisters would be married to the same man. Petit likened it to Jacob and his two wives, Leah and Rachel.

NOVEMBER 1837

Petit was living at the Yellow River Reserve of Chief Alexis Menominee. His wife was Angelique Sagike, and together they had several children, the youngest was three-year-old Mary Ann.

There were over one hundred wigwams and cabins, not including the tepees belonging to a few guests. Petit's cabin was at a location called Chichipé Outipé, which means "Duck Head." Subsequently, he had received the Indian name Chichipé, the Duck. Lizette Angelique, the nine-year-old daughter of the Chieftess Mas-saw and Andrew Goshlieu, a French Canadian Catholic, gave him the name because some of the Indians believed he laughed like a duck. Indeed, his French tongue may have made him sound like a duck.

From the first day he arrived at the Yellow River Reserve, the natives welcomed him as their father. They came to him saying, "We were orphans, but you have appeared to take the place of our father who died. You will preserve for us the way of prayer taught to our ancestors by the blackrobes of old. We pray you will not be our last blackrobe." The children gathered about him as ducklings to their mother. What humble innocence. If only the people of this country could have come to know them as he knew them. Such humility.

Life at Menominee's village centered on community life and faith in God. At sunrise Petit rang the church bell and the Indians made their way from the woods and their cabins and wigwams to the log chapel. The clapboard-covered, wood-shingled log chapel was thirty by forty feet and stood in the center of the village on the north bank of the largest lake. The loft in the west end of the chapel was where Petit slept.

Chichipé Petit's interpreter was the seventy-two-year-old lay missioner, Mademoiselle Angelique Campeau, who ministered with Father Stephen Theodore Badin for many years among the Potawatomi. Under her direction, the Indians recited morning prayers and she delivered a sermon. They then sang a few hymns and celebrated Mass. Petit preached his sermon, and Campeau would translate it into the Potawatomi tongue. They would conclude with a Pater and an Ave and sing a Marian hymn. Afterwards they quietly left the chapel.

This holy woman was, indeed, one of the most edifying missionaries. Often Petit heard confessions through the day—with her interpreting—until vespers in the chapel at evening. After evening prayer they ate supper then gathered for a catechism lesson. Petit exhorted them to live the life of grace and gave them his poor blessing.

One of his closest Indian companions was the twenty-five-year-old Nanweshmah, Abram Burnett; his is a fascinating history. His grandfather was a French Canadian and his grandmother was a sister to the Potawatomi Chief, Chebass. His mother was Conezo-qua and father Shau-uque-be. Nanweshmah was born in northern Indiana along the Tippecanoe River.

In 1821, at eight years of age, Nanweshmah Burnett's father was killed in Michigan. Nanweshmah was then taken in by the Baptist missionary, Isaac McCoy, and a year later he was enrolled in the Chocktaw Academy in Kentucky where he learned English. In 1827, he left the academy at age fifteen. From that time on he had lived with his tribe bridging the gap between Americans and Potawatomi as an official interpreter for the tribe. He and Petit conversed most in the native tongue. He had yet to be baptized, but admitted he was partial to Catholicism and if he were to become Christian he would ask Petit to administer the sacraments to him.

Nanweshmah had recently been appointed Indian interpreter for the U.S. government and was part of the first official delegation of Potawatomi chiefs who traveled to Washington City to petition the U.S. president to allow the Indiana Potawatomi to remain.

Nanweshmah assured Petit that many of the Potawatomi believed he had been sent to them as an answer to their prayers. Petit had baptized nearly thirty Indians, over half were adults, and had blessed nine couples with the sacrament of holy matrimony. He had also administered over 120 first communions as well.

Many of the natives, while deprived of the sacraments due to Father DeSeilles' death, had practiced spiritual communion with all the ardor of pious longing. Petit felt that the conversion of these good people was wonderful: they would leave their homes and go far away to be with those who desire to be made Christians, to teach them what they must know in order to know Christ. Some of the people who could read traveled to the outlying Indian villages solely for the purpose of teaching prayers and the catechism.

If it were necessary to retrace everything Petit's heart had felt, paper would not have sufficed. His soul was overwhelmed by the sweetness of the Lord's favor and he did not know how to thank Him or the bishop, His servant, for having granted him this wonderful beginning in the holy ministry.

Not that sometimes there did not arise certain clouds, certain anxieties, but they are calmed by prayer and trust in God. These good Indians had given Petit their confidences so entirely, they surrounded him with so much filial attachment that it was only by weeping and rending his heart that he could tear himself away from their touching farewells, carrying off in his heart something of the sentiment that he knew nearly two years ago when he left his family in Rennes.

The communion of saints was a doctrine that the Indians readily understood for they believed that their ancestors' spirits lived on after death and watched over them. The natives lived each day as if it was to be their last. Overall, life was a struggle between good and misfortune, light and darkness. Planting and harvesting crops and celebrating fertility, birthing, and dying were all concrete experiences of the sacred and the sacramental.

The men and boys were taught to be in control of their emotions; this was important for a hunter and warrior. The native peoples might have appeared somewhat somber and grave, but they truly were most happy and cordial.

The habits and customs of the Indian culture were otherworldly. They were generous and hospitable with their meals and gatherings. They offered Petit the pipe of peace as if he was one of their own chiefs. The smoking of tobacco was a religious ritual for the men. They were intrigued by Petit's briar pipe; their pipes were made of clay and were called calumets.

At the ceremonial gatherings, a few of the older Indians wore their best clothes. Many of them could still recall the Battle of Tippecanoe and other skirmishes with whites.

Feasts of corn, beans, pumpkin with goat milk, pork, chicken, wild turkey, rabbit, squirrel, passenger pigeon, turtle and boiled turtle eggs were some of the favorite dishes.

The Indians played games such as stickball, spears thrown at a moving disk; football with a feather-stuffed, deerskin-covered ball; quoits, a game in which flat iron rings were pitched at a stake, similar to the game of horseshoes; Yuh-youh-tche-chick, played with a ball and curved stick like Lacrosse; and moccasin, a game of chance similar to the shell game. They also played wink, a staring contest where the first person to "wink" or blink lost. Oftentimes they gambled at these games. But they especially liked to wrestle.

Around the campfire, time stood still. The conversation and tobacco were entertainment enough, though the drums, music, song, and occasional dance fully complemented the evenings.

At the cribs of the young, "dreamcatchers" were fashioned to ward off evil. Petit tried to explain that the talismans were superstitious. But one of the unbaptized Indians, Chief Pepishkay, answered: "They are no more superstitious than your holy water and prayer beads."

There was one anomaly among them—some of the chiefs practiced polygamy. Petit could not see a way clear to dispense with the laws of marriage. Several of the chiefs had postponed baptism due to their irregular marriages.

Boys and girls passing into adolescence spent time alone fasting and praying to the Great Spirit and asking their ancestors for guidance. This practice was not so different from the Catholic custom of praying to patron saints.

Young boys were taught how to use bows and arrows, shoot rifles, and hunt and fish. During the winter, the boys bathed in the icy lake or river to build endurance. They also had a vision quest after puberty. Each boy was to go into the wilderness alone and fast and pray for several days until his guardian spirit appeared to give him his personal medicine and mission.

There were also legends among the people of a Mandidog or a Kegangizi—an evil water monster or sea serpent, a great fish with horns that inhabited Lake Manitou (Devil's Lake) and underground rivers. Some at Menominee's village believed there is a water panther at Twin Lakes that feeds on human flesh. The Indians sprinkle offerings of tobacco on the lake to appease the mysterious creature's anger. Whether such leviathans dwelt beneath one of the lakes was questionable, but for the Potawatomi they existed.

At the end of the lower Twin Lake at Yellow River Reserve was a grist mill called Barber's Mill. People went there to grind their corn; wheat had yet to be introduced here. There was a dam across Yellow River and a sawmill near Plymouth. There were several taverns near Twin Lakes that provided food and shelter for settler and traveler alike. One of the most popular taverns was Grove Pomeroy's, located at the intersection of Michigan and LaPorte streets in Plymouth. Osterhaut's was two miles south of Plymouth while Hickman's Tavern was south of Twin Lakes.

One of the largest cities in the Diocese of Vincennes was Chicago, Illinois. It was the site of Fort Dearborn where an Indian massacre took place in 1812. The fort still stood. Over four thousand people lived in Chicago. Some people believe it would one day be a major center of commerce and trade.

Meanwhile, Petit learned of a tragic incident in the lives of members of his tribe. Chief Aubbeenuabbee, in a drunken fit killed one of his wives. His oldest son, Paukooshuck, was urged to avenge his mother's death according to tribal law. He waited until Aubbeenuabbee was drunk and buried a tomahawk in his skull. Another story had that he stabbed his father in the back with a long knife and run him through. Paukooshuck then became the chief of the village, but he had since begun to drink to excess. The act of patricide was ever on his mind.

There was no question that there had been enough bloodshed between the races. The older Potawatomi regretted the shameless murder of women and children by Potawatomi warriors in the Fort Dearborn Massacre. They also regretted the loss of life in the Battle of Tippecanoe. Yet many Americans still feared that the Potawatomi would return to their warrior past and avenge the memory of their ancestors.

Yet Petit asked, "Is God's mercy ever exhausted?" Many of the Potawatomi had forgiven the Americans and had asked forgiveness from them as well.

The hospitality of the Potawatomi people knew no bounds. Petit enjoyed the tobacco of the peace pipe with Chiefs Menominee, Pcheeko, Macketomoah (Black Wolf), I-o-wah, Mukkose, Notawahah, and Pepinowah. The rest of the tribe looked to them for their wisdom. Chief Mukkose was especially known for his honesty and integrity.

Chief I-o-wa's younger brothers were Majoquis, Weesaw, Weewissa. Their mother was Kaukemazoqua; she was over a hundred years old. She often recalled when the first American settlers arrived in Indiana; she also related the initial fear that she and the tribe experienced.

Chief Pcheeko and some of the other Indians had American flags hanging outside their wigwam in an attempt to allay settlers' fears that the Potawatomi were on the warpath. Another Indian was Kawkawkay. Though not a chief, he was one of the patriarchs of the tribe. He had fought in the battle of 1811 at Tippecanoe and was an old man. He always wore red and carried a tall staff to help him walk. The man walked everywhere; in fact, he refused to ride a horse and had never ridden one.

"I might as well walk in the woods to die," the snaggle-toothed Indian told Petit at the campfire after vespers one evening. "None of the younger men in the tribe listen to me anymore. I'm just an old dog. I might as well be dead. I don't know why I'm still alive."

"God still has a purpose for you," Petit assured him, "Even if it is simply to pray for your people. Kawkawkay, no human life is worthless."

One of the older chiefs was Po-ke-queh (One-Eye); he had taken an arrow in the eye as a child.

Joseph Barron was a Frenchman in the employ of the traders, Ewing, Walker & Company, and had married an Indian woman. Barron was born of French parents in Detroit about 1765 but since encountering the tribes he was more Indian than French. He was seventy years strong, with a slender build, dark eyes, and long, gray hair tied back in a black-ribboned ponytail. He had a pallid complexion, heavy eyebrows, large nose, high forehead, and bald crown. He could sing, dance, and wrestle, but particularly fascinating was his ability to speak seventeen languages: French, English, and fifteen different Indian tongues. His French and English were good, though he could not read or write in any language.

Another Indian family that Petit had become close to was Andrew Goshlieu and his dark-skinned, brown-eyed wife, the Chieftess Mas-saw, and their daughters, Lizette and Mauri. Goshlieu was a French Canadian and was employed as a trader with the Ewing, Walker & Company. Chieftess Mas-saw was quite good at euchre and poker. She could rake men of all their money. She had a large, two-story log house with two rooms on each floor. The daughter Mauri, though only fourteen, was already married to a white man Henry Taylor, also known as Yo-ca-top-kone. He was a trader with the same company of his father-in-law. Mauri loved Henry and was amused when he would don Indian apparel and sing and dance at the pow-wows.

Chieftess Mas-saw and nine-year-old Lizette were seated next to Petit one evening around the fire. "Father Chichipé," Lizette began, toying with the string of beads about her neck, "will you always be our Father Blackrobe?"

"Why do you ask?" Petit removed his pipe from his mouth.

"Chief Weewissa's mother, Kaukemazoqua, believes you are our last blackrobe." She turned to directly face him. "The last blackrobe of Indiana."

Petit replaced his pipe and said nothing as he stared into the blazing campfire. His thoughts were on the imminent threat of the Indian's removal from their beloved Indiana. The distant howl of wolves and a hoot of an owl distracted his thoughts.

He was interrupted from the evening pow-wow when Yellow Butterfly, an Indian girl, approached him with a desire to confess her sins. She was ashen in color. Yellow Butterfly had experienced a dream that she considered a portent of her death. Chichipé Petit discouraged her from placing too much faith in premonitions. In her dream she was left behind as the village burned; she dies and is abandoned by the tribe. Petit blessed her and sent her back to bed. She returned to her wigwam and he to the pow-wow. A thunderstorm ended the festivities earlier than expected and Petit returned to his cabin.

In the middle of the night, two Indian children, each with a torch, came to Petit's cabin and awakened him. Yellow Butterfly was violently ill with convulsions. Petit wrapped a woolen blanket about himself and went forth with his own torch in his hand. In the dubious light, the children took him by the hand and led him through the lightning and rain to her wigwam in the woods. By the time they arrived, the girl had fallen unconscious after falling into the hearth in the center of the hut.

Petit gave her Extreme Unction and when he started to depart, the family begged him to stay. He slept on a mat near the fire. In the middle of the night, he was awakened by the silence; the rain had stopped and the moon was looking down from on high, revealed by the hole through which the wood smoke escapes.

By morning, Yellow Butterfly's condition had worsened. She was cold to the touch and her lips were blue. Petit tried to console her mother. He said the prayers for the dying and granted her final absolution. He departed for a time in order to eat. He prayed vespers and Compline at the chapel with the tribe. Around midnight, a single rifle report was heard; her father had fired his rifle to alert all in the village of his daughter's death. This was a common custom among the tribe. One of the young Indian boys, Little Crow, came to tell Chichipé Petit the news.

Petit dressed and rang the death knell. Many of the Indians assembled in the chapel to pray the office of the dead. The following day Petit said a Requiem Mass for Yellow Butterfly before laying her to rest.

Petit observed caravans of pioneers in their horse-drawn wagons moving through the wilderness—most likely on their way to buy up Indian lands from the government at a $1.25 per acre.

A resident of Indiana was called a Hoosier. According to some, the word meant "an unusually large and uncouth frontiersman." In some sense, Petit believed the definition applied, given the number of free-for-all melees, men dueling with swords and pistols, and killing helpless creatures—even fellow humans. The American settlers and pioneers were well-armed with rifles, pistols, knives, and swords.

In some of the most vicious duels with swords, ears were sliced off, eyes gouged out, and others run through completely. There had also been vicious murders in the woods accomplished with a rifle or an axe. A recent funeral near Logansport was a requiem for a murder victim killed in a duel over a woman. Another day two men were killed, one of them had been stabbed working the canal, and the other was a merchant killed in a shootout over a gambling debt.

On one occasion, while walking and praying in the woods adjacent to the river, Petit had encountered some wanton roughs engaging in the savage sport of a gander pull. Pity the poor, pathetic goose whose neck was greased with lard and hung upside down by its feet from a large tree limb fifteen to twenty feet above ground. The roughs mounted their horses, rode under the bird, and grabbed its head in an attempt to twist its head off. The one who managed to survive the flapping, squawking, pecking rage of the bird and snap its neck was hailed the victor.

When the men saw Petit in his cassock, they made inappropriate gestures and crowed out jeers against the Catholic religion. Their sacrilegious banter centered on Petit for being both a Catholic priest and a Frenchman. He minded his own business of prayer, trying to ignore their murmuring and made his way beyond their gathering, but not before hearing a mock chant of, "Hocus, pocus...Frock, go home."

Fulfilling his missionary duties, Chichipé Petit also made his way to visit the shanty communities of the Irish canal workers who were digging the Wabash-Erie Canal. The laborers digging the ditch, as it was called, were Irish immigrant laborers. Many were dying of malaria.

Petit worried that he may contract the swamp fever, but it was a risk he must take to bring Indian souls to Christ, and in the case of the Irish, bring souls back to Christ.

The intense malarial fever leaves half its victims dead. There were those who blamed the disease on stagnant water or bad air while others claimed it was transmitted by birds, flies, or mosquitoes. The habit of eating raw fish was a likely factor in their illnesses as well.

Others suffered from cholera since the drinking water was tainted with human urine and excrement owing to the lack of sanitation and poor hygiene of the male workers. Dung from the horse and mule teams went straight into the drinking water.

Exposure to the contagion caused profuse diarrhea and vomiting, followed by dehydration and shock. Death often came within hours of the first symptoms. Regardless of the causes of death, Petit fulfilled his mission kneeling before temporary altars made of barrels and crates, hearing deathbed confessions, administering the Last Rites to men stretched out on straw mattresses, and presiding at funeral Masses in the Indiana forest.

Were the diseases signs from God? Were the illnesses a plague from God, Divine Judgment being visited upon the Americans for their government's treatment of the Negro and the American Indian? Some of the abolitionists thought so. Some of the native tribes claimed that the Great Spirit had called down a curse upon the white man as an act of vengeance; while many Americans blamed the Indians and the immigrants for the nation's economic woes.

While pondering the physical scourge amid the wretched living conditions and severe heat, Petit granted absolution of spiritual maladies and anointed the dying. At the same time, otherwise healthy, whiskey-bloated Irishmen engaged in bare-knuckled savage brawls or melees with clubs and swords, oblivious to the squalor about them. Whole shanty towns of fifty to a hundred men assembled to battle one another in a barbaric game dubbed Gaelic football. After a day-long game, bloody and unconscious bodies could be found strewn along the banks of the canal's tow path. Grown men, drunken and angry, fighting over a bundle of cork and chicken feathers. Many of the Irishmen are Catholic in name only, in bondage to the whiskey and prostitutes that the American canal entrepreneurs and financiers provide them.

As he administered the rites of the Church, the ditch bosses would ring a bell and distribute the morning pay to the Irishmen: a gill of whiskey for each. In the face of such widespread drunkenness, it was not hard to understand why Father Badin took the pledge to only drink tea and water; he hoped to set an example for the Irish laborer, mere white whiskey slaves to their American lords.

JOURNAL

November 1837

1-2: visited St. Mary's Lake
3-26: remained at Chichipé Outipé
26-27: South Bend
28-30: Bertrand, Michigan

A calumet full of sweet tobacco, a simmering stew of beans, corn, and squash, a plate of fresh game, sassafras tea, a bonfire, and my circle of native Potawatomi children performing their songs and dance to the accompaniment of the drum—I prefer all this—and more—to the feasts of "civilized man."

I feel a singular attachment for everything which concerns the natives. When I travel in the woods, if I see an Indian cabin, even an abandoned camp site I feel my heart beat with joy. If I discover some Indians walking along my path, all my fatigue is forgotten. Their smiles greet me from afar—nearly all of them know me, and even those who have not been baptized call me their father. I who am only twenty-seven years old! Some of the men are four times my age and yet I am their father. Such affection refreshes me as if my own family was welcoming me.

When I am on a mission among the whites, my Potawatomi worriedly count the days of my absence, and I too consider my arrival at Chichipé Outipé as a feast day. What joy, what handshakes, what blessings before and after evening prayer! When darkness comes, they cannot seem to leave my wigwam. They seem to be nailed there as I recount the story of salvation history!

Ah, when I am away from them it is a weighty cross. If they be removed from Indiana—God forbid—they will be under the protection of Our Lady, Notre Dame. And I pray I would be allowed to accompany them.

I am told that I am what the Americans call an "Indian lover." Well, if that is what I am, then so be it. Our Blessed Lord said, "Blessed are you when they utter all calumny against you, for whatsoever you do to the least of my people that you do unto me." How least can one be if not a savage? Yet these savages are not savage. They are kind and loving.

Were I not here to bring the message of Christ to them, I would believe they could teach me His ways simply by their placid life. They seem to be closer to God than some of our French clergy—and certainly they are closer to Christ than some of the Americans who are seeking the Indians' removal.

The Potawatomi people are missionaries themselves. If only a few French and American Catholics would imitate their example of charity. The natives take the word of God with them wherever they go, teaching others the catechism and speaking of the love of Christ. Their lives are like living examples of the lives of the saints who lived on sparse provisions day to day and spread the Gospel.

Already the Indians take my hand and thank me for devoting my life to them. One of the older men of the tribe told me—with tears in his eyes—that he would never forget what I have already done for his people. "You console us," he said. "What will we do once the white man leads us into exile? To whom shall we go?" The question was wrenching. My heart is with this people—indeed, the Potawatomi people are my people. I believe if I continue to spend time with them, I myself shall become Potawatomi.

I love to walk through the village and see their smiling faces. On the last day I was among them, they gathered round me in silence and asked my blessing. As I departed Menominee's village, I had the same feeling I had the day I left Rennes for the final time. Even though I was only going away for a short time, it was as if I was leaving home. Indeed, I was leaving home; the Potawatomi are my family now.

There are other mission sites for me to visit here: St. Mary of the Lake, South Bend on the St. Joseph River, Pokagon's village, Bertrand, Michigan City, and other Indian settlements in northern Indiana and southern Michigan.

I practice the Potawatomi tongue when I ride, praying the

rosary in the natives' language. The sweet smell of wood smoke from the wigwams and cooking fires of Chichipé Outipé permeates the forest.

God has long called to me in the silence. And this is where He has called me.

CHAPTER 19

CHICHIPÉ OUTIPÉ

My ministry at Tête de Canard or in the Potawatomi tongue, Chichipé Outipé, (Duck Head) has become dear to me. I consider myself singularly blessed as I exercise the holy ministry to the savages. I actually find that word disagreeable, for the Potawatomi Indians are not savage by any means. The true savages I have encountered so far are the Americans who ply the Indians with alcohol and sell them superfluous trinkets in order to take what little money they have. The Indians have no idea of the worth of cash, and they wind up frittering away what little wealth they have. The Americans are also spoiling the land with fences while laying the forests low.

My greatest fear is that the United States government will destroy the culture of my people. For they are my people now; I am their blackrobe. The U.S. government seeks to remove all native peoples to the west of the great Mississippi River. I am forever caught between hope and fear. The U.S. Indian agents intend to do all in their power to aid in the removal. It is a dark cloud hovering over the good I am trying to do.

Should the government have their way, the Indians' faith will dry up and they will be left to languish under an unknown sky where I, their father, shall be unable to follow. All the same, I shall do all in my power never to abandon them.

If they leave, then I wish to accompany them. I will do all in my power to join them. God alone knows how my heart grieves the prospect of their departure. As long as the Indians remain in Indiana, I shall be their missionary. Their attachment to me, and I to them is stronger than ever. Yet some days the fear comes over me that I shall see this mission destroyed. Ah, were I but free! When they go westward to the Mississippi, they would not be without a priest!

Amid my clouds of anxieties I am heartened by prayer and trust. As we enter the Advent season, my command of the Potawatomi tongue is progressing. More and more I go without the aid of my translator, Mlle. Campeau. Nanweshmah says I already speak as a true native.

One of the Indian chiefs, Black Squirrel, came to Petit for confession. He was a good Christian, yet he was in an irregular marriage. The situation was thus: before he was baptized, he married a wife, yet they were not agreeable. He sent her away and married another, Floating Cloud. Before he died, Father DeSeille had told Black Squirrel to dismiss his present wife and return to his first wife. Black Squirrel refused to go along with the recommendation. DeSeille then forbade him from entering the chapel and receiving communion until the marriage situation was rectified. This situation persisted for a year. Even when Black Squirrel presented himself for confession, DeSeille refused to hear his confession as long as he refused to return to his first wife.

With the advent of Petit's arrival he had ascertained that the first wife of Black Squirrel was actually his brother's widow. This made it possible to grant a dispensation owing to the irregularity of that union. Petit called Black Squirrel and his present wife, Floating Cloud, to the chapel where he instructed them that they should fast and pray—and refrain from conjugal relations until Sunday when he would marry them. They came early that morning for confession and Mass. After Mass he blessed their union with the sacrament of holy matrimony. Black Squirrel, gloomy and sad before, was alive again.

It was one of the greatest joys Petit had ever experienced. *Omnia ad Majorem Dei Gloriam* (all for the greater glory of God).

7 DECEMBER 1837

The Potawatomi were preparing to protest the treatment they received at the hands of the U.S. government. The Yellow River Reserve Treaty of 5 August 1836 was again in question. Chief Menominee refused to sign the treaty. He argued that the treaty was indeed illegal—a "whiskey treaty"—because the Americans gave the Indians whiskey to get them to sign and agree to remove, and the treaty was in no way applicable to his people, who had sold nothing. Chiefs Menominee and Sun-go-waw (another chief who had converted to Catholicism), Nanweshmah (acting as interpreter), and an American attorney were preparing to leave for Washington City. If the government was just, then they would certainly redress the wrongs committed. Some of the Indians who signed the treaty did not even live on the Yellow River Reserve. Other chiefs who did live there had not signed—Chief Menominee in particular.

Petit wrote the bishop that if this folly of Indian removal wasn't challenged and the president made to see the egregious injustice of it all, then the most edifying congregation in the entire diocese would be lost beyond the Mississippi. Petit exclaimed, "My heart bleeds at so much injustice. If this is allowed to happen, then will it not likewise be heinously unjust to sacrifice the innocent to the guilty by keeping silent?

"If the Indians cannot find a way to go to Washington themselves, I could go with a power of attorney from them."

If the bishop would allow it, Petit was quite up for it. Not that he wanted to leave his missionary post; it would be a trial to be away from the Indians for the weeks it would require.

Petit's mother had written to assure him that there were French benefactors ready to dispense the necessary funds for the Indians' cause. She had already sent him 400 francs. This would enable him to make the trip at his own expense. How could he abandon them without an attempt to protect them? After all, they were the original inhabitants of this country.

Petit entrusted the matter to the Holy Virgin and prayed the bishop would allow him to make the journey. He would promise to keep his absence from the diocese as short as possible.

Madame Clark, a Protestant lady, came to him in tears seeking the sacraments for her and her entire family. When he inquired as to why she and her family desired to become Catholic, she explained that it was due to the holiness exhibited by the native peoples. She was also repulsed by the Protestant congregations' almost unquestioning acceptance of the governmental policy of Indian removal. She spent a great deal of time explaining how the U.S. government seemed to have convinced many Christians that some of God's children were unworthy of defense against injustice. Petit commended her on her principles: "When basic human rights are violated, the Church cannot be used to further a particular political agenda. In France we have seen all too well the negative effects of the union of altar and throne. Many Christians in America are politically engaged to a fault; they are Americans first and Christians second."

Petit's horse, Pierre, had been ill. Some of the French residents at South Bend told him that Pierre must be eighteen or nineteen years old. Indeed he was on his last leg. The last time he rode Pierre, the horse could not go more than ten miles. Madame Coquillard, the wife of Alexis Coquillard, the agent with the American Fur Company, promised him another horse. Mme. Coquillard was a Good Samaritan among the Indians.

13 DECEMBER 1837

The bishop wrote Petit expressing his concern that his young priest may be blurring the lines between his spiritual role and his former life as a lawyer. Petit prayed his bishop would forgive him, but Petit believed that even one act of injustice threatened all justice and all people. Bruté was concerned that Petit's influence may encourage the Potawatomi to disobey the government's orders to remove if their appeal was not granted. Though Petit had not told them to disobey, he believed it would be a grave injustice if they were removed. If it did happen that the government required them to be removed, he vowed to do all in his power to prevent all out war with the American soldiers.

He would assist the Indians in removing west, but he could not deny that such removal would be a grave act of inequality in a nation that prides itself on its Declaration of Independence that declares all men are created equal, endowed by their Creator with the right to life, liberty, and the pursuit of happiness. His vow of obedience to his bishop would likely preclude him from accompanying them west. In case the worst occurred, he must be prepared to part ways with them though it would be a great sorrow in his heart.

Meanwhile, Petit gave $140 to the Indians of Chichipé Outipé. Chief Menominee would need it for his journey to Washington City. Petit also promised to assist Chief Menominee in writing a memorial—a written petition that was to be presented to the legislative and executive branches of the U.S. government. He hoped it would aid in briefly explaining their case so that when Menominee went before the president, he would be able to make him understand the facts of their situation completely. Menominee would deliver it, and Petit's name would not appear anywhere on the document. It was a simple and logical exposé of the facts. Petit tried to prove legally that not all the Yellow River Potawatomi signed the treaty in question, and the ones who did sign either did so without knowing what they were agreeing to or they were not even of the Yellow Reserve.

Petit made no accusations against anyone. After all, not all the Indian agents were prejudiced, even though most of them had been labeled so. He believed he could remain silent no more. Some of his fellow priests may have feared he was becoming too political, yet all he had done was write a letter for an illiterate people. This is a service that can hardly, with charity, be refused them. The poor Indians have been deceived by lawyers, Indian agents, and interpreters. They have been made to say what they do not mean, and so Petit happily volunteered to write their communiqué.

As it is, the treaty was not a law as Petit saw it. What the Indians sought was for the president of the United States to declare the treaty fraudulent. The president had the power to execute it or refuse to sign it into law.

"I fear I am still too much of a lawyer and not enough a priest," Petit prayed. "Just when I think I have cast aside my former life, the voices of the weak, demoralized, and oppressed rouse in me the thirst for justice. Yet is that not also priestly? Who else but the priest can raise his voice against an unjust aggressor?"

In the midst of such inner turmoil, the Indian children enjoyed snowball fights with their missionary father. Young Foxtail, one of the newly baptized, took great joy in wrestling Chichipé Petit to the ground and baptizing him with ice and snow. If only his mother and brother could know how much he loved his mission, his children.

Petit set about to do the work for which he was ordained and packed his saddlebags, mounted his horse, and rode north to Pokagon's village. Pokagon's village was sixty miles north of Chichipé Outipé. Chief Pokagon fasted on Fridays and led his community in prayer each morning and evening. They would reverently make the sign of the cross, kneel, and recite the prayers and commandments in their native tongue.

Chief Pokagon, dressed in his ceremonial robe and feathered turban, delivered a sermon in Petit's presence. "You will not be abandoned. The God of your ancestors, who dwells in the heavens, will send you blackrobes. Jesus gave to the world a great chief of religion to teach men the truths which He brought down from heaven and which He Himself taught on earth. The Savior Jesus died nailed to a cross but arose on the third day and ascended into heaven. During his earthly ministry he established a great chief who was to reside in Rome, the capital city of the world across the sea.

"This great chief himself was also crucified testifying to the truths which Jesus had taught. This great chief was Saint Peter, the rock on which Jesus built His Church. Jesus promised that His Church would ever remain and the powers of hell would never prevail against it. Jesus gave Saint Peter successors who would instruct the world's people in His way of Salvation."

After the prayers, Father Petit raised his hand in blessing and dismissed the gathered tribe. Pokagon then turned to Father Petit and asked, "Father, tell the truth. Will the blackrobes remain with our children always? Or will you too go away? It is our hope and prayer to always have the blackrobes among us."

"That is my hope and prayer as well," Petit replied.

Petit had much to reflect upon as he packed his belongings and rode to Bertrand and South Bend. He wrote Bishop Bruté:

14 DECEMBER 1837

Dear Bishop Bruté,

I am ashamed of myself, Monseigneur, and I fear you find me still too much a lawyer. I should perhaps have cast that spirit far from me, and yet it was at a time when the weak and oppressed people had no sure defense against the oppressor other than the priest's voice. Could you give them a letter of recommendation to the attorney and statesman, John Ewing of Vincennes? He is an elected member of the U.S. House of Representatives in Congress.

The Potawatomi want me to accompany them east to Washington City in the spring so as to present their case before the highest authorities in this land. Of course, I am no longer an attorney; I am a priest. Consequently I shall leave the decision to you. My dear Monseigneur, if you find me in too much ardor and zeal for the savages, you will excuse me, will you not? For though I have known them only a short time, there is an inconceivable tenderness for them in the bottom of my heart which the good Lord will bless, I hope. Might it not turn out that this will give me the happiness of offering to Him the pain I shall feel in leaving them, if you wish it so?

Monseigneur, I may be mistaken, and I often am mistaken through ignorance, but I hope the good Lord will pardon me, for he reads in my heart a great desire to do well for his glory. And thanks a thousand times to you; you will pardon me, too, for I know your fatherly indulgence for your devoted son and priest, Benjamin Petit.

I had a conversation with a Protestant woman desiring to become a Catholic; she is a believer and is well educated. I do not think it will take too long. From listening to her, she is practically a Catholic already in thought and sentiment. She came to Mass today in spite of the extreme cold and icy roads. More ladies came from as far as Bertrand, Michigan—a seven-mile distance. They tell me of other Protestants who desire Catholicism. It would be a pity to abandon this post. If I am not to remain here, please try to send another priest here.

Your Obedient Son,
Benjamin Petit, missionary priest

15 December 1837

"The crows cry with envy every time they hover overhead as I ride poor Pierre," Petit told Nanweshmah. "The horse is as good as dead. I might as well ride a tortoise. The idea of a journey on this poor creature is hopeless. I am sure he was at one time a good horse, but his time has come to retire. If ever there was a carcass, he is one."

The government agents had not prevented Petit from taking up residence in the old house from which Father DeSeille was expelled.

Petit continued to feel such an attachment to the Indians, such ardor of spirit. For though he had only known them a short time, there was an inconceivable tenderness for them in his heart, which the good Lord will bless, he hoped. Might it not turn out that this charity would give him the happiness of offering to God the pain he shall feel when he must leave them. Or will they be forced to leave him? Or shall they leave together? These were unanswered questions.

With the bishop's approval, Petit would take up residence in the house on the lake at South Bend. He thought it appropriate since Father DeSeille was there and it was a more central location in the midst of his mission churches. It was only twenty-seven miles from Chichipé Outipé at the Yellow River Reserve.

The vicar general of Detroit, the younger brother of Rev. Stephen Badin, had given Petit permission to celebrate the sacraments in the Michigan territory. He would therefore celebrate Christmas Midnight Mass at the village of the Frenchman Joseph Bertrand. His trading house was a few miles south of the old Carey Mission on the St. Joseph River just on the other side of the Indiana border in southern Michigan.

The day after Christmas he planned to ride to Chichipé Outipé and celebrate Christmas with the Indians. He was quickly learning the native language and to his own amazement hardly required the services of a translator. It was as if this was his specific calling by God, for the language almost came naturally, though the natives continually laughed at him in jest and said he sounded like a duck.

Petit had also befriended Alexis Coquillard, the French Indian trader who lived near St. Mary's of the Lake near the St. Joseph River. Mme. Coquillard was most charitable with her money.

Many Protestants were coming to see Petit, inquiring about the Catholic faith. Even with the extreme cold and all the snow and ice, they came. Some of them wished to become Catholic owing to the Protestant endorsement of Indian Removal. Many of these Protestants have lived among the Indians for years and did not wish to see their neighbors removed. He waited to see what would become of the Cherokee nation. Most Indians believed that if the Cherokee were removed then the Potawatomi have no chance of remaining.

26 DECEMBER
CHRISTMAS

The good bishop wrote me before Christmas. He is concerned for my health since I am unaccustomed to the climate. It is likely my mother has again written him with her concerns. I admit I am surprised at my health. The week before Christmas I left Bertrand and rode twenty-four miles in the midst of a snowstorm—not on my dead horse—but in a sleigh pulled by Mr. Bertrand's horse. The sleigh overturned nine times—superb! We laughed like children. We finally arrived at our destination—Chief Pokagon's village—around two o'clock in the morning.

I finally went to sleep after three a.m. and was up by seven the next morning. I was as fresh and fit as you can possibly imagine. I remember a time in my life when I would have coughed, grown pale, or fainted with exhaustion, but I was not a missionary then: that makes quite a difference. I said Mass, gave another sermon, and then heard confessions all day. The next day I said Mass and gave Extreme Unction to some of the sick and returned to Bertrand.

On 23 December, nearly seventy of Pokagon's Indians arrived at the chapel at Bertrand. Petit heard confessions until sunset. The next day Mr. Bertrand took him by sleigh back to South Bend where Petit celebrated high Mass for a mixed congregation of French, Americans, and Indians. Afterwards he returned to Bertrand where he baptized seven (three of which were Indian adults), heard confessions until eleven p.m., and celebrated midnight Mass with sermons in French, English, and a smattering of Potawatomi. The next morning he was at St. Mary's of the Lake for confessions and High Mass/

After these Masses, sermons, and confessions, Petit was indeed very tired. That afternoon while in his cabin at the lake he fell asleep in the armchair by the fireplace. "Thank heaven for the generosity of these good Catholic families," he wrote the bishop. "Were it not for the Bertrands or the Coquillards, I do not know if I would be of any service to the Lord."

Petit was so tired at Christmas that he hardly felt any devotion. The reason behind his melancholy was the knowledge that the Yellow River Treaty would expire in August of 1838. At that time Menominee's people would have to remove. It was his own dark night of the soul.

As for his horse, Pierre, the time had come for him to be put out of his—and Petit's—misery. He asked the bishop for a new horse. "It is a necessary possession in such a wilderness. In many instances I walk rather than bother with the miserable creature, but one can neither walk the long distances nor trudge through all the snow without exhaustion. Mme. Coquillard has promised me a new horse, but for too long have I depended upon the generosity of the Coquillards and the Bertrands; I do not wish to abuse their kindness any longer. A missionary requires a good horse. I regard it as necessary for his ministry."

Mr. Joseph Bertrand, the founder of the trading post on the east side of the St. Joseph River that bore his name, had just returned from the Mississippi River where he conducted a group of Indians who were required to relocate there owing to a treaty agreement. He was not impressed with the territory. Mr. Bertrand was married to Chief Topenebe's daughter, Madeline.

"My Potawatomi are not easily fooled by the government's promises; the Indians do not believe in the alleged benefits of removal," Petit told Bertrand.

Meanwhile, Petit prepared to go to Chichipé Outipé to preach a mission for the Indians. If the bishop would allow him to leave the diocese in the spring for the U.S. capitol at Washington City, he was prepared to defend the rights of the natives. Regardless whether he was with them or not, Chief Menominee was preparing to leave soon with a delegation from the tribe. Petit did not know if they all would be able to travel; they were having difficulty allocating the money for the trip. They were ready to give him power of attorney. The bishop had yet to decide whether he would allow Petit to go east. *Omnia ad majorem Dei Gloriam.*

Petit wrote his mother to express his joy of service.

The natives are my people, my family—a family that I love very much. When I am away from them my heart is torn. I am never happier than when I am with them, and I feel as if I will die if I am ever separated from them.

My children: Chieftess Mas-saw and Andrew Goshlieu; their daughters Lizette and Mauri; Mauri's husband, Henry "Yo-ka-top-kone" Taylor, the displaced English trader turned Indian; Chief Alexis Menominee and his wife, Angelique Sagike, and their children; old Chief Ashkum; young Chiefs I-o-wah and Mukkose and their respective bands; the catechists Angelique Campeau and Chief Sinagua; Arrowhead and Turtle Woman and their sick child, Little Tree; the soldier Thomas Robb and his Indian wife, Sin-is-qua (Pebble), and their six-year-old daughter, Nancy, and infant son, Wash-Shing; Sin-is-qua's sixteen-year-old daughter and her husband Captain Richard Reed; the old head man, KawKawKay (No Horse); even Paushuk, the salacious sinner; and Pepishkay, the sincere skeptic; and all those in need of redemption; the young men, Wolf-Nose, Fox-Tail, Chipmunk, Flapping Crow; and the women, Sunrise, White Fawn, Red Leaf, and Demoskikague (Little Girl). Several of the young braves have their hearts set on Demoskikague, but I believe I know which man she has set her heart on: Nanweshmah. As the natives say: the medicine between them is good.

JOURNAL

December 1837

1-10: South Bend
11-18: Bertrand, Pokagon's Village, Bertrand, South Bend.
19-21: South Bend
22-23: Bertrand

24-25: Mass at St. Mary of the Lake

26-27: South Bend

December 28 – January: Bertrand, Pokagon's Village, Bertrand, SouthBend, Chichipé Outipé.

February 1838: Chichipé Outipé. 28 adult baptisms, 7 children baptized, 5 marriages, 107 communions. Received a new pair of moccasins.

> *The evening pow-wows of winter consist of conversation and storytelling directed to handing on the tradition of the tribe and their ancestors. I believe Providence desires me to remain with my Potawatomi family.*

CHAPTER 20

EPIPHANY

5 JANUARY 1838

I am at Chichipé Outipé in the bosom of my Indian church. The mission is laborious, but what consolation! I shall not repeat it—it is always the same miracle—an incredible succession of conversions among these poor natives. There are close to twelve hundred Christians among them and what fervor! What touching simplicity! The spiritual ties which the ministry forms are sweet and strong, like all the manifestations of the love of God, whom we serve.

Chief Sinagau, Petit's first catechist, was known for his remarkable wit, eloquence, and deep faith. He had been very ill, nearly unable to walk and in great pain prior to my arrival. When his Indian neighbors and his own family prepared to leave for Chichipé Outipé chapel, he desired to be with his people and with his ardor for Christ that he insisted that he be placed on his horse so he could ride to Mass. He wept with pain as he clung to the horse. After he arrived and was helped off his horse, he was doubled over, barely able to walk. With great difficulty he leaned on his cane and dragged himself to the chapel.

During the Mass, there was a commotion but with my back to the congregation I was unsure what was happening. As I turned to distribute Holy Communion, Chief Sinagau stood before me, perfectly erect and without the assistance of his cane. The natives proclaimed it a

Christmas miracle. A few hold me responsible for the seeming cure, yet I have assured them that it is the Lord Jesus, and not I who is responsible for the chief's recovery.

The whole village here is still recounting the event, of which several converts have been made. Chief Sinagau continues to teach and the entire community venerates him as a beloved Indian missionary. I regard him as a true blackrobe; a holy and lovable man of God.

On 31 December, I was asleep on a straw mat in my cabin when I was suddenly awakened by a discharge of musket fire. I arose and ran to my door expecting the worst. The door was being shaken by someone on the outside. When I opened it my room was immediately filled with a crowd of Indians—men, women, and children. They had come to wish me a happy new year. They knelt around me for my blessing. Then they pressed my hand in firm handshakes. It was truly a family celebration. I led them to the chapel where we prayed. Then they asked my permission to do the same honors to Chief Menominee and I-o-wah and some of the others. I granted it without reluctance! What innocence!

Ah, I love them tenderly as a father loves his own children. If you could experience the love and piety of the natives, you too could not help loving them. When I enter their wigwams or cabins the men and women surround me while the children climb on me. The fathers and mothers and elder children gather together, piously make the sign of the cross and, with a trusting smile, come to press my hand. No one could help loving them as I do.

They gather about their fire, sing hymns, say their prayers, recite the catechism and the scriptures, and share stories from the life of Christ or the apostles. There is no way for me to give you all the details of their life; if I were to begin, I should never finish. I am truly too happy when I am with them. They live a virtual monastic lifestyle— save celibacy. All things are shared in common and they live in obedience to one another.

Yet my constant prayer is for God's protection. The ever continual fear that the U.S. government will soon remove them west of the Mississippi taints the hope I have for this country, yet I entrust my hope and fear into the hands of the Lord!

FEBRUARY 1838
LENT

The bishop replied to Petit's last letter and informed him that he would not be granted permission to leave his missionary post to travel east to Washington City. He also informed him that due to his deteriorating health, he was leaving for New Orleans where the air is better. In his absence, the vicar general Rev. Celestin de La Hailandière had once again assumed administrative authority over the diocese.

As in any community, the call of a pastor involves him in the intimacies of human relationships. One such relationship was the question of marriage. At Menominee's village on the Yellow River, one of the common problems dealt with chiefs who had two wives. It was the custom of the Potawatomi that when a brother died, the oldest brother is expected to take the deceased brother's wife for his own for reasons of support; it was considered a sacred duty. This was the qituation of one of the chiefs.

After the chief and his sister-in-law had been married for four years and with a child of their own (plus the five from her previous marriage with his brother), the two wished to become Christian. Petit believed the husband to be of good character. The man had vowed to be her four children's father and he exhibited the virtues of both a good husband and a good father.

Since the bishop was away, Petit wrote to Father de La Hailandière asking for his opinion. Should he grant a dispensation in this situation? In Petit's legal mind it not only seemed possible, but also seemed to be the right thing to do. The two had married believing they were fulfilling a duty. Their union appeared to be a firm bond as well. The Indian ways were different and preaching the Gospel required a missionary to take into consideration the difficulties the Indian culture sometimes presented.

As it was, the first wife would have nothing to do with the chief now that he had been married for four years. She desired to marry another man and Petit gave her permission. Such dispensations are granted to the Chippewa of Michilimackinac and L'Arbre Croche, Michigan. Petit prayed that Rev. de La Hailandière would agree with his assessment of the situation since both parties wished to be good Catholic Christians.

Meantime Petit purchased a new horse. He named him Tom. As for his former horse, Pierre, one of the Indians sold him to an American settler for eighteen dollars. The American who bought him worked him a few days and brought him back asking for a refund of his money. The Indian refused. The horse, poor Pierre, fell over dead after the Indian refused the settler's demand. "No doubt the horse died of grief," Petit said, "and I am glad of it. If there is a happy valley where horses run wild and free in the afterlife, as the Indians believe, I pray Pierre is there."

JOURNAL

10–26 Feb: South Bend, Bertrand, South Bend. Lent begins. 26 Feb–20 March: Chichipé Outipé. Ash Wednesday February 28.

I fell from my horse, Tom. I consulted with Father Claude François; François had hoped that I would have been granted permission to go to Washington and plead the Potawatomi case.

20-27 March: South Bend

27 March-2 April: South Bend, Goshen, and Turkey Creek.

God's Mercy extends through generations

Oh, my dear Indiana Indians! They are so unlike the savages that the Americans paint them to be! I know who the true savages are here in the United States. Many of the Americans have hearts as dry as cork and only think of two things: land and money! They treat the Indians with hatred, disdain, and injustice, and are driving the natives from their ancestral homelands!

If you could know or feel the love that engulfs me when I am with the Indians, then you would understand my position. It is to them that I am completely devoted as a servant—all for the love of Christ and His Church.

Even when I traverse the twenty-five miles from Menominee's village to South Bend, my heart aches until I shall return to them. Riding horseback in the extreme cold and two feet of snow has had no effect upon me. It seems very strange indeed that I haven't experienced any of my health problems. It is as if my mission here with the Indians has burnt away all dross and invigorated not only my soul, but my body as well! The only complaint I have is that my eyes are weary from the bright sunlight reflecting off the blanket of snow.

I sleep on a mat just like my Indians and have not noticed the cold. My boots are torn and pierced through with holes, but I have yet to suffer from the cold. I even had to remove my mittens a time or two because I was too warm. I feel like a prince among these people. Recently I was afforded the opportunity to celebrate Mass in M. and Mme. Coquillard's parlor. That evening they allowed me to sleep in one of their feather beds, but I did not sleep well. I believe I was too comfortable. It is as if I can no longer enjoy any earthly comforts. My one comfort is doing the will of the One who has sent me here among the natives. Blessed be His name.

My mother has written to tell me she is sending me a pair of riding breeches and leggings and extra underdrawers. I should so welcome those amenities. One must admit there are some necessities. A twenty-five-mile ride on horseback contributes greatly to saddle sores. On more than one occasion I have bruised my haunches. This past month I could not sit for nearly seven days. It was quite awkward hearing confessions while standing. Some of my native children thought it quite humorous that my backside was bruised and chafed. Happily I can laugh with them now; the injury has healed. I pray that my posterior parts will not suffer too much from my next missionary trip.

There are many little things one must overlook in life. To scorn these amenities readily is to have seen the empty promises the world offers. The good Lord makes me feel the sweet joy of serving Him, and sometimes my heart overflows with joy and my eyes with tears as I think of my happy fate.

CHAPTER 21

BAPTISM

MARCH 1838

Oh, how my heart is proudly Indian. Is it not strange how God disposes all things through His Providence? How well I know that all things work together for good to them that love God. I have learned the language so well, it still remains a mystery to me how I have done so quickly. The settlers here are amazed, and one of the women has likened it to a Pentecostal event. I am not so sure I would go that far in the comparison.

Indeed, I have a father's yearning for them and what melancholy engulfs my heart when the shadow of the reality of Indian removal eclipses the sun of joy. What profound anguish oppresses my soul when I think of having to behold their being forced to depart their beloved Indiana—without a priest! A thousand Christians deprived of the solace of the sacraments and the Word of God, which they love so much, in a country which proclaims to be Christian!

A number of the women of the tribe stood out as leaders. The Chieftess Mas-saw was highly regarded among her people. On 4 March, she and her daughters, Mauri and Lizette, were baptized. Mas-saw was outspoken and not afraid of speaking her mind to the chiefs. She also had quite a mind for business. She was married to Andrew Goshlieu, the French Canadian Catholic. Mas-saw eloquently argued that women should be allowed to own property and learn to read and write. She was also quite the card player. It was Mas-saw's nine-year-old daughter, Lizette, who first called Petit Chichipé.

Vicar general Monseigneur de La Hailandière wrote Petit with his opinion regarding the hoped-for dispensation for my Indian couple. He refused. Petit planned to broach the subject with Bishop Bruté once he returned to Vincennes. He was not convinced that the bishop was of the same mind as his vicar general. Christ taught that the Sabbath was made for man, not man for the Sabbath. The same could be said for the law: the law was made for man, not man for the law. Canon Law was not necessarily the first priority in the Indiana wilderness. Petit thought perhaps that is why he was not named vicar general.

It was the Lenten season and Petit and his flock fasted every Wednesday and Friday—no meat and only one full meal. On Sundays they feasted.

The Indians were also preparing for the spring planting season. Though the natives were at relative peace, Petit was not. He was uncertain whether his mission would be destroyed. There was not much hope and much to fear in that regard; he had received a letter from Chief Menominee as well. He and the Potawatomi delegation were in Washington City to present their case before President Martin Van Buren. However, legislators tried to keep them from meeting with the president for a time. Fortunately, a friend of Bishop Bruté's interceded for them, enabling them to have a private meeting with the president. However, no promises or assurances were made concerning the future of Menominee's band in Indiana.

Petit placed them under the care of the Blessed Virgin, and if Providence permitted that the Potawatomi be allowed to remain, he intended to give the name of *Notre Dame* to the mission. *Fiat voluntas tua* (Thy will be done).

Father Mueller, the priest at Fort Wayne, happened through

on his way to Chicago. He was surprised to hear Petit speaking and chatting with the natives and singing hymns in their own tongue as if it was French or Latin. Petit was astonished himself. Mueller said Petit spoke as if he was a native. After the two priests had visited the Indians in their rush huts and took part in an evening pow-wow, Mueller amended his statement: he said Petit was one of them. Completely. "What an honor," Petit exclaimed. *"Nin Maketakônia Chichipé Outipé. I am the black-robe called the Duck's Head. Deo gratias."*

APRIL JOURNAL

2-3 April: Bertrand

4-8: South Bend. Confessions and Communion in anticipation of Easter.

9-10: Masses

12: Holy Thursday

13: Good Friday

15: Easter Sunday

11-24: Chichipé Outipé

25-26: Tippecanoe

27- 30: South Bend

1-3 May: South Bend

Christ is risen. Indeed. Alleluia.

15 APRIL 1838
EASTER SUNDAY

Despite the joy of Easter, my concern is for the Potawatomi delegation in Washington City. I have heard no news from them. All I know is that our business is under consideration. What will be the outcome? I wait and pray.

Bishop Bruté returned from his trip and was feeling better. He has also relieved Father de La Hailandière of administrative control of the diocese.

Petit baptized an American woman whose husband was a French Catholic—that is, a non-practicing French Catholic. Petit planned on blessing their marriage despite the husband's refusal to come to confession. Why is it that the converts to the faith are often the most zealous?

Petit made a trip to Leesburg some forty miles distant. He was called there for the funeral of a Catholic originally from Maryland, Mr. Norris by name. Norris and his whole family were Catholic, but for the past twenty-one years, they hadn't seen a priest or received the sacraments. Petit found only two other Catholic men in the region and both of them came to the funeral. One was an Irishman, a Mr. Horan, and the other was a Frenchman. All the others in attendance for the funeral were Protestant. They were highly suspicious of the rites Petit performed.

In the homily, Petit condemned private interpretation of the scriptures, defended the practice of honoring the saints, extolled the sacraments of the Eucharist and Confession, explained the doctrine of purgatory, and spoke of the wholesomeness of the practice of praying for the dead. There were not a few heavy sighs and grunts of disapproval. Perhaps he spoke out of turn when he asked those gathered to pray for the repose of the soul of the deceased. In retrospect he believed it was not well considered to speak thus to Protestants. One of the men looked as if he was ready for fisticuffs.

In Leesburg, Petit also happened to see several Potawatomi people from another band. They were not attending the funeral, nor were they likely to have been so inclined. They were not Catholic nor were they Christian. Instead, they were intoxicated. Two of the Indian men were struggling with a dagger and they were both naked. The larger of the two thrust the other man through the upper arm. When Petit tried to intervene, the wounded man boasted that he did not need God nor did he need to abstain from spirits. He then began to ridicule the Christian faith and laughed at Petit.

Another man of their number then spoke. He agreed that liquor was bad for the Indians, but he wanted to engage Petit in a bet. Petit attempted to reason with him that many a life had been ruined through gambling. The man said he would come to confession when he was ready to confess. He was amazed that Petit could speak his native tongue so well.

Soon thereafter three drunken Indian women came along and invited Petit to their wigwam. He said nothing to them; his soul was sick with pity for them. All he knew was that he loved the native peoples so much, especially those in most need of mercy. He loved their language, their customs, and their simplicity. He prayed the good Lord to bless him as an instrument for their salvation: this was his sole desire: that His holy will be accomplished in him and through him.

Some of the Protestants in the South Bend area claim that M. Coquillard gives him a yearly payment of $100 for a license from the Church allowing him to sin as he pleases without jeopardizing his soul! Petit told them that if he had paid him $100 that he had yet to see any of the money.

A Baptist woman living near Chichipé Outipé asked to be baptized as a Catholic. Her husband opposed it at first but then acquiesced.

From 14 through 16 May, Mlle. Campeau and Petit heard confessions and preached at Pokagon's village. There Petit heard his first confessions without her assistance as interpreter. He understood almost everything now.

A good number of Irishmen were moving into the area looking for work on the canal project. They said if a priest settled at South Bend, then they would settle there. If the priest remained at Yellow River, they would settle near there. For them no reason existed for their decision other than proximity to a priest and the Church. They accepted the natives as brothers in the Lord.

25 April 1838

Mother has written me again. She fears for both my safety and my health. How I love her. She cannot fathom my joy at living in a log hut in the midst of a savage people of the wilderness. I have tried to explain to her that they are not savage. She has inquired whether I will be returning to France any time soon. How does one explain the call of Christ? I have written her back requesting that she send me a good French alarm watch with a double case.

My beloved home is the village of the Indiana Indians now. My grand habitation is built of logs. Daylight streams through the spaces between the logs—as does the wind and the elements. My fireplace is large enough for a quarter of a cord of wood.

I have no rugs, only wooden planks. The planks are not secured, so when I walk they tremble underfoot like loose piano keys under a musician's fingers. At night I place a blanket on the floor near the fireplace and throw a mat down. I cover myself with another blanket and sleep as well as I should on the most sumptuous couch in the world.

My life as a missionary has removed from me worldly desires. My living, always going from place to place, has rendered me a passerby on the earth. Never before have I ever had such freedom of spirit. I believe I can truly say that I wish to die, if God wills it, without ever having felt tired of life. Amidst my labors, my health has been fortified. I imagine myself ministering here for another forty years, and then heaven! Then again, perhaps I only have forty days more, and then heaven. I willingly accept one or the other—it matters little which—provided I am in good favor with God.

And yet, with a joyful heart, I am now ever conscious of the sad prospect of my Indian mission's early destruction. A letter from Chief Menominee and Nanweshmah arrived this week. The impending darkness continually seeks to gather like storm clouds on the horizon of my life. I know the bishop has asked me to resign myself to the political reality of Indian removal, and I am aware that all has been done to avert the removal, but even after meeting with President Van Buren, their efforts were without salutary effects.

I do believe my poor Indians do have one more chance in staving off the federal government's troops: recourse to a court of law. Will they succeed? God only knows. As for me, I must dry their tears if, or when, they go into exile. I must remove the altar and dismantle the church and lay low the cross that marks their graves in order to spare the sacred from being profaned! And then I must say farewell to those whom I love and who love me so much, never to see them again!

And these Christian souls will waste away without the Word of God and the aid of the sacraments of which they partook with such love, and languish under a strange sky, where I, their father, will not be allowed to follow though I will long to dry their tears of exile.

Ah! I shall do everything in my power to keep from abandoning them! If they leave, I want to go with them at least as far as the reserves along the Mississippi River. Otherwise, many of my Christians, my children, will die without a priest to absolve them of their sins. I pray the good Jesuits will soon establish their missions there.

God alone knows all my heartaches—for three months I have been seeking to know and do His just and merciful will in regard to all of this.

MAY JOURNAL

5 MAY 1838

A tragedy occurred at Chichipé Outipé late last night. I was awakened from sleep to the screams of women. I immediately rose, threw my cassock on, grabbed my pistol, and went to investigate. As I made my way through the village, the natives were standing around the dead bodies of two young men; each man had a tomahawk buried in his skull. The story was that the men had been drinking whiskey and were fighting for the affections of the woman Demoskikague. (During Lent she had expressed interest in the faith and is currently taking instructions for her baptism; she is also promised to marry Nanweshmah. He too has been taking instructions in the faith.)

The grief of both men's families was felt by all; I attempted to console the parents of both boys but to no avail.

There were other Indians who claimed that Paukooshuck had been drinking with them and was also arguing with the men over the woman. Chiefs Pepishkay and Ashkum, two of the more outspoken Indian chiefs, believe Paukooshuck might have been the one who murdered both men. Of that I am uncertain; however, he was no where to be seen this morning at the funeral.

These murders only serve to fuel the American fears that the Indians are savages. With free will comes not only the power to do great good, but also great evil. What sadness, what a blight upon the Easter season! I took the opportunity to preach about the evils of liquor and anger. The tribe is in mourning.

That night, around the campfire, Nanweshmah retold a story that involved Father Badin and Angelique Campeau. In June of 1832, Topenebe, a twenty-five-year-old Potawatomi chief under the influence of alcohol, killed a young brave Nananko at Pokagon's village. A council was held where Topenebe surrendered himself. The family of the murdered man produced their knives and tomahawks and, according to tribal custom, Topenebe fell prostrate in their presence and waited for death.

Chief Pokagon delivered a speech hoping to spare the tribe of another death, but those ready to avenge Nananko heard nothing. As they were about to execute justice, the female interpreter, Angelique Campeau, stepped forward and said in the native tongue, "Kill me instead and be satisfied."

All were shocked. None of the Indians expected such an offer, especially an offer from a woman. Father Badin rose in response to his companion's offer. He stepped forward and spoke in the Potawatomi tongue. Nanweshmah produced a journal where Father Badin's words were written:

To all the chiefs, indeed all my children of the Potawatomi Nation, my brethren in Christ, I am your father, the old French priest, one of the last blackrobes. You know how we French blackrobes have always been the friends of the Indians. Listen to me. I wish for all of you to be happy. What I say I say in truth. Love one another, and forgive, if you wish God to forgive you, who has often been offended by your drinking whiskey and in many other ways. If you forgive not others their offenses against you, I will not forgive your offenses against me.

My children, Jesus, the Son of God, became man and was put to death by wicked men. When they were crucifying him he was praying to God for them. He did not wish for revenge and their deaths. He said, 'O God, my Father, forgive them;

they know not what they do.' If we do as Jesus has done, we will be happy with him and with God, the Father of all men—red and white.

My children, I speak to you as a father speaks to his beloved children. What I tell you is truth. God has sent me to instruct you; he has commanded me to teach you what His son Jesus Christ taught. Be assured that my heart cherishes you all equally, the least no less than the great. God shows no partiality.

I have already spoken too long, but I must say one word more. Open your ears. Open your hearts. No man, by killing Chief Topenebe, can restore Nananko to life nor give happiness to his soul in the other world; only great mischief would be done by adding sorrow to sorrow and tears to tears.

My Potawatomi children, I, as your father, am confident that all wise men among you—indeed all men—will agree that what I have said to you is right and true.

According to Nanweshmah, Father Badin sighed and looked around at the assemblage before taking his seat again. His eyes were still on Angelique Campeau, standing in the center of the circle next to Topenebe. Topenebe had remained prostrate before the mother, brothers, and friends of the victim, Nananko.

The silence had worried Badin that his words had only agitated the Indians further and Mlle. Campeau's life was to be taken along with Topenebe's. However, finally the mother of Nananko stood and called for the elders of the tribe. In their conference, the Indians conceded that it would be best to spare Topenebe's life and refuse Angelique's offer.

Petit lamented the fact that the Americans had neither learned the lesson of the guillotine nor the cruelty of slavery.

15 MAY 1838

Easter kept Petit traveling from place to place to celebrate the joy of his Blessed Lord's resurrection. As a result he was remiss in keeping his journal and correspondences up to date. He visited South Bend, Bertrand, Chichipé Outipé, and other settlements along the Tippecanoe River. He celebrated a large number of baptisms, communions, and marriages. His heart loved so much to call his people his children.

There were days where he and Mlle. Campeau acting as his interpreter heard confessions constantly from morning until evening, though his command of the Potawatomi tongue was such that he truly no longer needed any assistance in interpreting. They hardly had time to eat. The only respite he had was in visiting the sick.

One such woman he visited was Mme. Coquillard's sister, Mrs. John Hendricks. She was the first person he had seen die. She was cognizant and understood him until the end. She even responded to the prayers for the dying. Her funeral was impressive. Many Protestants attended. She was buried in the Catholic cemetery near the lake at South Bend.

Petit performed forty-five baptisms and ten marriages at South Bend, Chichipé Outipé, and elsewhere. The hearts of the Catholic Christians were readily receptive to God's Grace. Another Baptist woman accepted baptism and the sacraments despite the fact that her desire was against the will of her Protestant husband. Petit only baptized her after her husband reservedly gave his consent.

He and Mlle. Campeau then left for Pokagon's village on the fourteenth of May. Mlle. Campeau was seventy-two years old and, thanks be to God, she was still strong. From the sixteenth to the twenty-fourth inclusive, they heard confessions and preached; his exhortation was well understood. He presided at five marriages and eighteen baptisms.

Chief Pokagon said to him: "We have been blamed without fault . . . . I pray that *waw-kwi* (heaven) will bless you and your influence most abundantly and hasten the day when all shall acknowledge that the white man and the red man are brothers, and that *ki-ji-manitou* (God) is *o-os-si-maw ka-ki-naw* (the Father of all)."

Petit had a case to decide: an Indian woman lived five years with an American. He was never baptized and was not a believer. She fell ill; Mlle. Campeau baptized her on condition that she leave the man. However, the Indian woman recovered and she returned to the man. Father DeSeille then refused her the sacraments as long as she stayed with the man. Petit did not believe the woman should be required to put him away. Saint Paul wrote in First Corinthians that if a woman has an unbelieving husband, and he consents to dwell with her, then let her not put him away. The faith of the believer will save the unbeliever.

This was all the more true in her case since she had not neglected her religious duties, but rather had urged the man to abide by the law of God. He had not yet asked for baptism, but their union was strong. Petit believed she should be reinstated with the community and be afforded the sacraments, especially of marriage. The only obstacle that he could think of was one of scandal. But was not the Gospel message one of mercy and forbearance? Why should she be made to believe she was in an illicit union when in reality she was not? She was willing to separate if he was unwilling to accept baptism. However, Petit did not believe he had the right to impose such an obligation on him. Canonical matters were complicated in the Indiana wilderness among the native peoples.

Meanwhile, an American Protestant continued to chop wood from their property. Petit had politely asked him to refrain from such action and pay for the wood, but the man persisted, claiming that the Potawatomi would not be there much longer. He desired the land and said that an Indian agent had promised him the land near the lake, Petit then warned him that he would seek legal counsel in order to make him stop. He laughed. Petit then told him he was trained as a lawyer. He dared Petit—a foreign pagan—to take him to court. Petit detested lawsuits, but what would stop the greed of the Americans? After all, someone must stop the depredations. *If I am mistaken, the bishop will scold me,* Petit thought. *Perhaps I deserve a scolding.*

Petit gave the Indians the two hundred dollars that the bishop had given him for his planned trip to Washington City. Since he was prevented from going, he thought it appropriate to give it to them. There was no doubt that it had cost them much to travel east.

Petit still wished that he had been allowed to go to Washington City. He was not questioning his bishop's authority, but the Indian question was, he believed, far from being settled. And it was for this reason that he desired to travel east. He feared that the issue would be decided prematurely simply for political expediency.

Yet Petit still prayed daily that the mission there would be allowed to remain. As it was, the Potawatomi did not wish to leave, and the government had no authority to use force. And even if the land was taken from them, the majority of Indians would remain and purchase land and farms.

One of the older Indian women, Kaukemazoqua, the mother of Chief Weewissa, took Chichipé Petit by the hands and told him that she had received a vision. In her vision, he was to soon go away to the Great Blackrobe and "we shall see you no more." He knew that there was always the possibility that the bishop could send him elsewhere or he might be expelled from the country due to alleged interference in Indian affairs. Petit assured her that if he was transferred, the bishop would send another missionary father in his place. She somberly replied: "Others may come, but you are becoming a Potawatomi; soon you will be nothing but Potawatomi."

Her words pierced him through; her penetrating gaze somehow reached inside him. He could not get their interchange out of his mind. He was still unsure what it all meant. She was believed to have received the gift of prophecy from the Great Spirit. As a child she survived a lightning strike and ever since she had been revered among her tribesmen as having second sight.

He also received word from Nanweshmah that the government continued to make plans to remove the Indians from Indiana. Nanweshmah informed him that another agent assigned to the removal party was Judge William Polke. Polke was supposed to be a decent man. He was the brother-in-law of Isaac McCoy, the Baptist missionary who raised Nanweshmah. At one time, Polke himself served as a Baptist missionary at Carey Mission.

The other men assigned to the removal, Col. Abel Pepper and Brigadier General Amaziah Morgan, were not sympathetic to the Indians' cause. Despite some promises and hints of concession, Petit feared that the sword of Indian removal was hastening ever closer to sever his people far and wide from their beloved homeland.

JUNE JOURNAL

3 June: Pentecost

31 May – June 23: Chichipé Outipé.

The Indians gave me another pistol. I purchased a straw hat. Some traders have announced that they oppose the Indian removal; but alas they only do so because they lament the likely loss of business.

CHAPTER 22

THE WORK OF GOD

1 JUNE 1838

Perhaps you think a missionary is a saint. On the contrary, I admit that there are many a day or week where I scarcely can meditate or pour out my heart in prayer. After hearing confessions, saying Mass, praying my breviary and psalms and rosary, I collapse on my mat. My sleep is like that of a child's, calm and without interruption. I awaken refreshed, ready to begin another day of ministry. This thought consoles me. A day's fatigue is not in vain; rather it is all for the glory of God. To God alone I give myself entirely. He is merciful and kind enough to accept my sacrifice of labor as a continual prayer. In the words of Saint Paul: "Pray always." I am ever reminded of the admonition of Saint Benedict: "Ora et labora (pray and work)."

There are many moments when, in spite of the weariness of soul which fatigue brings, my heart is filled with joy and my eyes are moist with sweet tears. Oh, it is so good to be in a world where one has nothing to do but work for God!

Deo gratias! Thanks be to God!

An English painter named George Winter who is sympathetic to the Indian cause, has been painting portraits of the Potawatomi. He lives at Logansport and asked me to sit for a sketch and painting. I reluctantly agreed.

I baptized Demoskikiague on 17 May and she took the

Christian name of Marie. She is a beautiful person. She is to marry my companion and interpreter, Nanweshmah.

10 June 1838

I baptized Abram Nanweshmah Burnett on 5 June and celebrated his marriage to Demoskikiague. There was much celebrating among the tribe. Demoskikiague is the woman the two young Indians fought over until they both tomahawked each other to death.

I am taking advantage of a rare leisure moment here at Chichipé Outipé. The good Lord has entrusted many spiritual blessings to the mission and my heart. Since Easter I have baptized eighty-three natives and at Pokagon's village I baptized fifteen. On 3 June, Pentecost Sunday, 166 of my beloved Potawatomi received Holy Communion.

We returned to South Bend and rested before continuing on to St. Mary of the Lake. There we celebrated Pentecost with the Indians.

Oh, these Indians are not savage as the Americans portray them to be! They are far, far less savage than most of the coarse American woodsmen. If these Christian Indians are removed west, who will continue to give them the help of religion?

In His Divine Providence the good Lord has seen fit to give me a command of the Indian tongue and completely eliminate the need for my interpreter now. On the eve of Pentecost, I asked the Lord to give me the gift of the Potawatomi tongue and He granted me my request. I consider it a miracle. I even read and write their language sufficiently enough without the aid of Mlle. Campeau. The Indians themselves have expressed astonishment at the ease with which I acquired command of their language. I too am very much surprised! I love the people and their language very much; indeed their tongue is musical.

The Indians say that I have become one of them, a beloved blackrobe missionary, as in the days of old, a true Indian missionary. My temperament agrees with theirs, and I know that I am more Indian than any of my brother priests would ever desire to be. This is nothing against their good will, but it is a fact that none of the other priests wish to trade places with me. The Potawatomi are whom my heart loves.

Later I was hearing confessions before Mass when I was struck to hear the chant Veni, Sancte Spiritu[1] and the Litanae Sanctorum[2] from the lips of my natives—and in their native Potawatomi tongue. The Indians' voices are uniquely dark and resonant; the prayer of the chorus was as holy as, if not holier than, any European choir's Latin Gregorian chant.

Mlle. Campeau is greatly fatigued, and now that I have command of the Indian language, she may soon retire, her mission complete. I understand the language sufficiently enough to give advice in confession. I can even speak with them about everyday matters such as hunting, fishing, and farming. The Lord blesses the work and efforts of poor missionaries; perpetually having to employ an interpreter is quite incongruous to the zeal of a missionary

My Indian child, Corn Stalk, died. She was a sweet child who had been sick for some time, and the example she left through her death reminded me of the stories of the lives of the saints. She understood me to the end. I sought to comfort her in her death agony; instead, her purity assured me of the grace of God and she taught me how to live. After her funeral, her body was wrapped in a blanket and placed in a tree.

---

1 Come, Holy Spirit (a prayer associated with the feast of Pentecost).
2 The Litany of the Saints.

I also traveled to Chief Louison's village over forty miles away where I baptized some of the Indians and heard confessions from morning until evening. The chief and all his people were astounded to hear me speaking their tongue. The chief heralded me as a true blackrobe, as in the days of old. I was humbled by his words and gratitude. I thought I would never be allowed to leave their village; the Indians made me stay for their pow-wow and every villager, man, woman, and child shook my hand and thanked me for coming. Then they called down God the Father's blessing upon me.

I was edified when a French lady, Madame Mouton, came to Chichipé Outipé with her son and two daughters. They traveled eighty miles from Bertrand to spend time with the Indians. Madame Mouton went to confession and her children all received their first holy communion with several of the natives. They were inspired with the example of the Indians' faith and reverence. In turn, the Indians were humbled that she and her family desired to be with them. When the time came for the Moutons to leave, the children wept and begged their mother to let them stay at the village. The Indians welcome with great charity those who desire to pray with them. The fraternal affection in Christ is mutual among the Indians and the Catholic settlers.

20 JUNE 1838

The Indians are particularly under the influence of Grace! The good Lord treats me as a spoiled child; I have been thus favored all my life. It is truly a blessing to be placed in the midst of souls like these. The ties of the ministry are like family ties; not that there are no difficulties, for they exist everywhere, but the spiritual consolations outweigh them all. Indeed, the faith here is thriving.

I am praying that my good bishop will soon come to the

outpost and give confirmation to the Indians who are prepared to receive it. I have written the bishop asking that he
come soon. However, the bishop replied that he fears the
American governmental authorities would see in his coming a
Catholic conspiracy and an attempt to prevent the Indians
from departing.

A letter arrived today from Washington City. Lamentably,
the government refused to rule in the Indians favor. The president said, "I do not wish to speak of it. Your names are on the
treaty; your lands are lost." He wouldn't even speak of their
remaining. Chief Menominee said the Secretary of War
argued that their names were on the treaty, therefore, their
lands were lost. When Menominee and his attorney tried to
show the fraud, the president dismissed them outright and the
secretary saw them to the door. Menominee was told that they
didn't need his signature because, as they saw things, he wasn't
even a rightful chief. Secretary Cass even claimed that
Menominee was neither a chief nor a Potawatomi.

The people of the highest rank in the legislature have given
their advice and the Indians are following it. The case is to
come to trial soon and will be heard in the federal court at
Indianapolis. Their lawyer declares that the Indians are sure
to win. I am unconvinced now that the president has given his
decision. Oh, how I wish the bishop could prevent the
removal! Yet if he were to interfere, he would be charged with
high treason and I would be deported.

The Indian agent for northern Indiana, Col. Pepper arrived at
Chichipé Outipé mid-afternoon. It was horrendously humid as
Petit emerged from the chapel at the sound of a horse and rider.

Pepper refused to shake Petit's hand and instead leveled a
blistering accusation. "The savages are plotting a rebellion and

many are among the Indians here at Menominee's village," Col. Pepper insisted as he tied his brown horse in front of the chapel.

"I can assure you that there is no such plot," Petit replied, as he filled the bowl of his pipe with tobacco. "These people are peaceful."

"I will not be contradicted by a French frock," Pepper shouted at Petit. "Just as I was convinced of the priest DeSeille's treachery, so now I am convinced of yours! You are impeding these Indians' progress."

"Progress?" Petit asked.

"Yes, progress." He produced a document from his vest pocket. "The law of 1834 says, 'Heavy penalties will be incurred by anyone contravening any treaty established by the U.S. government or questioning the humanness of the U.S. government's Indian policy.' So there."

"I am not convinced that it is the policy of the U.S. government to be content to simply remove or relocate the Indian people, but rather to extinguish their nationality."

"You, priest," he said, doubling his right fist, "are an alien and represent a subversive foreign power."

"Subversive? Come now, Colonel, one cannot chain the word of God."

"And if you stand in our way I will have no alternative but to have *you* placed in chains and taken to Washington City." Pepper jiggled his revolver in its holster.

"But to remove the Indians is a grave injustice," Petit responded in kind.

"According to whom?" Pepper laughed through his teeth and removed his soft brimmed hat, wiping away sweat from his brow.

"Why can't this band remain?" Petit ignored Pepper's previous question and worked to light his pipe.

"If this band remains, then other bands will want to remain.

And if one band is allowed to resist, then soon all bands will resist. And all our efforts will have been in vain!"

"The government's policy is rooted in bigotry—" Petit was cut off.

"As a colonel, I will see to it that you are silent regarding their remaining. Your meetings with the Indians must be solely of a spiritual nature. If you wish to remain in the United States, then you must prove yourself a U.S. citizen. Don't make me arrest you for disturbing the peace among the Indians, attempting to alienate them from the U.S. government, and inciting hatred between the two races. Suppose the white settlers should attack the Indians before they are removed from Indiana? There would be no one else to blame for the resistance but the French black-robes."

"When you attack the Indians, you attack us." Petit's chest throbbed with emotion as he took his pipe from his mouth.

"Then the blackrobes and all you papists must also be removed." He looked down his crooked, sweaty nose at Petit.

"You insult the name of Christ and His Church," he replied, clenching his teeth as the feelings of indignation surged within him.

"One of our Indian agents with the emigration, Judge William Polke, has attempted to reason with the Indians, but they pay him no heed," Pepper continued, ignoring Petit's words. "Polke is too sympathetic with the Indians—he even speaks the tongue—so they continue to build and farm under his very eyes. It's driving him frantic. When he tries to speak, the Indians reduce him to silence and argue forcibly that they will not go."

"Some of the Indian scouts who have traveled to the proposed emigration lands west of the Mississippi River have returned with wretched tales." Petit returned his pipe to his shirt pocket underneath his cassock. "They report that the land is infertile and water scarce. Some of the Americans attempted to bribe the Indian scouts into saying that the land is fine. The braves flatly refused the money and declared the truth rather than deceive their brothers and sisters." One of the scouts, the young Indian, Arrowhead, had died from a fall from his horse on his way back to Indiana. The tribe already knew the cost of removal."

"Who are you going to believe? Me or these savages? I was sent here to give you this information," Pepper reiterated the warnings. "You've been warned before." Pepper untied his mount and left Petit in a cloud of dust.

The Potawatomi children looked on wondering why Col. Pepper was so angry.

Later that evening, the Indians were subdued as they gathered around the fire. Over the sound of the drumbeat, Petit heard some of the angry chiefs discussing the matter in council.

"The white race is an evil monster from the sea," Chief Pepishkay argued, recalling the words of Tecumseh, "He is always hungry and what he eats is our land. Yet you can no more own the land as you can own the sky above or the air we breathe. We belong to the land, and the land to us. The whites are already nearly a match for us all united, and they are too strong for any one tribe alone to resist. Unless we support one another with our collective forces, they will soon conquer us, and we will be driven away from our native country and scattered as leaves before the wind.

"Shall we give up our homes, our country bequeathed to us by the Great Spirit, the graves of our dead, and everything that is dear and sacred to us without a struggle? I know you will cry with me: Never! Never! War or extermination is now our only choice. Which do you choose?"

Petit was caught between two worlds just as Christ was.

1 JULY 1838

The first time Petit met Brigadier General Amaziah Morgan was upon Petit's return to Chichipé Outipé from Pokagon's village. The well-armed, uniformed U.S. soldier stopped Petit on the road just north of the village. Morgan spoke in English, though he did know a few words in Potawatomi. The right side of his mouth looked as if it had been sliced with a dagger or sword; he was unshaven and smelled of whiskey, tobacco, and perspiration.

"Are you the gentleman living at the chapel?" he asked.

Petit replied that he was.

"I am an assistant to the Indian agent, Colonel Pepper," Morgan said with a lisp and slight stutter as he removed his hat to brush away flies. "I shall be here for some time as I conduct the affairs of state. I would like it very much if you would depart west with the Indians. The government and everyone involved would be delighted if you did so."

Petit held Tom's reins and descended. Morgan dismounted his steed and swaggered in his steps with a peculiar slouch, his left shoulder slightly higher than the right. He informed Petit that Col. Pepper was on his way.

The two men walked together the rest of the way back to the village's chapel. They tied their horses to the hitching post outside the chapel.

Within the hour, Col. Pepper arrived at the reserve and joined General Morgan. Pepper was accompanied by a Miami interpreter. Petit chose to speak in the native tongue when the Indians were present.

Despite Morgan's initial introduction as a general, Col. Pepper referred to him as Captain Morgan; Pepper emphasized that he was Morgan's superior officer. Upon the revelation, Morgan glared at Pepper.

Petit excused himself as he went to the chapel to pray. In the interim, the two soldiers and the interpreter met with Chiefs I-o-wah and Pepishkay.

Petit was kneeling before the simple crucifix and crude altar praying his rosary when Col. Pepper entered the chapel with his hat on and a lit cigar between his teeth.

"Sir, I consider you an enemy of the American Republic and its government," Pepper said with the cigar still in his mouth. "You are interfering with the orders to carry out the Indian removal policy."

"Arguing for people's freedom does not make one an enemy of America," Petit replied with deliberate conviction as he rose from the kneeler.

"Are you here as a lawyer or a missionary?" Pepper sighed and rolled his eyes. Smoke wafted from his cigar.

"I am knowledgeable of law, and I have practiced it in the past," Petit answered looking Pepper directly in the eyes, "but today I am a priest and occupied with the ministry. Such are the orders I have received from my bishop. As for the emigration, I have never said anything for or against it, though I admit, I shall never say anything in favor of it. Instead I shall leave it alone. As for my acting as a lawyer, I gave that up when I decided to become a priest. I shall never practice law again—unless I am personally attacked or my rights are challenged or the rights of—"

"Sir, I have certain allegations against you," Pepper interrupted, removing the cigar from his mouth.

"I would like to hear these allegations, sir." Petit bristled as he placed his rosary in his right pants pocket. "And would you please remove your hat? This is the house of God."

Pepper looked around as if reluctant to remove his hat. "You know what the accusations are," Pepper said as he bared his head.

"Are they the same accusations that have been made against Mlle. Campeau?"

"There are witnesses to prove that Mlle. Campeau was encouraging the natives to hold back."

"And she has defied you to produce them," Petit replied. "And you have yet to bring forth any such witnesses."

"I know both of you and your bishop have encouraged them to remain." He flicked some ashes from his cigar onto the floor.

"You may think you know that, but it is not true," Petit said, glancing down at the ashes. "Were it true, then none of the Indians would have ever left Indiana."

"Don't dismiss me, Reverend." Pepper squeezed his hat in his left and replaced his cigar. "I thought by properly approaching you as a gentleman, we might resolve things agreeably. I thought you were a man of good sense. I would not have imagined that you were so subversive."

"And I thought you were a man concerned with justice."

"Your poor barbarians with their stupefied intellect, drunkenness, and laziness—" Pepper began to elaborate before being cut off mid-sentence.

"The poor barbarians you describe are not the Potawatomi I know," Petit said.

"Can't you understand that civilized white farmers have driven away the game, making the Indians' removal an absolute benefit for all involved?" Pepper said.

"Yes, unscrupulous white traders have contributed to the degraded condition of the natives by cheating them out of their annuities and providing them with copious amounts of whiskey."

"The hatred of these Indians runs deep, priest."

"Yes, the hatred *for* the Indians."

"I'm through arguing with you. Can't you see that unless they remove, the day will come when they will want to avenge the deaths of their ancestors?"

"You know nothing of my people," Petit replied.

"Reverend, I have no intention of thwarting you in the exercise of your ministry. None of the American officials will deprive the Indians of your ministry as long as they remain here."

"Colonel Pepper, the Constitution of the United States guarantees me that right."

"Are you an alien or a citizen?" Pepper asked, seemingly ignoring Petit's last statement.

"I am a Frenchman," Petit replied.

"Well, then, you are not subject to U.S. law, but you can be ejected from the Indian Territory—and deported from the country."

"Is that a threat?"

"Only a warning. Presently." Pepper chuckled. "The priest who came before you was evicted from the territory for being an agitator."

"He was not an agitator."

"That's your opinion." Pepper puffed on his cigar.

"Regardless, Father DeSeille has since died a premature death. Some would say a *questionable* death."

"Yes," Pepper chuckled and removed his cigar. "We have heard the ridiculous rumors that the priest was poisoned. Why do the Indians distrust us so? They seem to always think we are lying to them."

"Are you in earnest?" Petit asked. "The answer is very simple. During the last few years, many men posing as agents have come to the Indians and grossly lied to them. Now the Indians believe every agent sent to them has been paid to deceive them.

"For example, Captain Morgan asked me to announce to the Indians that a priest had already been assigned to accompany them west. This was not true; there is no priest. As it is, Mr. Morgan is dishonest. To some he says one thing and to others another. He even told some of the Indians that a certain Bishop Flaxen was assigned to the Mississippi Indian territory. This was a complete fabrication. There is no such Bishop Flaxen."

"Don't divert my attention. Is it true that you have told the Indians to remain?"

"No. I have never told them they should remain."

"Very well, however, with your legal background may I assume that you have never told them to leave either?"

Petit hesitated to answer. "I don't believe it is my position to instruct them to depart until every legal option on their behalf has been exhausted."

"Their legal arguments *are* exhausted. I am sorry I have to be the harbinger of such news: the time has come for the removal to begin."

"I will only believe it if I hear it from the president himself."

Pepper said nothing as he produced a document from his shirt pocket. He handed it to Petit.

It was the order for the Indians to remove. President Van Buren's signature was at the bottom of the page.

Petit hung his head low. Col. Pepper dropped his cigar, crushed it out on the chapel floor, and walked outside.

Petit said nothing more as he returned to his lodge where he collapsed on his mat. Tears were not enough to express his sorrow.

4 JULY 1838

I now face the sad fact of my Indian mission's destruction. I must dry their tears when they go into exile. I must destroy the altar and church and lay low the cross which stands watch over their graves in order to spare the sacred articles from profanation. Then I must say farewell to those whom I love and who love me so much, never to see them again! And these Christian souls will waste away without the aid of the sacraments of which they partook with such love, and they will languish in a strange land without a missionary.

I am here at St. Mary of the Lake on retreat of sorts in obe-

219

dience to Christ's words: "Come away to an out-of-the-way place and rest awhile."

Despite prayers rising to heaven, it appears that this is the end. The salvation of numerous Christians will be greatly imperiled if injustice prevails here. I have put the Indians under the protection of the Holy Virgin, and I do it every day. 15 August, the feast of her glorious Assumption into heaven, is the date set for them to know the final decision regarding their removal.

As long as the savages remain in Indiana, I shall be their missionary. The moment is coming when I shall see the mission's destruction. From time to time a ray of hope gives my heart a passing serenity. I entrust everything, however, to God's hands. God can work all things together to the good for those that trust in His Providence

I believe that if any decent-hearted American was to come and stay with the so-called savages, he would soon learn what I have learned: the natives are deeply religious, loving, and happy. Unfortunately the Americans fear the natives because of what happened in the past. Many Americans had relatives and friends killed in Indian raids years ago and cannot let go of their grudges and fear of all Indians.

Ah! If I were free, when they go west of the Mississippi they would not go without a priest! I would go with them. I have so little time left with them and so much to do among them. My white congregations are so far from giving me the same happiness as my poor redskins! Ah, the beauty of their souls!

Today some of the American settlers were fishing in the lake. They gave their catch to the Indians, perhaps wishing to become reconciled. Even some of the settlers who previously had acted like arrogant barbaric invaders have exhibited a previously unknown gentleness. Some have chosen to move away, others have befriended the Indians. One of the settlers explained that a new wave of settlers is moving westward; these new settlers will fill the territory and make removal inevitable. He said this with a tear in his eye.

There is some encouragement in the midst of this sea of woes. One of the Indian braves, Red-Tailed Hawk, a pious eighteen-year-old, has expressed an interest in continuing his education in Vincennes. He speaks well and can read and write English. I believe he could become a schoolmaster. God willing, he may even have a vocation to the priesthood.

8 JULY

I went to Logansport in the company of Mr. Pierre Navarre. He owns a trading post at South Bend and is married to a Potawatomi woman.

14 JULY 1838

Chief Menominee, Nanweshmah, and the others have returned to the village here at Chichipé Outipé. I have never seen such dejection in a people. There is no further recourse. The president has ordered the U.S. Army to enforce the Indian Removal Act.

They have also relayed the unbelievable news that on 26 May President Martin Van Buren sent seven thousand U.S. soldiers to begin the removal of the fourteen thousand Cherokee people from their eastern homelands of Georgia, Tennessee, North Carolina, and Alabama. The Cherokee were arrested and driven from their homes. Soldiers bore rifles with bayonets and forced the people to cram into wagons, treating them no better than unwanted sheep or cattle. The soldiers did not hesitate to use violence in apprehending the Indians and burning their villages once the people were seized. Many of the Cherokee not already on their forced march are in holding pens and stockades awaiting removal.

With word of the Cherokee removal I know now that it will only be a matter of weeks until my beloved Potawatomi will be removed in the same manner. Who will be their advocate in the face of all the wrongs committed upon their people?

With this knowledge also comes the sad news that my horse, Tom, died unexpectedly this afternoon.

More and more squatters began advancing on the Potawatomi reserve and Menominee's village. The settlers were moving westward, felling trees in their path, clearing the woods, scraping the hillsides, gouging them of all vegetation and wildlife, and piling the wood high in a huge bonfire. The natives lamented such a wasteful conflagration, such amount of wood would have easily been months, if not years, worth of fuel. "No thundering cyclone had ever caused such widespread devastation," Menominee declared one evening around the fire as he decried the loss of the forest.

With the beauty of the woods disappearing, so were the birds and game. Petit believed it a harbinger of the natives' removal.

CHAPTER 23

UNDER SIEGE

17 JULY 1838

Colonel Pepper, Captain Morgan, and Judge Polke arrived to implement the removal, or the emigration, as the Americans call it. Polke has also been made the Superintendent of Indian Affairs. Pepper and Morgan both indicted me as the party primarily responsible for embolden-ing the Indians' obstinacy in the face of removal. I replied to them immediately refuting their claims. I also wrote their superior, Lewis Sands, and announced my intention to reg-ister a formal complaint against them to Washington.

This is so painful, today more than ever, but God con-tinues to protect us. The colonel and his men are carrying forth the removal with a temerity and tenacity to which most of the Indians will yield although there will likely be a remnant of the tribe that will remain obstinate despite Col. Pepper's caveat that to remain would be a clear viola-tion of the treaty's provisions and U.S. governmental poli-cy. He warned that he and his men would be obliged to use force against any Indian who refused to leave when the time comes.

Chief Menominee reiterated their refusal to leave and pleaded with Judge Polke, "Sir, the president was imposed upon. The treaties are lies."

Col. Pepper claims that I am guilty of a personal affront and insult upon the president and the American government. He warned me that he has full authority to use force against the Indians. I assured him and his men that there will be no occasion for violence, as the Indians have no desire for war. He said that was only my opinion. He continually refers to the Potawatomi as poor, barbarian savages who refuse the ways of civilization.

He does not know my people.

Chief Menominee exhorted his band to remain and resist the government and the white settlers who would advance on their land. Unfortunately, some of the men have given in to despair and the demon of alcohol, which is generously supplied by some of the white settlers.

24 JULY 1838

Lo and behold! Captain Morgan paid me another personal visit this morning at Chichipé Outipé. He was hesitant to enter my tent, first inquiring with my Indian companion, Abram Burnett, whether I was too angry to speak to him. Morgan apologized, telling me that the week before he and Pepper had spoken on the spur of the moment without properly reflecting upon their words or the matter. He admitted the impropriety of his demeanor and sought reconciliation with me. At the same time he reminded me that the government intends to force the natives to abandon their reserve.

These Americans treat me with great consideration, but I am no idiot. They are highly suspicious of me. They all desire for me to leave with the Indians. I believe they would all be delighted for me to move west so as to forever remove the thorn from their side. I assured them I would gladly sojourn with my people, but I also counseled them not to hope too much since I have to answer to my bishop. Given his enormous diocese he is unlikely to allow one of his few priests to go west.

I am tired, but in good health; my spirit is troubled, yet I trust in His mercy; and my heart is filled with anxiety, but I

am calm enough to submit to His will. I pray the good Lord
to allow me to travel west with the Indians. Nevertheless,
Bishop Bruté will have the final decision.

Why do I desire to follow them west? I love them. I should
like to follow them until I place them in the hands of another
Catholic pastor. If a large number of these Christians, recent
converts, move west alone and are thrust into the hands of
American Protestants, their tender faith may be corrupted
through arid preaching and lack of appreciation for their
Indian ways. All the fruits of Fathers Badin and DeSeille and
Mlle. Campeau's efforts would be lost.

Imagine if our French brothers were to learn that we
allowed the Indians to depart in exile without a priest accompanying them. They will be greatly surprised—even shocked—
and the fact will be unique in the history of Catholic missions.

My presence would be their protection during the journey. I
have learned that the American authorities would likely place
me in charge of the emigration party for they know that the
blackrobes are respected among the Indians, whereas the
American agents are not. Although if I were to assume the
post, I fear the Indians would think I had somehow conspired
to deceive them from the beginning and betrayed their trust.

The Indians do not wish to depart, and they have such an
aversion to going west that for me to even speak of it is to
expose myself to the loss of their confidence. They are the ones
who will have to make the decision, not I. Whatever their
decision their religion ought to protect them. Nonetheless, my
bishop will not allow me to leave the diocesan territory.

And my heart aches as I think of how they will be treated
like dogs and mistreated. The diocese would lose nothing by
my absence; I would still be tending my flock. A maternal tenderness will be needed to console and protect my new-born
Christians. Misfortune awaits them if they are abandoned.

The bishop may relent, after all, and allow me to go with them. I would return within a year's time after placing my children, my tender children, safely in another pastor's hands. The time there would not be wasted since the fatigues of charity offered to God have value through Jesus Christ.

The immense territories conceded to the Indians have also been opened to the missions; therefore, the missions may prosper greatly through God's Providence. Certainly the bishop could not refuse me this request. Otherwise these poor children will be reduced to the plight of exposed infants and, humanly speaking, completely destitute of aid. A good father would not do such a thing and my bishop is a good father. Those are many of the reasons for my request; there are still many more.

Whatever the decision, I wait, hope, and pray. Whether here or west of the Mississippi, I wait for the word of the Lord: Speak, Lord, your servant is listening.

If the bishop agrees to send me west, I pray he will make his decision after the Indians have made their decision. I should not want my departure to be the reason for their departure.

Some of the Indians still have private lands and can settle on them, but whether the Americans will allow it is a question yet to be answered. Sadly, many of the Americans will not tolerate Indian neighbors.

I think of other missionaries busily erecting new churches and chapels while I will unhappily within a few days destroy this church from which so many fervid prayers rose to heaven—this altar where hitherto I have so many times received my Savior and around which I have so often seen such a large number of these good Indians crowded together to worship and receive their Lord.

I have been informed that on the fifth of August an American settler will take possession of the mission site. He plans on using the chapel as a stable. I should like to see the house of God destroyed before such an act of sacrilege.

As for the removal, I deeply desire that such a hideous cup pass far from me—and them. Nevertheless, I will accept the bitterness of this life and every day I will offer it to God, for them and for me.

Meanwhile, the brother-in-law of William Polke, the Baptist missionary Isaac McCoy says there are French Catholic priests in the Indian Territory. Perhaps they are Jesuits from St. Louis.

4 August 1838

Concerning the fate of the tribe, Chief Pash-po-ho was conflicted. He opposed removal, but since he feared being killed by the Americans he was willing to go west. However, he feared that if it be known, then some of his own tribesmen might kill him for siding with the U.S. government. Unfortunately, Pash-po-ho sought relief to his quandary by imbibing in liquor. He began to neglect himself and his customary neat appearance.

The majority of the Indians carried on as if they were to remain. They were well aware of the Cherokee in the east being driven from their homes and being placed in fort stockades. With fourteen thousand Cherokee to be removed from the states of Georgia, Tennessee, and North Carolina, the Cherokee removal would require a great deal of time and preparation. Unfortunately, the U.S. government couldn't wait for them to leave and herded them into holding pens prior to their march west.

A few of the Indians wrapped their rifles and guns in deer hides and had hidden them in the woods. They knew the enemy was on the march. A few had had premonitions and bad dreams. Even Petit had had one but he dared not recall the specifics, half fearful that it was prophetic.

Petit took Chiefs Menominee and I-o-wah and Joseph Barron aside at the evening pow-wow. "Have you told the children yet?"

"No," Menominee answered. "We will hold a council so as to determine how best to tell them. But then how does one tell the children that they are to be removed? Our language doesn't even have a word detestable enough to describe *removal*. How does one tell a child that he must leave his homeland and sojourn as a refugee, not because of a famine, flood, or fire, but because of the prejudice, bigotry, and hatred of one race against another?"

"Certainly many of our people will die, especially the very young and the elderly. They cannot travel such a great distance without adequate provisions. I refuse to believe that the American government will be able to procure enough food and water for my people despite their promises. I know how well this government keeps it word."

The Yellow River Reserve Treaty of 1836 had now expired. The treaty required the Potawatomi to leave Indiana within two years, and the time had arrived.[1]

"I fear I am still too much a lawyer," Petit prayed, "but how can one not be concerned for justice in the face of so much injustice." He could not sleep. He walked up and down the road in the light of the crescent moon. The brightness of the stars and constellations never seemed so brilliant in the velvet sky.

---

1 President Jackson appointed Colonel Abel C. Pepper to negotiate the purchase of all Indian land for the government. In 1836 Pepper negotiated nine treaties with the Potawatomi. He purchased 135 sections of land for $95,360 at $1.10 per acre. The Potawatomi could remain on the land for two years. At the end of the two-year period it was understood that the Indians would remove west. Chief Menominee had refused to sign the 1836 treaty and would not remove. August 5 was the expiration date for the Yellow River Reserve.

There was a strange silence the following morning, as if nature itself was holding its breath. When Pepper and his dragoons arrived, many of the men were carrying swords as well as rifles, revolvers, and bayonets.

Colonel Pepper wanted Father Petit to go west with the Indians. If the Potawatomi must be removed, Petit desired to go west; however, that decision was not for him to make.

5 AUGUST 1838

Today was the expiration date for the Yellow River Reserve. The emigration agents harassed, accused, and threatened the Indians while attempting to flatter Father Petit. To avoid the troops and armed force or forced seizure of the reserve, Petit insisted that the Indians would offer no resistance to removal.

Col. Pepper invited the governor of Indiana, David Wallace, to visit the village. Pepper called for a council and mediated between Chief Menominee and the governor. Nothing was settled. As the governor and Col. Pepper made it clear that the time for removal had passed, Menominee refused to leave and maintained that he had never sold his land. Menominee said his village was a haven of hope for the landless Indian. When Pepper demanded that the tribe remove, Menominee, dressed in his ceremonial garb, leather leggings, white silk shirt, and his red and black blanket draped over his left shoulder, predictably protested.

His eyes were moist with tears as he adjusted his turban and feathers. He rose to address the assemblage: "The president of the United States does not know the truth of what is happening here. He, like me, has been imposed upon. He does not know that you made my young chiefs drunk and got their consent and pretended to get mine! He does not know that I have refused to sell my lands and still refuse.

"The president would not forcibly drive our people from our homeland, the graves of our tribe, and our children who have gone to the Great Spirit, nor allow you to tell me your braves will take me tied like a dog, if he knew the truth. My brothers, the president is just, but he listens to the words of men who have lied, and when he knows the truth he will leave us to our own.

"I have not sold my lands. I will never sell my lands. I have not signed any of your treaties, and I will not sign any. I am not going to leave my lands and neither will my people. I do not care to hear any more about it. The Great Spirit has heard all things and will remember what has been said and done. The treaties are lies. Our lands belong to us; we will not go west."

Menominee had spoken.

Chief Pepishkay rose and spoke: "The Prophet Tenskwatawa, the brother of Chief Tecumseh, once said 'The Americans are unjust; they have taken away our lands which were not made for them.' Now I see why he is called the Prophet."

Petit had done all he could to defend the rights of the Potawatomi when he spoke with Col. Pepper. "Many of these people frequently attend Mass and go to confession regularly. They have the faith of children, yet it is a most edifying faith. They know their prayers and have memorized many of the stories from scripture. I have become their father; they are my own children. Do you not see what would happen to them if they are deprived of their homeland?"

Pepper stared blankly at the young, zealous priest but said nothing.

"They were orphaned by Father DeSeille at his death—" Petit began.

"DeSeille was a liar! He betrayed our government to these savages."

"He betrayed no one. And the natives will do nothing without my advice."

"Then you must advise them to prepare to leave tomorrow."

"They cannot be expected to leave on such short notice."

"Listen, priest. I don't give the orders. We're following word from Washington. The Indians are to be removed. I can't change that. You break the news to them. Their chief is ridiculous. Besides, they've known for *two years* they would have to leave. That's not exactly short notice."

"Are you saying that you are removing the Indians because you *love* the red children?"

"Don't tell me *you* love them?"

"Sir, I *do* love them."

"Hmmm. The way you defend them tells me that there's certainly got to be something in it for you."

"They are my people. I have renounced everything and given my life for them. I have become one of them."

"You are more ridiculous than Menominee."

"The Great Spirit will bless them. They were not the ones who broke the treaty."

With that, Pepper spat on the ground and placed his hand upon his revolver.

"I am even now prepared to give my life for them."

Pepper laughed to himself and shook his head as he made his way to the governor. "You are a fool, priest."

"A fool for Christ," Petit replied.

Petit knew that the tribe faced a terrible reality. Save a presidential reprieve, the removal of the Potawatomi nation was inevitable. Even if the young men were to take up arms and assume their ancient warrior paints and wield their bows and spears, they would fall to the white man and his steady and aggressive advance westward. The council at Menominee's village dispersed.

Before the two-year period had expired and the Potawatomi were required to begin their removal, a white American squatter, Mr. Waters, had moved onto the reservation and had dared some of the Indians to make him stop building on the land. He goaded some of the young braves to prove their manhood.

Nanweshmah came forward and spoke to Petit and Chief Menominee. "The trouble started when Waters settled in the reservation and staked off 160 acres. He is trying to provoke a fight with the young braves here so the governor will be forced to call out the militia to restore order. Once a riot breaks out between the Indians and the settlers, the Indians will be forced off the land. Mark my words, there is a conspiracy afoot."

Meanwhile, Menominee emboldened his people and the Indians assembled that evening after their supper for a powwow. They were seated on blankets, downed logs, or stumps, while the men smoked their tomahawk pipes. A fire was built in the midst of the semicircle. Their musicians with reed flutes, drummers with buckskin drums, and many others with small rattles and shell bells of sorts, started playing. A young brave wailed aloud a song of the hunt and the joy of living in the forest as he began to dance around, hopping on one leg, alternating with the rhythm. The drumbeat was hypnotic as more of the male Indians joined in the song and dance, whooping and crying aloud a native mantra in the cathedral wilderness.

A few of the whites that had accompanied Col. Pepper tried to join in the dance, but the Indians laughed at them.

Then some of the women of the tribe, Chieftess Mas-saw, Mauri, Angelique Menominee, Demoskikague Burnett, and others, who had been mere spectators until now, joined in the dance. They were draped in red and black blankets decorated with colorful ribbons and wampum. Their dance and manner was far different from the men's dance; they barely lifted their moccasins from the ground, choosing rather to shuffle their feet along. Their blanket mantles nearly reached the ground. Many of the women wore multiple strings of beads, and large rings of silver dangled from the pierced lobes of their ears.

The dancing, chanting, singing, and laughing went on into the late hours. The Indians' ethereal chant, at times like that of bees and not completely unlike Gregorian chants, was hopeful and full of joy. This hardly sounded like a lament of resignation.

The next morning the Indians assembled in the chapel for Morning Prayer and Mass. Petit could see the sadness in the eyes of his people.

After Mass, Col. Pepper declared Petit's house and chapel to be the property of the U.S. government. Petit was also to be removed, an exile in his own diocese. Reluctantly, Petit dismantled the altar and stripped the church's interior amidst the Indians' sobs and his own tears. He bade his people farewell and prayed with them once more for the success of missions. Together they sang: *In thy protection do we trust, O Virgin, meek and mild.*

Some of the Protestant militiamen ridiculed the reverence for the Virgin Mary displayed by the natives. Petit could contain himself no further; to scoff at the Mother of Christ was tantamount to blasphemy. He turned to them and addressed them in perfect English. "Gentlemen, if you claim to be Christians, then Christ is your brother. Therefore, His mother is also your mother."

The men quieted down, but they still murmured against the Catholic faith. The blackrobes were looked down upon because, as the Protestants claimed, the Catholics impart their superstitions to the Indians and, worse, they even live like them by dwelling with them in their wigwams.

Yet Petit knew that by living close to the people, sharing their lot, the good and the not so good, their joys and hardships, and speaking their common human language, he had brought Christ to a waiting world.

Col. Pepper hushed his men and announced, "The corn harvest also belongs to the government. A certain Mr. Nash will take the Indians' cows and hogs and sell them. He has also been given control of the chapel; he plans to use it as a barn for his livestock.

Petit was heartsick.

His people departed in stunned silence.

It appeared that Father Petit's assurances of and hopes for a peaceful resolution were premature. Senator John Tipton arrived to survey the situation at Chichipé Outipé. The chiefs were obstinate. Petit was unable to intervene.

Col. Pepper had written the governor urging him to send an armed force of men to settle the issue once and for all.

Meanwhile, with no more options left, Father Petit left Chichipé Outipé and returned to St. Mary of the Lake.

15 AUGUST 1838

The feast of the Assumption of Mary. Petit celebrated Mass at St. Mary of the Lake. The congregation's reverential silence spoke for their bewilderment at the knowledge that their Potawatomi neighbors must remove.

Later the same day, while riding on a borrowed horse, Petit could not get the animal to slow and he was thrown from the beast. His ribs were sorely bruised and it hurt to breathe. Afterwards Petit became ill with a fever. He continually got worse. Providentially, the trader Pierre Navarre on his way to South Bend was able to transport Petit to South Bend to the Coquillards who promised to care for the young priest.

Mme. Coquillard believed Petit was suffering from melancholia. He was a priest, consecrated to his people by a vow of obedience, and yet he was deprived of his mission, made to sleep in a strange bed. The Coquillards displayed hospitality, yet he was homesick for his cabin in the midst of his people. His fever rendered him delirious at times and the bruises received from his fall from the horse were slow to heal. The doctor at South Bend forbade him from traveling or riding.

August 25

As Petit convalesced he had ample time to ponder the meaning of the Indian removal and his own purpose for being so closely involved only to lose his people in the end. His expulsion from Chichipé Outipé and exile to St. Mary of the Lake must be God's will, he told himself time and again. It must be God's will; how else could he live with his grief?

He was in more pain thinking of his beloved Indians. He resolved to think of them no more. He began to contemplate a new mission, to build a great cathedral at South Bend or in the wilderness over the tomb of Father DeSeille. Perhaps he should return to France and establish himself in Rennes or Paris. Or he could join the Jesuits in St. Louis.

His knowledge of law could benefit him greatly, even enabling him to earn a degree in Canon Law. He could study in Rome, ensconce himself among the hierarchy, and secure a bishopric and conceivably be named an archbishop and cardinal.

He had already done more for the Church than most would ever hope of doing and had earned himself a page in the annals of church history, if not American history. In effect, he was a living martyr. He had done all he could. The cause of the Indians was lost. Bishop Bruté's word was to be taken as the word of Christ. Petit would remain behind in Indiana while the Potawatomi would migrate alone without the aid of the sacraments. He had no further say in the matter. Even his fellow priests advised him to see the providential hand of God at work in the situation; the separation of the races seemed to be the destiny of America.

Petit struggled to make himself believe it all, but he couldn't. As the fire that burned within Jeremiah after he had vowed never to speak the word of the Lord, Petit's ardor, fervor, and passion for his mission engulfed him again. Like Jacob of old, he contended with his better angels. As Moses, he thought of ways to avoid returning to Pharaoh. And, like Peter, who had denied his Lord and later tried to avoid martyrdom in Rome by fleeing from the city until he was met on the Appian Way by the Lord Jesus Himself, Petit could not avoid thinking of his Potawatomi children.

His mind was fraught with fear for the future of his people and legal arguments in favor of the Indians' rights. By day, he lay in bed and prayed his beads with inattention; by night, he wrestled with his thoughts and nervously walked the floor. Even his appetite disappeared. He could not enjoy the comfort of his featherbed as long as his children of the forest were left as prey to the American authorities, and forced to sleep under an angry sky.

In ages past, American Indians had killed Jesuit missionaries for nothing more than making the sign of the cross. Yet he was forever indebted to the fervent spirits of the Potawatomi.

But his thoughts would turnabout again and again. "*I am free. Free of the Indian agents, free of the American troops, free of the Indians. I am free to leave—but to what end? Were I to remain in South Bend knowing that my people are no longer free and, in fact, are being marched off as convicts—some even in chains—then I have renounced my priestly vows and calling as an ambassador of Christ.*"

Some days it seemed a blessing to be freed from the responsibility, yet well he knew to think in such a manner was a malediction.

In the comfort and ease of the Coquillards' home, he seemed destined to receive earthly glory, all the while longing for reunion with his copper-faced natives. He did not belong in South Bend lying in a featherbed eating three meals per day. He was as home-sick for his people as a husband for his wife and children.

He was ill with fever and experiencing restless nights. One dream was vivid: he and his father were out for a horse ride. His father pulled the reins of his white and brown speckled horse. Young Petit pulled his horse up close to his father's.

"What is it, Father?"

"My son, promise me one thing."

"Yes, Father?"

"Promise me that you will not abandon your bride and her children."

"Benjamin? Father Benjamin?" Mme. Coquillard was stand-ing next to his bed with some hot tea. He was disoriented and slightly irritated that she had interrupted his dream.

M. Coquillard offered Petit a drink of whiskey to ease his melancholy and to raise his spirits. He flatly refused for two rea-sons: one, to be in solidarity with his people, and two, he would not attempt to salve his remorse, deny the burden of conscience, or mollify the reality of Indian removal.

He prayed for death and sought escape from all earthly con-venience.

September was marked with the colors of autumn as falling dry, dead leaves fell in the cool breeze and gathered at the doorsteps and in the windowsills of the Coquillard home. Acorns from a large oak tree peppered the roof and windows like hailstones, while the oak's limbs clutched its decaying leaves, reluctant to admit winter's approach.

"Oh, how can I think of my own safety and liberty while my people—my children—are deprived of both?" Petit asked aloud. "I shall find the means—and the strength—to rejoin them."

He wrote his mother and others in France requesting sums of money for the missions and asking for fervent prayers on his and their behalf.

26 AUGUST

Bishop Bruté has both cheered my heart and confounded me with his recent letter. He has violated his own order of neutrality regarding the Indian removal and has voiced his opinion in a letter to Washington arguing against the removal. Whether the bishop intended it, he has now cast a pall of suspicion over all Catholic clergy—a suspicion that already exists in this country. He even used my name in his letter, reminding the government officials of my work among the native bands as reason for extending justice to them by allowing them to remain. I am afraid, however, that any effort on their behalf is now in vain.

My quandary continues as to whether I will be allowed to go west with the Indians or not. The bishop wrote: "To sacrifice you to the savages, a new pardon from your family would be necessary." I replied that my family had given me entirely to God. Their initial reluctance has acquiesced to the Will of God. My mother has declared that it no longer matters whether I am here or there. They would not understand why I should abandon my children. What if they were to read in the annals of the Propagation of the Faith that the natives had no priest to accompany them in their exile? They would ask, "Where has their priest gone? Why are there no priests with them?" Such would be most unusual in the annals of missions; the Church has always given a consoler for the sufferings of her children. I asked the bishop's blessing on us all—the Indians and his priest. May God arrange everything for His glory.

Petit's health wavered while he remained at South Bend being cared for by the Coquillards. He was delirious with fever and headache pain; he couldn't even read or pray. He didn't sleep well for several days, consumed with anxiety about what was to become of his people.

Petit received word from Chichipé Outipé that on the night before some of the braves had chopped down the cabin door of the American squatter, Mr. Waters, and had threatened his life. Before daybreak Waters and some of his kin had set fire to twelve Indian cabins.

By morning, there was a call for the governor to send in troops to keep the peace. A courier was sent to notify Col. Pepper at Logansport in hopes he might leave for Indianapolis to report the incident to the governor. The hopes were that the governor would muster a militia of two hundred men.

28 August

Mme. Coquillard showed Petit the open letter from Senator Tipton asking for assistance in gathering a volunteer militia.

28 August

General John Tipton

"Gentlemen, I am authorized by his Excellency the Governor of Indiana to accept the services of 100 volunteers and organize them for service to prevent difficulty between the Citizens of the State [of Indiana] and the [Potawatomi] Indians. I know too well the gallant spirit which animates the militia of [Indiana] your county to suppose that any other stimulus is necessary to induce them to enter service of their Country than to know that their services are required.

Will you do me the favor to raise 15 men from your

county and meet me at Rochester at 5 o'clock of Thursday
morning next. Let them come armed and mounted if they
can; if not, bring the men and I will arm them there.
Make as little stir as possible in raising your men until the
moment of your departure. Do not speak of it publicly.
Start tomorrow at 12 or sooner and march a little by the
moon. Sleep at Chippeway. Don't fail.

Your Obedient Servant,
General John Tipton,
Indiana Senator

The senator also wrote Alexis Coquillard; Alexis showed Petit
the letter.

28 August

Sir,

It is in contemplation to effect a peaceable removal of
the Potawatomi Indians off the lands lately owned by
them on the Yellow River [also called Menominee's
Reserve]. I am authorized [by the governor] to accept the
services of 100 volunteers to prevent difficulty between the
Indians and the whites. I do not believe that force is necessary but I shall be on the spot on Friday next and would
be glad to meet you there. Come if you can and bring four
or five suitable men with you. I am confident that you can
do much to effect the objects of my visit.

Your Obedient Servant,
Senator John Tipton

Coquillard replied to Tipton that he could not volunteer due
to a family illness. Petit was thankful for Alexis's refusal to participate (though Petit wished Alexis had been more honest with

his reason for refusal) and celebrated Mass at the Coquillard home again even though he was still suffering from the fever.

The following day Governor Wallace of the state of Indiana called for the Indians to leave without resistance so that the new settlers could take possession of the lands. The natives were resolved to leave in peace and Petit assured M. Coquillard that the governor had no need for a military force; it would only create excitement and disorder. Petit longed to be with his people.

3 September

On Monday afternoon, Petit was resting in bed with a fever when Nanweshmah appeared at the Coquillards with troubling news: the Indiana militia had begun the removal at Chichipé Outipé. Senator Tipton and Col. Pepper had arrived at the Yellow River Reserve and had called a council with the Indians in the chapel. Nanweshmah served as translator. Pepper brought his own interpreter, Luther Rice Noah-quet, a Métis Indian. Within forty-eight hours, the chapel had been demoted to the status of a stockade.

Nanweshmah also had a letter for Reverend Benjamin Petit. It was from Senator Tipton who was encamped at Menominee's Reserve.

September 2, 1838

Dear Reverend Petit,

The unpleasant state of affairs here which no one can lament more than I do, has induced the governor of the state to request me to accept the service of one hundred volunteers, and organize them for service to prevent difficulty between the Indians and the whites. I find Colonel Abel Pepper the agent for emigration ready to remove the Potawatomi from our state to their new home in the west, where the government of the United States is bound to protect them and to give each of them three hundred twenty acres of land besides defraying the expense of their removal and their support for one year after they arrive.

I find all are willing to remove with a few exceptions among the number of whom is Menominee and Black Wolf, who being Catholics, desire to remain here with [you] their priest. I have told them that I would recommend to the president to defray the expenses of building a chapel and residence for yourself or any other priest who might wish to go and settle among and improve these people.

I suggest this for your consideration, entertaining no doubt that it is in your power to satisfy the dissentients[1], and to harmonize this whole matter that these Indians will go off quietly and peaceably this week. Provided you wish to do so, I will hope for a definite answer tomorrow.

Your Obedient Servant,
Senator John Tipton

Nanweshmah explained to Petit and the Coquillards that beginning on Thursday, 30 August, Col. Pepper's troops had been corralling the Potawatomi at Chichipé Outipé on the Yellow River Reserve. By Sunday, 2 September, nearly eight hundred Indians had been driven at gunpoint to Menominee's village and Senator Tipton had arrived with over one hundred volunteer militiamen from all around central and northern Indiana.

The soldiers were prodding the Indians along with bayonets at their backs even though many were sick. The natives were to be crowded onto wagons and forced to march. They were only

---

1 Dissenters; also regarded as hostile dissidents.

to be allowed to take what they could carry. The night before, twenty Indians had escaped and stolen several horses.

These pieces of news were like so many swords piercing Petit's heart.

Col. Pepper then invited the Indians to the old chapel under the pretext of a council; he also told them that Petit would join them later for one last service. Whether this was an attempt to coax Petit back is unknown, but it had always been Pepper's intention of getting Petit to go west with the tribe. Petit was convinced that Col. Pepper simply wanted him gone.

Petit also knew that the government wanted him to accompany the natives to the western country because the prospect of separation from their priest and religion was one of the main reasons that kept the Indians from consenting to their exile.

"Our people, despite their peaceable disposition and cooperation are now prisoners of war," Nanweshmah exclaimed.

"*War*?" Petit retorted.

"Yes. War." Nanweshmah lowered his eyes, sighed, and continued. "The armed militia has seized our people as enemy combatants."

"Enemy combatants?" Alexis Coquillard and Benjamin Petit repeated the words simultaneously.

"Yes, two caches of weapons were found in the cornfield and the woods at Yellow River. They belonged to some of Paukooshuck's men."

"Paukooshuck. I might have known he'd do something like this!" Petit slammed his right fist into his left hand.

Nanweshmah also revealed that a general named Amaziah Morgan was abusing the Indians, both verbally and physically. Col. Pepper told the Indians that Father Petit would be going west with them, and Senator Tipton assumed it had all been arranged.

Petit now realized that he and the bishop and the entire Potawatomi people had been betrayed by the U.S. government.

Although Petit had written Bishop Bruté seeking permission to go west when the removal began, the bishop had denied the request. In fact, Petit had received a full denial of his request. Therefore he resolved to not think any more of going west.

Father Petit prepared a reply to the Tipton:

3 SEPTEMBER 1838

To the Honorable General Tipton:

General I received your letter dated 2 September, to which I give today the answer which you requested me to give you. It is not the least of the world in my power to satisfy those whom you call the dissentients, and to harmonize the whole matter, because it is not let to my choice to go, or not to go west.

I am under the dependence of my bishop and at his disposal, as much at least as any soldier of your troops is at your disposal; I wrote to him for the subject of being allowed to follow the Indians, in the case, that most of them would be willing to emigrate. I received a full denial of my request. Therefore I must not think any more of going west, no matter how much I desire it.

Was I at liberty to go or not to go, in the case the Indians would be willing to go, it would be repugnant and hard for me to associate in any way to the unaccountable measures lately taken for the removal of the Indians. You had right perhaps, if duly authorized, to take possession of the lands, but to make free men slaves? No man can take upon himself the right to do so in this free country!

Those who wish to move must be moved, those who want to want to remain must be left to themselves. Colonel Pepper, in the name of the U.S. president, spoke several times in that way and he said that by the fifth of August those who wanted to remain would be allowed if they submitted to the law of the country (and assimilate). Of course it is against men under the protection of law that you act in such a dictatorial manner; therefore, it is impossible for me, and for many others to conceive how such events may take place in this country of liberty.

I have consecrated my whole life, my whole powers to the good of my neighbors, but as to associate myself with any violence against them, even if it were at my own disposal, I cannot find in me strength enough to do so. May God protect them, and me, against the numerous misrepresentations which are made against us.

I have spoken with the Indians concerning the determination of the governor to send a military force to protect the right of the white settlers according to the laws of Congress. The natives have expressed unanimously—and in the strongest terms—their determination of offering no resistance to removal. Therefore, I assure you, there will be no need for a military force. The presence of an armed force would (will) only irritate and agitate already ill feelings. In fact, it may well create excitement that would lead to disorder and violence.

I am sorry, General, I am not to be able to comply any further with your wishes.

Your most obedient servant,

Benjamin Petit,

Chichipé Maketakônia

Missionary priest

Nanweshmah departed for the Yellow River Reserve with Petit's reply to the general.

"Can you imagine the anxiety of not knowing what was happening to your people, your family, and your children?" Petit rhetorically asked Mme. Coquillard. Of course, she was sympathetic to the cause of the Indians, but she was also concerned for Petit's health.

For his part, Petit had wanted to immediately leave for Menominee's village after reading General Tipton's letter to M. Coquillard. After the revelations of Nanweshmah's visit he wanted to leave more than ever, but he was weak, had a fever, and was still sore from his fall from the horse. The Coquillards and the physician urged him to remain in South Bend. Petit reluctantly returned to bed though he did not sleep that night. Ever since his fall the pain in his ribcage persisted.

The following morning at first light the sun streamed through the curtain as a flurry of dust particles glistened in the shaft of light. The silence of the room was loud. He knew what he had to do.

Even though he was burning with fever and his chest felt as if every rib was broken, he flung the sheet and blankets aside and got out of bed. Either his illness had suddenly subsided or else he forgot his pain for the sake of his people. Regardless, with these new revelations, Petit surprised everyone, including himself, when he began to prepare to ride south that very hour. He dressed and hesitated briefly before putting on his gun belt and placing the pistol in its holster.

In spite of the physician's insistent warning for him to remain in bed, and Mme. Coquillard's motherly protests, Chichipé Maketakônia Benjamin Petit mounted his steed and headed south to Chichipé Outipé at Twin Lakes. With great haste, he rode hard as never before and prayed his presence would discourage a clash between the militia and the Indians.

CHAPTER 24

REMOVAL

4 SEPTEMBER 1838

May God have mercy on the people of the United States of America and her statesmen.

—◆◇●◇◆—

In the midst of the glory of autumn's dying colors, Petit arrived at Chichipé Outipé and found himself surrounded by armed horsemen. The militiamen refused him entry and guarded him with bayonet-tipped rifles, but his collar, cassock, and the cross about his neck indicated his purpose.

Once they admitted him past their ranks he saw his people being marched to the chapel to the sound of drum and fife; the combination of bare feet and moccasins conjured clouds of dust. He dismounted his ride, tied the reins at the hitching post, and entered the former chapel now reduced to a barn. Hundreds of his people were corralled in the building. The smell of animal dung and wet hay was noticeable.

He saw the natives' faces, devoid of color and emotion. Chieftess Mas-Saw and daughters Lizette and Mauri hurried to him as did Sin-is-qua (Pebble) and her daughters Nancy and Pea-Walk-O. Sin-is-qua was holding her infant boy, Wash-Shing. Her husband, Thomas Robb, and her son-in-law, Captain Reed had chosen sides. Robb chose to leave Sin-is-qua and remain behind; Captain Reed had volunteered to serve in the militia. Both men's allegiance to the American way was greater than their devotion to wife and children. Petit believed that the final act that severed both men from the tribe was when their wives were baptized into the Catholic faith.

One by one the women and children came to Petit with tears in their eyes. They took his hand, squeezing it in an embrace. The children, Nancy and Lizette, clutched him about the waist. It was as if they would never let go. Their desperate question of why this was happening weighed upon his conscience.

Andrew Goshlieu, the husband of Mas-saw, and the seventy-year-old Canadian born French Creole, Joseph Barron, made their way to Petit. Chiefs Menominee and Ashkum soon followed. The well-dressed Chief Pash-po-ho looked as if he had been crying. Meanwhile, the older Chief Pepishkay glared at Petit from a distance. The chiefs said nothing.

Nanweshmah and his wife, Demoskikague, then approached Petit. "Chichipé Maketakônia!" Nanweshmah said, startled to see him. "How did you get here? You are ill. What about the doctor? You shouldn't have—"

"Never mind me," Petit replied, shaking his head. "I was wrong not to leave with you yesterday. I must be here with all of you. I am your father."

In an uncommon show of emotion, Nanweshmah enfolded Chichipé Petit in an embrace and collapsed in his arms. Petit held him close. The sight of all the people, one hundred fifty or more, squeezed together like animals, nothing more than penned up livestock, infuriated Petit. The specter of such injustice made it tempting to hate the Americans.

Petit departed the chapel, returned to his horse where he took his Mass kit from one of the saddle bags, and stepped up to the rope leading to the small bell in the belfry atop the chapel.

The familiar ring of the bell of Chichipé Outipé called all the natives to worship and Mass. Some of the volunteer soldiers laughed at Petit as he rang the bell.

Petit returned inside the chapel, stood on the dais and exhorted the Potawatomi to avoid violence with the American settlers. Then he asked them to prepare to celebrate the sacred mysteries. Petit spread a cloth over a barrelhead for a makeshift altar and the people encircled him. They chanted the prayers in the Potawatomi tongue.

He felt as if he was presiding over a Requiem Mass; the entire people a corpse about to be laid to rest. Yet this people had no burial ground; they were being ripped from their lands, dug up by their ancestral roots. Petit was also painfully aware that he would likely never see any of them again. He was to remain in Indiana and, alas, Kansas was not in Indiana. Though, within two months time the Indians that gave Indiana its name would be in Kansas.

The Gospel was from Luke: the parable of the tenant farmers:

A man planted a vineyard, leased it to tenant farmers, and then went on a journey. At harvest time he sent a servant to the tenant farmers to receive some of the produce. But they beat the servant and sent him away empty-handed. So he proceeded to send another servant, but him also they beat and insulted and sent away empty-handed. Then he proceeded to send a third, but this one too they wounded and threw out of the vineyard. The owner of the vineyard said, "What shall I do? I shall send my beloved son; maybe they will respect him." But when the tenant farmers saw him they said to one another, "This is the heir. Let us kill him that the inheritance may become ours. So they threw him out of the vineyard and killed him. What will the owner of the vineyard do to them? He will come and put those wretched tenant farmers to death and turn the vineyard over to other laborers (Luke 20:9-16).

The readings were providential. During his sermon, Petit looked up and saw Col. Pepper standing in the back of the chapel near the door with several armed militiamen. Besides his fever and bruised ribs, he now had a severe headache.

He prayed for the Potwatomi's happiness in their new hunting grounds west of the Mississippi and for the success of the mission that would be established there. Gazing at his dying mission and hearing the heartrending sobs of women and children, Petit himself sobbed as he prepared to consecrate the elements of bread and wine.

As he bowed before the makeshift altar and prepared to raise the Eucharistic host, outside a hail of thundering musket fire was heard. The footfall of American troops surrounding the structure could be heard.

"Hoc est enim corpus meum . . . Hic est enim calix sanguinis mei . . . This is my body . . . this is the cup of my blood. . . ." His tears choked off his words as the dusky faces of his people reflected back at him in his silver chalice as he elevated it to heaven. " . . . which is to be shed for you."

At the end of Mass, he led the people in a hymn to the Virgin: *O Virgin, we place our confidence in Thee. . . .*

Only a few were able to finish the paean, the lament so deep.

Their prayers of supplication were interrupted by Col. Pepper's voice. "The time for removal has come, Reverend."

Petit covered the chalice on the altar and turned around. "This is unspeakable."

"Spare me the drama, Reverend," Col. Pepper said. "You and your people are moving west."

"You vowed that by the fifth of August those who wanted to remain would be allowed to as long as they adhered to the laws and customs of the United States."

"That I did say," Col. Pepper said, "but the law states that all of your Indians must move west." He placed his hand on his revolver. "Take it up with Governor Wallace and General Tipton!"

"It is against the principle of civilization—indeed a crime against justice—that you and your forces are acting in such a dictatorial manner. It is impossible for me—and others—to conceive how such things are taking place in a country that prides itself upon liberty and whose government proclaims that all men are created equal!"

Pepper stood speechless as did all the Indians.

"I have consecrated my whole life to the good of my neighbor," Petit said emphatically, his face turning red, "and to even think of doing any one of them violence, even in self defense, I cannot find the strength within me to do so."

More gunfire rang out and Pepper nodded to a volunteer soldier entering the chapel. It was General Tipton. Petit knew him as the senator and Tippecanoe Battle veteran. The armed men were shouting, which frightened and intimidated the Indians, especially the women and children. The terror of not knowing what was to happen next was agonizing, especially for the children. Some of the young braves moved toward the door as if in an attempt to leave. They reached for their tomahawks and knives, but the American militiamen lowered their rifles stopping the Indians; the soldiers then quickly confiscated the weaponry.

More and more of the Potawatomi people were pushed inside the chapel. While the Americans guarded the door, Petit and the Potawatomi all began to realize their impending fate.

General Tipton's first act was to take Chief Menominee prisoner. He placed his rifle's bayonet at Menominee's neck, against his right jugular vein.

The chief sighed aloud and prayed in his native tongue.

Father Petit said aloud in French, "*Mon Dieu*! Has it come to this?"

"How could any people have allowed things to come to this?" Menominee dejectedly asked, though loud enough for all those in the chapel to hear—even above the cruel laughter of the volunteer soldiers. One of the American volunteers stepped forward and aimed his flintlock rifle at Chief Menominee's left temple. It was Captain Amaziah Morgan.

"Rifles and bayonets displayed in the house of God is a shameful thing in a country that claims justice for all," Petit the lawyer argued. "*Sancta Maria.*"

"What are you going to do, priest? Call your anti-Christ pope to have him send in French and Spanish troops?" Morgan laughed and turned his rifle toward Petit. "Just stop your mouth before I arrest you like these savages. There are over a hundred militiamen surrounding the village."

Petit said nothing more. Morgan turned the rifle back on Chief Menominee.

Tipton commended the Indians for being so complacent and cooperative. Yet how could they have done otherwise? They had no further recourse; this was the end. The orders were clear: Tipton's men were to shoot the first Indian resistor.

The general then gloated that he and his men had discovered a cache of weapons hidden in the cornfield and adjacent woods. All of the weaponry has been collected and placed under guard in a covered wagon.

"Forty rifles in the corn and twenty more hidden in the woods near the river. You people were going to ambush us, weren't you?" Tipton looked at Menominee.

None answered. Petit looked around for Paukooshuck; he was nowhere to be seen.

"Love your enemies," Menominee said in the Potawatomi tongue. "Forgive and you shall be forgiven." He continued with his head bowed to the crucifix that hung from Chichipé Petit's neck, "Father, forgive them; they know not what they do."

When Petit exited the chapel, he saw over one hundred armed militiamen with bayonets and guns surrounding his children. He motioned to a few braves who were still clutching at their weapons. The American soldiers took their weapons and placed them under guard.

The braves did not cry. Neither did they curse their tormentors—the Potawatomi tongue had no curse words. They sat as if their hearts had been carved from their chests; their dry stares beyond this earthly vale of tears.

Col. Pepper asked Petit to join him; there was one Indian who refused to leave his wigwam. "Help us coax him out, Father."

Petit went with Col. Pepper and several other soldiers. They surrounded the wigwam and Noah-quet, Pepper's interpreter, called for the brave to surrender. Petit recognized the wigwam as that belonging to Paukooshuck. He was quite capable of violence—even murder. Suddenly, the flap opened and Paukooshuck sprang forward with a tomahawk held high in his right hand and a rifle in his left. But when Paukooshuck saw Petit and the rifles and bayonet at his neck he threw down his weapons, crossed his arms, and held them out to be tied—but not before spitting upon Col. Pepper's boots.

By mid-day, even more Indian people were crammed into the chapel turned stockade and chained together and handcuffed to prevent escape—contrary to General Tipton and Colonel Pepper's insistence that they wouldn't use handcuffs. A number of Indians were chained together and were forced to stand in the heat of the day outside the stockade. General Tipton even ordered the old Chief Menominee to be shackled. Menominee and the Chiefs Black Wolf, Pepinawaw, Kankakee, and Macatamoah, and the troublesome Paukooshuck were shackled together. Paukooshuck's face was bruised and bloody as if the soldiers had taken turns teaching him a lesson. The indignity the people suffered was hard to imagine. They were forced to relieve themselves inside the building and in front of everyone. The stench of human urine and excrement grew worse and the natives were growing hungrier and thirstier by the hour.

The patriotism of the American citizens was such that in order to secure the white citizens from violence and all-out Indian war from the Indians at Menominee's village, the last remnant of the Potawatomi tribe in Indiana had to be removed.

General Tipton's friend Spencer had died at the hands of the Prophet's Shawnee warriors at Tippecanoe in 1811 at the infamous Tippecanoe battleground. Tipton had never forgiven the Indians for atrocities of the past and he held all Indians responsible, guilty or not. Tipton married Spencer's widow. Tipton, an Indian fighter and Indian hater, considered it his ultimate patriotic duty to remove the Indians once and for all.

Petit approached the shackled chiefs. "I have lived too long to see my people come to an end such as this," Menominee declared. "The flap of the wigwam of my life is opening to the better land beyond. Soon I shall enter into the wigwam of the Great Spirit and there I shall stand firm and beseech Him to grant our people a future of hope. I shall plead with Him to protect my people from the great destroyer of your children and ours, the great dragon. Yet I fear that, in time, our race shall disappear. Generations yet to be born will likely hear of our race and ask 'where have they gone?'"

Petit held his cuffed hand. "What has become of that great command: 'Love thy neighbor'?" he would have wept had he not been so indignant at the troops.

"The land of the Algonquin, Potawatomi, Ottawa, Miami, Kickapoo, Chippewa, Shawnee, and Delaware is no more," Menominee continued. "Civilized man considered our races savage and yet he has treated us most savagely." He sighed. "The only way for a man to know the heart of an Indian is for that

man to become an Indian. What white man has ever done that?"
Menominee studied his calloused fingers and cuffed wrists for a
moment before glancing up at Petit. "Only our beloved
Catholic blackrobes have done so."

Petit had humbled himself to share in the Indian existence
and he said nothing as Menominee's chocolate brown eyes glistened with sorrow.

"Your eyes speak truthfully, *Maketakônia Chichipé*,"
Menominee said firmly. "You have become one of us. You are
Potawatomi."

Petit had long considered himself Potawatomi ever since first
joining the mission under Father DeSeille, but the word of
Menominee confirmed his every prayer and belief about his mission to the natives.

He left the chiefs and went to find General Tipton. How the
young priest longed to reason with President Van Buren and
Congress that the Indians were the aboriginal peoples, the first
inhabitants of the Americas. They were the true natives unlike
the white "nativists" who claimed the land rightly belonged only
to their ancestors and their posterity.

With his passion barely in check, Petit approached General
Tipton. The general was surrounded by a dozen of his soldiers,
including Colonel Pepper and Captain Morgan.

"How can Christians permit such horrendous suffering to be
inflicted on fellow human beings?" Petit pointed to Tipton.

"Those savages? *People?*" Tipton chuckled to his officers and
the other soldiers as he puffed on his cigar.

"They *are* people—*my* people!" Petit insisted. "When they
suffer, I suffer!"

"*Your* people?" Tipton removed the cigar from his mouth and
squinted his left eye.

"I am no longer French; I was never an American. I am
Potawatomi. *Maketakonia Chichipé* is my name."

"You're different," Tipton said as he rolled his eyes; Morgan and Pepper sniggered.

"Must we not hearken to the voice of the Master when he said, 'Whatsoever you do to the least of my people that you do unto me'? Will we not be judged harshly on the Last Day for allowing such an injustice to occur? And what of those who rendered the injustice?" Petit was at the point of tears. "As for those who call them pagan and unbelievers, they know nothing of this people," Petit stated emphatically. "The Indians believe in God and their manner of life reflects this beautifully."

"Reverend, you need to calm down," Tipton said to Petit. "They're only Indians."

"*Only* Indians? How can one remain calm in the face of such evil? Would to God that the American gentlemen abide by the words of Christ as readily as the Indians have! How can you claim the name of Christian and continually violate the promises of your treaties with the Indians? And now you are about to make free men into slaves. Divine justice will not sleep forever."

"You're breaking my heart," Pepper huffed as he lit up a cigar.

"Don't talk about justice to us, frock. This is justice," Morgan said with a smile as he grasped his flintlock rifle and held it up. "The Indians are in the way of progress. It's not like they're like us. They're uncivilized. I mean, are you even sure they're human?"

"Yes, they are human *and* humane."

"Well, if they're human, then so are the nigger slaves."

"Precisely. Spoken like a true minister of justice."

"Shut up, frock," Morgan shouted. "You French have never learned anything. Yours is a weak race; your kind intermarried with the savages. Had you managed affairs differently in your war with the British, this territory might still be called New France. Now just step aside and pray your beads, and let us men take care of this Indian business."

For a moment Petit felt like reaching for his pistol to shoot the men, but he silently uttered the name of the Savior and resisted the temptation.

"It may be your opinion—an uninformed opinion—that the Indian removal is uncalled for," Tipton replied, "but I am confident that nothing but the presence of an armed and mounted force, both for the protection of the citizens of the state and to punish the insolence of the Indians, will prevent bloodshed.

"While you were praying with them in the chapel, we found a batch of weapons in the woods and cornfield," Tipton exclaimed. "Sixty rifles are now in our wagons and none of the Indians will lay claim to them. I cannot doubt that the savages are under the influence of bad feelings—their worst passions have been aroused – and nothing will, in my opinion, prevent a serious difficulty but the removal of the Indians from Indiana. The removal of these poor, degraded beings from our state will bring peace, security, and happiness not only to our citizens but to the Indians as well. The relocation of the Indians will be for their future betterment—as well as our own.

"If it were not for our presence here," Tipton exclaimed, as if for all to hear, "I am certain there would have been bloodshed, if not an all-out massacre. Think of it, our armed force has affected in three days what your counsel and words had failed to do in so many months. Granted, I do not feel authorized to drive these poor degraded beings from our state, but I do so under the highest authority so as to restore peace and security to our own citizens. As it is, these Indians do not own one acre of land east of the Mississippi, but the government has granted them new lands and is now obliged to remove them west.

"However, this self-styled chief, Menominee, argues that they will only listen to the advice of their black-robed priest: Benjamin Petit. You, sir, have resided with the tribe since the quarrel first began between the Indians and the whites. Only recently have you left Twin Lakes and moved to South Bend. Therefore, I am inviting you to join the emigration and go west."

"I cannot," Petit argued, shaking his head. "I have already told you. My bishop will not permit it."

"What a pity," Tipton shook his head. "Were you to travel with the savages, I believe you might be able to produce a favorable change in their morals and industry. In the cause of civilization, you would be eminently beneficial to these unfortunate Potawatomi when they reach their new abode. They ought to be eager to proceed on their journey to their new homes where I am sure they will experience peace, security, and happiness." Tipton removed his pistol from its holster and examined the weapon.

"Their removal will be without bloodshed or maltreatment. Every attention will be paid to their health, comfort, and convenience. We will accomplish our task peaceably if we can, forcibly if we must. The Indians must remain quiet and obey the law. If they do this, then they will be protected from abuse. We will conduct them west without incident, difficulty, or bloodshed." He returned his pistol to the holster.

"You give the impression that I have power over the Indians and could, if I wanted, give a nod of the head and the Indians would rise up either in rebellion or obedience to the law," Petit replied. "I am subject to the will of my bishop just as your soldiers are subject to your command. I have also received word from the bishop: he has denied my request to move west with the Potawatomi. I must not think of it any more, no matter how difficult or heart breaking.

"General Tipton, regretfully I am most displeased with the repugnant methods of removal being employed against the natives. You Americans are not accountable to any authority other than your own. Though your government has the right to take possession of the land, there are those who wish to remain."

"Then you do oppose the removal?" Tipton asked as he turned to Pepper and Morgan.

"Indeed," Petit clenched his teeth.

"The truth is discovered," Tipton laughed.

"What if you and your household were held at gunpoint and made to march to a foreign place?" Petit asked. "Would you call it an emigration or removal?"

"Rev'rend, that isn't going to happen."

"I am an *émigré*," Petit continued. "They are natives. They are the true *native* Americans. Indian removal should strike at the heart of all you hold dear as an 'American' for it certainly strikes at the heart of all I hold dear as a Christian."

"I am a Christian too, but Indian removal is not a religious issue; it is a matter of America's national security. The two are separate matters."

"But Col. Pepper assured the Indians that those who wished to remain could do so, provided they agreed to submit to the laws of the U.S. government," Petit argued.

"The Indians are savage and as such are incapable of assimilation," Tipton retorted. "Besides, the governor is giving the orders and I'm in charge of carrying them out."

"So it's all a matter of duty. Removing human beings like unwanted vermin."

Two of the soldiers cocked their rifles behind Petit; he refused to be intimidated.

"These savages, as you call them, are human beings with hopes, dreams, faith, and intelligence just as you and I have." Petit's jaw tightened as he spoke. "Yet you and your men come here and terrorize women and children! I find it hard to fathom that such tyranny is actually taking place in a country that prides itself as founded upon liberty! I have consecrated my whole life to the good of my neighbor, and to imagine doing violence to anyone, well, I cannot find in me the strength enough to do so.

May God protect them and me, and may God take pity and have mercy on you and your men. With God as my witness, General, and with all due respect, I cannot comply any further with your wishes or demands."

"I don't need your respect or your permission to do what is necessary. You may doubt it, but more has been accomplished for the cause of civilization by our troops in a few hours than was accomplished through months of fruitless dialogue."

"This is an act of war!"

"No, their removal will prevent future violence *and war*. In the end, you and every other naysayer will come to see this as an act of charity on behalf of our military so that all citizens may enjoy peace and freedom."

"Not in my lifetime—or yours. This peace and freedom you claim is an illusion. Those who oppress are not free but slaves to sin. The unjust oppression my people are receiving is not the fruit of charity. Truth and love lead to peace and freedom, not violence and war. War is a defeat for all involved. You do not prevent a war with a war. Can you not understand?"

"Ah, spoken like a true civilian. You have never served in the military, have you priest? With all due respect, Reverend, keep to your scripture."

"I am!" Petit answered firmly. "Where is the charity in your troops' actions?"

"Charity? These Indians were hiding weapons. They were prepared to kill Americans. If you are trying to defend that, then you're just like 'em."

"I love these people."

"Blackrobe, if you actually *love* these savages, then believe me, this is a necessary measure."

"Measure? The only measure of love is to love without measure." Petit walked away before Tipton or any of the others could say anything else. He felt that one more word might propel him to violence. *O Lord, who will speak on behalf of the Indians? Who will be their advocate in the face of all the wrongs committed upon their people?* His unspoken questions, indeed prayers of lament, remained unanswered.

"We didn't believe they would do it," Chieftess Mas-saw exclaimed aloud to Petit. "How can you remove an entire people? It cannot be done."

He approached her and some of the other women.

"What do we take?" Demoskikague Burnett asked. "How does one leave her ancestral homeland? We do not desire to leave. There are blankets unfinished and deer hides half-tanned. Venison is on the fires and soup is being prepared—for what?"

Petit was stiff and weary, yet wide awake. What could he do? *Will my people despise me knowing that I am to remain behind while they go off to an unknown land alone? I can hardly gaze into the eyes of my people!*

Some of the Indian converts lamented, "Has the God of the blackrobes abandoned us? Where is God, Father Chichipé?" Worst of all were the children's plaintive cry, "Maketokonia Chichipé, why are these bad men making us leave? Where are they taking us? What did we do wrong?" They grasped him tightly. "Where is Jesus?" Little Lizette asked tearfully, as she clutched at her father's cuffed arm. Andrew Goshlieu was motionless.

Petit knew where Christ was: He was about to be led away, as once before, to Golgotha. "Lord, have mercy," Petit sighed aloud.

Mas-saw and Demoskikague held his hands tightly.

The people were then threatened that if anyone tried to escape they would be shot. General Tipton's men had scoured the woods for any Potawatomi holdouts. Assembling the Indians, he had nearly eight hundred Potawatomi under arrest. Father Petit led them in tearful prayers.

Many whites came to bid them farewell; some of them were

troubled in conscience now that the removal had become reality. Some of the soldiers were surprised to see several whites among the natives. The troops did not understand why they would not want to remain. "You're free to stay," Pepper attempted to reason with them.

"They are my people," the elderly Joseph Barron explained. "I am one of them." He and Andrew Goshlieu simply shook their heads at the Americans' misguided zeal.

Henry Yo-ka-top-kone Taylor, "White Legs" as the Indians called him, was standing next to his wife, Mauri. "We do not have to remove, but if she leaves I go with her."

"Then goodbye and good riddance to you and yours," a soldier answered with a laugh.

The natives were permitted, under guard, to visit the graves of their departed friends one final time, where they held another religious ceremony. Pepper and Morgan chided Petit, accusing him of only delaying the inevitable departure. Chief Menominee expressed his fear that the advances of civilization would soon obliterate their burial grounds from the face of the earth.

As the people bade their village adieu the American volunteer soldiers hurried them along. The shackled Chief Menominee defiantly collapsed to the ground and sat, refusing to move. Tipton aimed his rifle at the chief and forced him to get up.

The wigwams and cabins of the Indians were torn down in the sight of all, and, as if to heap humiliation upon humiliation, the men began to set fire to them all. One by one the cabins and wigwams were torched. The heat and flames seared; the crackling sound roared.

The last structure standing was the former chapel. Petit watched in incredulity as the village burned. In the presence of the volunteers who were laughing and joking about the Indians' plight, Morgan stood outside the chapel with a flaming torch.

"Nothing personal, Rev'rend," Morgan said to Petit, "just following presidential orders. President Jackson always said that if we don't punish the insolence of these Indians, they will eventually shed innocent American blood. Try to see things from my perspective. I had an uncle butchered by your savages." Morgan started for the chapel with the flame; he looked drunk with joy.

No sooner had he said the words, the chapel exploded in flame. Petit was as angry as he was grieved. The young priest recalled his own advice to the young braves who so desired revenge on the Americans.

"It's all for the best, Rev'rend," Morgan assured Petit. "Don't you agree?"

"Just following orders?"

"Uh huh. But don't give me no lip. You Catholics do your anti-Christ pope's bidding, no matter what he says."

"*What* are you doing?" General Tipton shouted as he galloped up on his horse. "Morgan, you Cretan! You were not to burn the stockade! It was to be used as a barn."

It was no comfort to Petit; all was lost.

Things were happening so quickly that Petit wanted to follow them on horseback. He feared for his people's safety, having no guarantee they would be treated with respect. One of the Indians asked permission to break ranks and speak with the priest one last time. It was Nanweshmah. Both he and his wife, Demoskikague, nervously held Petit's hands.

"Father, I have always believed what you have taught my people," Nanweshmah spoke in the native tongue. "Is this God's will? Why should this happen to us?"

Petit gave no answer but only lowered his head. With tear-filled eyes and a grief-stricken heart he knelt on his right knee. Some of the other Indians slowly made their way to Petit, dragging their shackles and chains behind them. Together they embraced one another.

The American volunteers did nothing to prevent it; they seemed genuinely shocked. The sight of the burning village and the missionary surrounded by his flock did nothing, however, to delay or avert the Indian removal.

Judge William Polke was horrified at the burning of the village. Polke rubbed his forehead and ran his right hand through his carefully combed whitening hair. His age had caught up with him in a slight limp as he favored his left leg.

The natives were stoically silent and stood with their hands over their mouths. Many of their white neighbors were weeping.

Tipton told Petit that he had to level their village to ensure that none of the Indians would return. "They have no reason to return now; nothing to come back to."

As the Indians were led away, some of the new white settlers could be seen harvesting corn from the Indians' fields.

Chiefs Menominee and Sun-go-waw and three of the other chiefs were placed in a jail wagon. The spectacle of the savages behind bars was not lost on some of the white settlers and curious onlookers. A large American flag was affixed to the front of the wagon and the shadow of the stars and stripes graced the wagon. Some of the soldiers taunted the chiefs for a time before growing bored. The Indians seemed lost in deep meditation or deep melancholy—or both. The elderly, children, and mothers with papooses strapped to their back were all made to march. Many of the natives were still barefoot. Petit was sickened to discover that only about half of the Potawatomi had shoes or moccasins.

The Indians thought that the leveling and firing of their village was the final act of humiliation. Not so. They beheld the last act of desecration to their homeland: as their three-mile-long caravan passed by their ancestral homeland, white squatters were busily harvesting the corn. Petit imagined that it wouldn't be too long before the settlers would be plowing and churning the remains of the Potawatomi ancestors sleeping in the good earth—making way for progress.

An American volunteer was assigned to every thirty or forty Indians as they walked single file. Many of the Indians refused to ride in the wagons out of fear. They had never ridden in a wheeled carriage.

All of this was too much to bear for Petit. He so desired to accompany the caravan west but his bishop instructed him to refrain from acting impetuously and obey the governmental decree, even if they both disagreed with it. It had only been four years since a convent had been torched in the eastern U.S. and anti-Catholic rhetoric was easily fanned into flame when priests or bishops openly challenged American policy.

Paukooshuck had been taunting the troops against the wishes of Chiefs I-o-wah, Pepishkay, and Menominee. As the party progressed in its march, Paukooshuck must have irritated General Tipton one too many times; the general reared his horse and smashed the butt of his rifle square into the quarrelsome Paukooshuck's face.

Petit was furious and his hand came down on the handle of his pistol.

William Polke saw it and put his hand on Petit's shoulder. It prevented Petit from getting into fisticuffs with Morgan.

"What is it, priest?" Morgan asked. "Do you think you're Moses? Are these your people? I can hear you now: 'Let my people go!' Well, you just get back in line before I whack you a good one. You'd best listen to Judge Polke here. He's a good Christian. But then you Catholics ain't Christian, are you?"

Petit held his tongue and prayed: *Father, forgive them; they know not what they do.*

Henry Yokatopkone Taylor, the husband of Mauri, stepped forward to defend the honor of the priest. "Sir, have you no respect for this man?"

"Listen to you!" Morgan sneered. "Going Injun and leaving your own kind."

"*She* is my *wife*," Yokatopkone said, motioning to Mauri.

"So you married an Injun, did you now? What a sorry excuse for a man."

Yocatopkone stepped forward, but Morgan hit him in the gut with his rifle butt. Yocatopkone fell to the ground. One of the young Indian men, Little Crow, moved toward Morgan in response only to receive the same rifle butt to the ribs.

Some other Indians moved forward only to find themselves staring at the edges of bayonet blades; the Indians flinched, doing their very best at controlling themselves. They glared at Morgan and the other soldiers as if waiting for the opportunity to tomahawk them to death. Meanwhile, Yocatopkone was slow to get up.

"I see the hate in your eyes, you savage bastards!"

Tipton appeared again, pulling the reins of his neighing horse. "All right, Captain. That'll be enough."

Morgan tipped his hat to Petit and mounted his horse joining the general. "Let's get this show on the road, soldiers!" he cried out. "Move 'em out!"

With such a great number of Indians in custody, and with nearly 150 horses, and twenty wagons, Tipton planned on only traveling ten to fifteen miles south on the Michigan Road due to the extreme heat and lack of water and necessities.

Tipton was furious to discover the incompetence of the War Department and the Indian agents who had planned the removal. "They had more than two years to prepare for this!" he exclaimed. There was seemingly no plan, and the removal was being poorly executed. The contractors who had agreed to provide provisions of food and blankets had also failed to meet the requirements of their agreement. The caravan would have to stop in Logansport to secure more food, provisions, horses, and wagons for the caravan. Tipton was also surprised at the level of poverty among the Indians. They were destitute of blankets, shirts, decent shoes, and other amenities. He planned on spending three thousand dollars at the Logansport trading post to purchase enough clothes, shoes, and blankets for the tribe.

Some of the older Indians were ill, and about fifty of them stayed behind. One of the soldiers agreed to remain behind and travel with the Indians when they are able. Some of the old and sick were allowed to ride in the wagons as were many of the women and children. The others were on foot or riding ponies and guarded at the rear by militiamen with bayonet-tipped rifles. Many of the mothers and fathers were already carrying their hungry, frightened, weary children.

Petit painfully watched the tribe disappear into the horizon as the smoke from the burning village enveloped him. He was as a mother mourning the loss of an only child.

4 SEPTEMBER 1838

The Americans have made good on their promise to remove my beloved Potawatomi people from Indiana. The weeping and wailing of the Indians cannot be adequately recounted in mere words. The human tragedy of such inhumane treatment of the aboriginal peoples of this land is incomparable. And all of this "removal" was performed by a people that claim the words of the United States Declaration of Independence which boldly proclaims: "We hold these truths to be self-evident, that all men are created equal, endowed by their creator with certain inalienable rights, of which are the right to life, liberty, and the pursuit of happiness."

These red men, women, and children were denied their God-given right. How could a Christian people allow for such an act of cruelty? How could the majority of decent American citizens meekly stand by and allow fellow human beings to be "removed" as if they were nothing more than bothersome insects or unwanted animals?

General John Tipton believes the removal is not uncalled for. The presence of armed forces is for the protection of the citizens of the state and to punish the insolence of the Indians. He boasts that the armed forces have affected in three days what counsel had failed to do. According to Tipton, the Indian problem had to be resolved and removal was the solution.

The Americans seem to rejoice over all the wrong things. Isaiah's words were never clearer: "Woe to those who call evil good and good evil" (Is. 5:20).

The overwhelming experience of desolation and defeat has crushed their spirits. Yet the words of the psalmist give me hope: "The Lord is close to the brokenhearted; those whose spirit is crushed he will save" (Ps. 34:19).

The exile has led the Potawatomi into deep reflection. As Menominee departed he asked: "Are we a people apart from our land? Do we own the land anymore than we own the sky above?"

CHAPTER 25

WESTWARD

My Indians are to experience their own Babylonian Exile. Yes, there is a desire to take revenge and kill the Americans as my people ask: "Where is God in all of this? Where is the Christ? Was all that the blackrobes taught for naught? Has God abandoned us? Is the Christian God all-powerful after all? What does the Great Chief in Rome have to say? Can he intervene? To these and all their questions I am silent. Everything familiar is gone. There is no hope of return. Their desolation is my own.

After the people had been driven away, Petit saddled his horse, packed his belongings in the saddle bags, and prepared to make for Chicago since the bishop was there on a pastoral visit. He would once again seek permission from the bishop to leave Indiana and accompany his beloved Potawatomi people west.

When Petit arrived at St. Mary of the Lake, the slumped figure of a black-robed priest atop a horse appeared, seemingly out of nowhere. It was Bishop Bruté. Petit believed that Providence wonderfully ordered all things; this was a miracle. The bishop proceeded to lavish all the consolations of a father upon the soul of his spiritual son.

There were stories of saints who had the gift of bilocation and Petit wondered whether his bishop, the beloved Bruté, was one such saint. Of course, Bruté brushed aside any comparisons with the saints. He explained that he had just returned from Chicago where he had yet to place a resident priest. He had then gone on to South Bend where he learned about the Indian removal and Petit's absence.

Bruté was scheduled to be in Logansport on 9 September for the dedication of the new church there. He had left Vincennes a few days early in order to travel north to visit the Indians. His heart was heavy with grief at the removal of the Indian bands. Long had he desired to minister to the aboriginal peoples of America just as his French heroes of old, the Jesuit Blackrobe Isaac Jogues—Ondessonk—had done in the seventeenth century, and how the other blackrobes from that time on had lived in the midst of the various tribes, spreading the word of Christ among them.

The fifty-nine-year-old bishop had a terrible hacking cough, and the discharge from his cough looked dark and bloody. His slumped position over the mane of his horse was due to a hernia condition. It was inoperable and the bishop knew it was one of his crosses that he would carry for the rest of his life.

Petit did not believe it was his place to try to dissuade the bishop from such strenuous horseback travel. Long had he known that this bishop—first among men—would spend himself to the end, his flame burning brightly until the candle had been fully consumed. Such was this last of the blackrobes, the diminutive missionary bishop from France.

The Indian removal was foremost on his mind. "Nearly a thousand souls that have been entrusted to my care will soon be gone from our midst," Bruté lamented. "I have heard violent tales of the volunteer soldiers who are herding the Indians off to an unknown land and an unknown future. I should have done more on their behalf."

Petit then described how Chief Menominee and some of the other chiefs were shackled and jailed.

5 September

On Petit and Bruté's journey south toward Logansport (but before they overtook the caravan), the two men were met by Angelique Campeau and Nanweshmah. The two had ridden north to relate the anguishing details of the removal march so far. The papooses strapped to the mothers' cradleboards were either dead or dying. Many of the women, children, and older Indians could hardly walk and were forced to climb into cramped and loaded wagons.

Others bore the soldiers' cruel taunts and abuse. Some of the Indians fought like demons till they were overpowered and roped like wild boars; some went into hiding, others escaped to seek refuge in Michigan. Thankfully, there were also decent American soldiers who took pity and prevented the mayhem from turning to bloodshed. Even some of the soldiers were beginning to question the wisdom of removal.

In fact, at the end of the first day, twenty troops, either homesick at the prospect of being gone for more than two months or disenchanted with their heartless task of driving humans like cattle stole twenty of the Indians' ponies and deserted Tipton's command.

Campeau and Nanweshmah had come for Petit. They did not know that they would also meet their bishop. His presence seemed providential. If the government's authorities and the soldiers were to see the bishop of the diocese ride into the emigration's encampment, certainly they would cease their abuse of the Indians. Perhaps they would even be allowed to return to their former village and be allowed to remain. Petit realized the hopes for their return were in vain, yet he still prayed for a miracle.

Bishop Bruté was visibly vexed. He didn't want to irritate the strained relations between the Catholics of the country and the governmental authorities. He was forever haunted by the memory of the French Revolution and the subsequent Reign of Terror, which drove Catholics into exile and employed the guillotine against the ministers of the church. Anti-Catholic, anti-immigrant sentiment was seemingly everywhere. Bruté weighed things in his mind. Petit waited to learn whether his superior would allow him to ride west with his people.

Bruté and Petit traveled south with Nanweshmah and Campeau as far as Lake Manitou where they pitched their tents and spent the night. The stories of the Lake Manitou sea serpent fired Petit's imagination as he told the bishop the tale.

The legend of Lake Manitou, also called Devil's Lake, was taken seriously by the tribe. A huge monster in the form of an eel or serpent was believed to lurk beneath the surface of the water. The Indians would not hunt along its shore line nor would they fish from it. Some of the Indians said that at certain times of the year, schools of fish could be seen swimming away from something in the water. The Indians believed the fish were fleeing from the evil spirit that dwelt there within the giant serpent. There were also white settlers who reported seeing it. It was supposedly some sixty feet long, its head three feet wide, and its eyes were as wide as dinner plates.

Many people from Logansport were fearful that it might emerge and come to their town. One day, a party of twenty men armed with harpoons and spears came to fish the leviathan creature out, but nothing fitting the description of a monster was ever lifted from the tarn. Such was the tale that Nanweshmah and Petit told the bishop.

The next morning the bishop thanked the men for keeping him awake with the thought that a monster would crawl forth from the lake to devour him sometime in the night. Yet the only monster that Petit had encountered was the inordinately patriotic Americans who fervently enforced the insidious Act of Congress that mandated Indian Removal.

After an examination of conscience, Petit knelt before Bruté and confessed his sinful thoughts toward the U.S. government and its officials. He also confessed his temptation to abandon his vocation and pray for death. He then asked for the courage, grace, and obedience to accept whatever decision the bishop would make regarding his request to go west with the natives. The bishop reminded him to first ask for the courage, grace, and obedience to obey God's will.

6 September 1838

The next day Bruté, Petit, Nanweshmah, and Campeau overtook the caravan just north of Logansport. The Indians were encamped along Horney Creek.

The conditions had worsened. The bishop straightened in his saddle when he rode through the midst of the tribe's encampment. Those Indians who had the strength came out of their tents and tepees to receive his blessing and have him lay hands upon the sick and dying. Two physicians of the city were rendering what aid they could to the sick. Many were near death with exhaustion and dehydration.

The scarcity of water was impeding progress since the distance between watering places either too small or too great. The government was still lagging behind in supplying food and other provisions. The summer season had been extremely dry, a veritable drought in much of the Midwest. Rivers dwindled to brooks, lakes stagnated, and ponds dried up. Malaria and the dreaded typhoid fever had affected both whites and Indians. Cholera was also a major concern.

A Catholic doctor of Logansport assisting with the sick and elderly offered to accompany the Indians west. The idle wagons were soon overcrowded with the sick and suffering. The desolate and unadorned Potawatomi people were near despair.

When Bruté encountered the caged chiefs, he was indignant

and asked that Chief Menominee be released. The guard unlocked the handcuffs and shackles but only gave the chief an hour of freedom. "Those are the orders, Rev'rend," the guard explained.

Petit watched as the two leaders, Bishop Bruté and Menominee, walked to the edge of the encampment and stood together on the brow of the hill overlooking the sad valley. Petit wondered what the two men discussed under the starlit sky.

The next morning Bishop Bruté openly wept at the news of the death of two of the Indian children.

7 SEPTEMBER

After morning prayers, Mass, and the burials of the two children, Bruté and Petit mounted their rides and rode to the hill outside Logansport, observing the sprawling mass of people spread through the woods awaiting that morning's bugle call and subsequent press westward. Both men sat in their saddles looking upon the pathetic sight. Bruté said nothing; his jaw was locked and his gums clenched—had he had teeth they would have been clenched. His penetrating gaze was fixed upon Petit who was next to him.

"How can men do such things to such helpless people?" the bishop turned and asked.

"I do not understand. These people are everything to me," Petit declared. "Without them, where will my priesthood be?"

Bruté was silent as he looked off into the distance as if contemplating eternity. Then he spoke: "I was thinking of sending you to Chicago, but now I am unsure." He paused for nearly half a minute before resuming his thoughts. "A dear friend from Maryland, Mother Elizabeth Ann Seton, once said to me: 'We want to make things happen according to our plans, our wishes, but we must not imagine that we can take things into our own hands and wrestle them away from God. In God's Providence, we shall come to know His plan in His own time. Therefore, let us not anticipate God's timing—for His timing is perfect—and patience on our part is essential to our discernment of the will of God.'" Bruté looked at Petit and continued. "Trust in God means being willing to abandon our own will for the will of God—even if we do not know what the will of God is.

"God is not with us *despite* our trials—God is with us *in* and *through* our trials. And God will see us through and bring us peace and joy even in the midst of adversity and suffering," Bruté smiled slightly. "All those beneath the Cross of Calvary who gaze at the face of the Crucified One share in His sufferings and one day will rise victorious from the grave. As far as God's will is concerned, I do not believe it was God's will that the Potawatomi be removed. Not all things that happen are God's will. Yet we know that there is nothing that can thwart the will of God. God achieves His will through the cross." Bruté looked away.

"The evil will of men must not be confused with the will of God. An evil situation can give us an opportunity for doing good; it can also reveal the goodness in men. God may permit evil as a means for a greater good, but God never directly wills evil as an end. God is mystery. We do not see clear to God's ways. Sorrow and pain are real, yet if we turn to God in trust we will not be disappointed. His love and care will guide us into His light, though it may seem to be darkness. Therefore we have no fear of being lost in the darkness. In His will is our peace."

Bruté turned to Petit. "Initially I denied your request to go west in order to avoid any and all suspicion that the Catholic Church and her ecclesiastical authorities have connived with the civil power's unjust measure in forcing the Indians westward. Nevertheless, now that the deed has been done, I must reconsider.

"Truly I have found that a person cannot truly discover himself until he has given of himself," Bruté continued. "You will now have the opportunity to do what I was never permitted to do. I am hereby authorizing you to go west with them. *Ite; missa est* (Go, this is your mission). Go with the Potawatomi; you have your mission. But, always, in your agony, remember Christ's." Bruté paused and raised his hand in a blessing. "You have my blessing, and may God have mercy upon you and all the Potawatomi people."

Bruté did not want to give anyone the impression that by Petit's traveling west the Catholic Church approved of the inhumane removal of Indian peoples. On the other hand, General Tipton had asked Petit to join the emigration party. And it appeared that either Tipton had spoken with Bruté or else Bruté had realized that Petit's presence may very well serve the cause of the natives. In the very least, perhaps the military officers and soldiers would be less likely to injure or harm them unnecessarily if a priest were traveling with them. The same could be said of the Indians: Petit's presence might prevent them from committing an atrocity against the Americans.

General Tipton was adamant that the Indians leave immediately and keep moving to cover as much distance as possible each day due to the approaching winter. Petit feared that by the time the Indians arrived in the western territory many of the Indians would be dead from exposure.

Anyone seemingly concerned for the welfare of the Indians was suspect by those who favored removal. Those who supported the Indians right to remain could be labeled a traitor. Many a politician wished the Indians would simply disappear. Petit believed that many of the Americans were already working for that day by supplying the Indians with enough liquor to kill them.

Whether or not Tipton's intentions were genuine, the

Indians would likely receive much better treatment with the presence of the missionary priest along the trail west.

By nightfall, a three-year-old child had died. Bruté and Petit joined the Indians at the burial.

8 September

I have received permission from the bishop to accompany the emigration party. The bishop actually sent me west with orders to see to their protection. It is amazing how Providence orders all things. The bishop was returning from a visit to Chicago and was scheduled to consecrate the church in Logansport. The two of us journeyed together south from South Bend. Reports reached us that the Indians were being driven with bayonets prodding their backs. A large number of the Indians were sick and were crammed into baggage wagons and several had already died of extreme heat and dehydration. These pieces of news were like swords piercing my heart.

The bishop grew indignant when we caught up with the removal party. They all came out to greet us and receive our blessing. Yet it was they who blessed us. Over three hundred of the nearly nine hundred Indians were languishing with illness. Physicians from Logansport and the surrounding area were coming to their aid.

Some of the Americans were indignant and warned General Tipton that I had more power over the Indians than he did. Meanwhile the Indians' smiles returned amidst the desolation of exile. Once more our family was together.

Due to illness, scarcity of water, and lack of provisions, Tipton ordered that the caravan would remain outside Logansport until supplies arrived. So far five children under three years of age have died here at the encampment.

Some of the Indians escaped during the night. The conduc-

tor, Judge Polke, is resigned to the fact that not all the Indians will be accounted for in the end. And even more may die before we reach our destination.

"O God, come to our assistance. O Lord, make haste to deliver us."

9 SEPTEMBER

Bishop Bruté consecrated the church at Logansport. I stayed with the Indians in their encampment just outside Logansport. I said Mass on an improvised altar under a great tree. That afternoon the bishop visited the camp. I went out first and knelt for his blessing. All the natives followed in turn. Then we processed to the altar where we sang vespers in the Potawatomi tongue; some of them prayed from books, others from heart. I intoned the Veni Creator in the Potawatomi tongue. The good bishop then confirmed twenty of my good savages. That afternoon we prayed the rosary and upon its completion the bishop gave the benediction.

That day was a wonderful triumph for the Catholic Faith: the whole town came to the camp, astonished at the Indians' reverence and edified by their holiness. The bishop called them his true Christians. The Indian children Mary Ann Menominee, Lizette Goshlieu, Nancy Robb, Fox Tail, and Flapping Crow hovered about me and the bishop.

That evening the bishop gave Extreme Unction to two more dying children and an older Indian; they all died in the night.

At the death bed of one of the children, Petit maintained his calm exterior disposition while within he fought to swallow his emotion. The memory of his own father's death flooded him with a grief that he thought he had long since arrested and appeased. The bishop, still kneeling, wiped away a tear from his left cheek. He reached for his breviary, opened the gilded pages of the book, and fumbled with the ribbons for a moment or two before reciting the office for the dead. When he finished with the prayers, Petit and the bishop slowly departed from the tent.

10 SEPTEMBER

The following morning, Bishop Bruté celebrated a Requiem Mass before the burial. The Potawatomi wrapped their dead in white muslin and secured the body upon a log funeral bier carried by six bearers. Men carry the dead men and women carry the dead women. The dead children are carried by their mothers. The dead are then buried in shallow graves and at the end of the service, all in attendance take a handful of soil and drop it upon the corpse.

As Petit observed the bishop performing his pastoral duties, the image of Jesus the Good Shepherd came to mind.

The English painter, George Winter, was among the crowd of onlookers. He spoke with Petit, appalled at the treatment of the Indians. He sketched a drawing of the assemblage of Indians gathered around the altar and gave it to Petit. He also wrote a short essay to accompany it:

Many melancholy and touching thoughts passed through the mind and these questions presented themselves, as the indistinct and fast fading forms of the party were lost to the view. Has the Redman in his dealings with the White, witnessed the practice of the immutable principles of justice and integrity which a holy religion teaches? Has he been taught virtue and divine reverence in example or by precept? To these startling inquiries let the page of history respond. Could the poor and degraded aborigine give his history to the world, it could but speak in emphatic language—the continual series of oppressions of the White man, from the day he first put foot upon

the aboriginal soil; and surely would the gilded emblazonry of
Freedom's boasted escutcheon be tarnished in the sight of
Philanthropy and Justice.

Bruté confirmed many of the Indians and sealed them with the gift of the Holy Spirit; and many more took communion, food for the journey. Petit feared that for some of the Indians it may well have been *Viaticum* (Eucharist given to a person in danger of death).

Judge Polke and two other soldiers returned from looking for fugitive Indians. They found several bands, most notably Chesaugan's band. He and his family had fled Menominee's village when Tipton's men arrived. Logansport was as far as he and his family were able to get before being apprehended. It looked as if the soldiers took better care of the three stolen horses and two ponies than they did of the women and children in Chesaugan's band.

A foreboding of difficulty seized the Potawatomi as they awaited their orders from General Tipton. Eight hundred fifty-nine Indians were now on the roll; many more from the surrounding area had been added to the number, even those from Wamego's village at the Fulton-Cass County line.

Before setting out on the journey west, Chichipé Petit prepared to leave the encampment to return to South Bend for his possessions. He was interrupted by a scratch at the flap of his tent. It was Mlle. Campeau. She had come to inform Petit that she was returning to the north, to live her last years among Pokagon's people in southern Michigan. The removal was far too painful for her and she was not in the necessary health required to travel such a great distance. Petit embraced and kissed her and said a blessing over her: "If we never meet again, may we joyfully be reunited in heaven."

With permission now granted by his bishop, Petit saddled his horse and hastened to South Bend to pack his belongings; he would need enough provisions to last until March of next year.

That night he pitched his tent halfway between Logansport and South Bend. The next day when he passed through the leveled village at Twin Lakes near Yellow River he paused at the smoldering remains. He spurred his horse on in haste but not before catching a glimpse of the former burial ground and field, plowed under and staked off in plats. Some new settlers were tilling the sacred soil even as he rode past; a few of the spirit houses were upturned.

He arrived at South Bend about noon. There were several sick people there who asked him to hear their confessions. He was surprised to find Chief Black Wolf's aged mother staying at one of the Frenchman's homes. He had recalled Black Wolf saying that he thought his mother had fled to Pokagon's village. Instead, she had only made it as far as South Bend.

On the day of her son's arrest, she had been so startled by General Tipton and his men's musket fire that she hid in the woods. She survived by eating a dead pheasant. She had wounded her left foot and could no longer walk. Providentially, an Indian who had eluded the authorities discovered her and put her on his horse. He transported her safely to the Frenchman's house.

Petit heard confessions and said Mass before leaving to catch up with the emigration party of Indians. Upon his departure, Mme. Coquillard said, "I feel as if I will never see you again." Petit packed his Mass kit and chalice, folded his vestments, gathered his pipes and tobacco pouch, and tin cup and placed everything in his traveling bag. He was filled with anxiety, so concerned for the well-being of the Potawatomi.

CHAPTER 26

THE TRAIL

II SEPTEMBER

I am journeying west in pursuit of my Potawatomi people.
All things are possible with God.

Petit had a six-hundred-mile journey to the other side of the Mississippi River ahead of him. Once there he hoped to establish a more durable mission among the Indians, which afterwards he would leave in the hands of the Jesuit fathers. He prayed that in this remote quest the good Lord would sustain him and not allow him to stumble.

He thought he would retake the caravan at Lafayette, but the emigration party was further west than he expected. He began to follow the trail of the three-mile-long procession. Wherever they had passed, the brush was beat down, animal dung littered the way, and millions of flies buzzed about. Regrettably he also saw fresh graves along the way.

No doubt their faith was being tested. He recalled the last time he saw all of them alive. The children of the forest departed their childhood homes; hesitant to glance behind, they mourned their beloved memories. Petit recalled the warriors looking heavenward as if imploring aid from the spirits of their departed chiefs to redress the wrong being committed against them.

Petit spurred his ride on in haste to comfort and counsel his people. All the while his cough worsened, his fever returned, and his chest and lower back were still sore from his fall from the horse.

12 SEPTEMBER

The sight of smoldering campfires and freshly hewn graves marked the miserable path of removal and death. Petit counted the graves, the anguish unbearable. How could they be so far advanced? The soldiers must be lashing them in hopes of making their sojourn as short as possible.

The days went by and every day he met settlers who relayed to him the sight of so many bare-footed Indians, refugees in their own land, a three-mile-long train of sorrow. The heat of the sun was grueling, the humid air stifling, and when there was a breeze the air was filled with dust.

Petit's horse was hungry and sick and the merchants were charging a high price for feed. The information he was receiving from settlers along the way was that the emigration party's teams of horses were wearing out. Many of the soldiers were sick or had had enough of the conditions, the doctors were nearly out of medicine, over 150 of the Indians were weary with exhaustion, the wagons were overcrowded with the sick, and worst of all, the children and elderly were dying.

The further Petit rode, the scarcer water was becoming. He feared that unless there was rain sometime soon, the rest of the march would be fraught with much pain, suffering, and death. Meanwhile, his horse continued to fail. Petit tried to overtake the caravan in Indiana, but with the troops moving the Indians in haste and his horse slowing to a mere trot, he was making no headway. Finally the horse collapsed.

He tried to secure a stage going west, but couldn't find one, so he wound up having to take one traveling south to Perrysville. From there he borrowed a horse from Michael Young, a young

Catholic gentleman who then accompanied Petit west toward Danville. Several of Young's friends and acquaintances joined him in the ride simply out of curiosity.

As Petit rode to catch up with the caravan he came across their campfires, still smoldering with hot embers. He reckoned that the Potawatomi were about a day's ride away. He camped along a filthy stream near the Indiana-Illinois state line.

The next day he neared Danville, Illinois. The merchants there were demanding enormous prices for forage and provisions. The sickness in the country was almost unparalleled. In fact, in every town there were those infirm, rendered invalid. A storekeeper told Petit that four Americans died in Danville the day before; Danville only had a population of about eight hundred people.

As he grew closer to Danville, he encountered a group of Indians who were under guard. They were too ill to continue. They informed him that despite it being Sabbath rest and despite the vocal protests from Chief Menominee, General Tipton and his officers Pepper and Morgan were forcing the Indians to march.

Petit remained with the sick. By morning, four of the Indians had died: a child, two women, and an elderly man. He buried them and rode ahead to rejoin the emigration party. Petit resolved to be with the Potawatomi by nightfall. The injustice impassioned every fiber of his being.

16 SEPTEMBER

I witnessed the tragic sight: my poor Christian children marched in a crooked, three-mile-long column, guarded by soldiers who, with the aid of bayonets, hastened the Indians' steps under the burning noonday sun, amidst clouds of dust. The dragoons, armed officers, and soldiers, hastened and insulted the stragglers with severe gestures and bitter words. My poor flock of Christians was being driven like a scapegoat into a land without milk and honey.

At the head of the march the flag of the United States was carried by a mounted dragoon. Mounted officers followed the flag, and then came the horse-drawn jail wagon that held the chiefs. The jail wagon was followed by hundreds of the Indians walking along the north bank of the Vermillion River while the wagons continued on the left.

The thousand people and over two hundred horses had stirred up so much dust that the hot, dry wind had become a wall of sand and grit. Despite the conditions, the soldiers were still hurrying my poor Indians along at gunpoint. Every Indian was suffering from fatigue and many of the bare footed trailed behind the horses and wagons. Next were forty baggage wagons, in which numerous invalids, men, women, and children, too weak or infirm to walk, were crammed. The sick were lying in these wagons under a canvas that was meant to shield them from the dust and heat, but only served to smother them. Almost all the babies were dying; the mothers wept silent tears.

At the sight of Petit's arrival, Dr. Jerolaman, a Catholic physician from Logansport, whom Petit had first met while the Potawatomi caravan had stopped there, approached him with tears in his eyes. "My God, Father, they're killing them. I can't believe they're enforcing this! I have been tempted to put some of the sick out of their misery. May God forgive me."

The authorities ordered the Indians to a halt about six miles out of the town of Danville. When General Tipton gave the order, many of the Indians who were marching collapsed where they were, completely exhausted from the extreme temperatures and lack of water. They were also thoroughly dejected from their treatment

They pitched camp at Danville, Illinois. The Potawatomi were nearly too weak to greet Father Petit.

He returned the horse to Mr. Young. Judge Polke then presented a horse to Petit. As it turned out, the horse belonged to a young Indian, Red Bird. The Indian approached and said, "Maketakônia Chichipé, I give you my horse." Petit offered him the opportunity to ride but he refused stating that the honor was his to offer.

Petit joined Nanweshmah and Demoskikiague that evening. Demoskikiague did not bear her customary beautiful smile. She was pale, her lips discolored, and she had a cough. She said nothing, her large, dark eyes heavy with fatigue.

Young Lizette and her parents, Andrew Goshlieu and Chieftess Mas-saw, came to Chichipé Petit when they heard of his arrival. They bore solemn news. It was only then that Petit learned that one of the graves he had passed was that of Henry Taylor, Yocatopkone, the husband of the fourteen-year-old Mauri had died since leaving Menominee's village. Mauri emerged from her tepee and collapsed in Petit's arms and sobbed. Andrew explained that the blow to the stomach that Henry had received at the hands of Morgan may have caused his death. "He complained every day that the pain was worsening. Soon he couldn't even stand, let alone walk. We placed him in one of the wagons, and when we pitched camp at Winnemac's old village we found him dead."

He also learned that Kaukemazoqua, the frail and crippled one-hundred-year-old mother of Chiefs I-o-wah, Weesaw, and Weewissa, had died on the trail in Lafayette. She had begged to be left behind; her sons told Petit they had considered tomahawking her in her sleep to end her misery. Petit thanked God they were prevented from acting on such a misguided notion of mercy.

It was a scene of desolation with the sick and dying. Nearly all the children, weakened by heat, had fallen into a state of complete languor and depression. Petit baptized several newly born babies, whose first breath was from exile to heaven. He also baptized three newborn babies that evening. He feared they would die by morning. Two other unbaptized infants had already died along the trail that day and were hastily buried without the Rites of the Church.

He made his way to General Tipton's quarters. Tipton expressed satisfaction upon seeing him. With a condescension that Petit did not expect, the general arose from his chair, which was the only one there, and offered it to Petit.

Tipton approached him privately and commended him for his missionary efforts. "I never would have imagined saying this: a French Catholic priest did something good. These Indians of yours act like they've got good morals. Your unflagging efforts and passion in civilizing these poor savages will be eminently beneficial to them when they arrive in their new homeland."

General Tipton then boasted that he had distributed over $5000 worth of goods to allay the discontent among the people in hopes of improving their spirits.

Petit cautioned him, "This will only prove temporary. Discontent can never be assuaged with material possessions, no matter how many or how great; the longings of the human heart can only be satisfied with a spiritual good: the presence of God.

"Many of the white settlers have 'buried the hatchet,' as the saying goes, and are not in favor of what the U.S. government or your troops are doing." Petit had said the words before he realized it.

General Tipton turned to Pepper and Morgan, "This man

has more power than I." There was an uncomfortable silence before Tipton spoke again. "I believe I have never rendered my country a greater service. Together we have saved the Potawatomi from extermination."

Petit said nothing but considered how the Indians' civilization in Indiana had been destroyed by the policy of the U.S. government. Tipton then ordered that Petit be given a tent for the journey. That night was the first he passed in a tent since leaving Indiana.

The flies were horrendous by day and the mosquitoes dreadful by night.

17 September

The death count continued. Early the next morning Petit celebrated Mass for about three hundred of the Indians who mourned the death of three more of their number during the night. Three wooden crosses marked their graves as the rest left Danville and continued west.

The dead were wrapped in blankets and Petit presided over the burials. Under a milk-pale sky, the sound of shovels digging the dusty, hard earth matched the desolate landscape. Bodies were wrapped in white muslin and laid on a rude wooden bier. Hickory vines were tied around the corpse to keep the body on the wood.

At the gravesite, one by one, the Indians would take a handful of dirt and toss it on the body as they recalled the scripture: "Ashes to ashes and dust to dust, shall you return." Even the unbaptized partook in this ritual since it was already part of their tradition, possibly since the beginning, or else introduced by the early black-robed Jesuit missionaries.

Mourning lasted nearly four days. A simple piece of cloth attached to a stick would mark the graves. In the case of the baptized, a simple cross would mark the grave and a piece of cloth would be attached. The Indians deeply regretted leaving the remains of their loved ones behind in unconsecrated, unfamiliar ground. The Indian cherishes the memory of the departed.

Oftentimes, blankets with unblinking eyes staring into oblivion refused to stir in the morning. The worst were the babies, many born only to die.

The people were silent about those who had died as a result of the forced removal. Petit was troubled by this uncharacteristic silence; the resentment was high. The sins he heard in confession expressed anger toward the Americans.

Petit took the time to pray with the tribe. "God has promised: 'Have no fear. I shall provide for you and your children' (Gen. 50:21).

"When Saint Paul was discouraged and abandoned, the Lord Jesus told him, 'My grace is sufficient for you, for my power is made perfect in weakness.'

"The apostle continued: 'I consider that the sufferings of this present time are as nothing compared with the glory to be revealed in us . . . . We know that all things work together for the good for those who love God, who are called according to His purpose'" (Rom. 8:18, 28).

If God is for us, who can be against us? Who shall separate us from the Love of Christ? Shall tribulation, or distress, or persecution, or famine, or nakedness, or peril, or the sword? No, in all these things we are more than conquerors through Him who loved us. For I am sure that neither death, nor life, nor angels, nor principalities, nor things present, nor things to come, nor powers, nor height, nor depth, nor anything else in all creation, will be able to separate us from the love of God in Christ Jesus our Lord (Rom. 8:31-39).

The two things that the Potawatomi did have was their faith in God and their beloved Blackrobe Petit The God of the blackrobes had not abandoned them. Christ had not abandoned them; He was with them, on the road to Calvary, continuing to carry His cross up the hill of Golgotha.

The Catholic Potawatomi believed that the Great Spirit they had worshiped for centuries had revealed himself in the Person of Jesus Christ. Now they recounted how often that their God had saved them in the past and how He would not abandon them, even now in the face of their removal and death! They prayed, they sang, they praised God even in the midst of their great sorrow. Heartbroken they longed for the green grass and forests of Indiana, but they began to resign themselves to the fact that they would never again dwell there.

It was through the humiliating experience of being poured forth into emptiness that the people began to see that they too were experiencing their own Passiontide, their own crucifixion. Indeed they were entering into the Paschal Mystery of Christ. They too would die in order to rise. The experience of the early disciples on the road to Emmaus was their own. Was it not necessary that the Messiah should suffer and die? Out of that crushing defeat and ignominious death Christ rose again and ascended into the heavens. This was now their hope.

They emptied themselves of their inordinate attachment to the land. They too had become pilgrims, ever searching, ever on the move, never at home.

Petit, recognizing that he too was a fellow pilgrim, declared "We are journeying toward home . . . our heavenly home."

He unsheathed his knife and stripped away the bark from downed tree limbs. Tying the limbs with rope, he fashioned crosses and placed them on the fresh graves. The soldiers then blew the bugle, got the Indians on their feet, heaped the sick into the baggage wagons; everyone else mounted their horses or ponies. At departure, Petit saddled and bridled his new horse, mounted the animal and prepared to continue westward.

General Tipton no longer had jurisdiction over the removal party since they had crossed the Illinois border, but he had yet to relinquish command to Judge Polke. Some of the Indians took turns as the standard-bearer, carrying the cross in procession, raising the standard high.

Provisions were again scarce, physical conditions were worsening, and the natives were exhausted. Dr. Jerolaman, now assisted by Dr. Buell of Williamsport, was treating sixty Indians sick with fever, four with diarrhea, and three with scrofula. Of those, eight were near death.

The Chiefs I-o-wah and Ashkum, on horseback, led the line of hundreds of Indians on foot followed by men, women, and children in single file. After this cavalry came a file of baggage wagons filled with luggage and Indians. The sick were lying in the wagons, rudely jolted, under a canvas that deprived them of air—for they were as if buried under this burning canopy. Several died in this manner. Soldiers on horseback brought up the rear.

For his part, Petit rode up and down the length of the caravan to keep watch over his flock. It was difficult to behold. The caravan was only able to cover six miles. They camped at Sandusky's Point. He busily helped the Indians gather twigs and sticks for their campfires.

Many more of the Indians were growing ill. Two children and one adult died there while one child was born. Petit was weary from burying innocent children, children who once laughed and played in the Indiana forests, condemned to die all on account of their copper skin and tribal ways.

18 SEPTEMBER

The emigration party remained encamped at Sandusky's

Point due to so much illness and heat. Meanwhile, General Tipton prepared to turn over command of the march to Judge William Polke of Rochester, Indiana. Polke had been appointed by the government to lead the Potawatomi to their western territory. Polke convinced Tipton to allow the Indians to rest outside Danville for two days since their sorrow and suffering was so great.

19 September

Despite the presence of two physicians, our six-year-old Little Tree died in Turtle Girl's arms. It was a pathetic sight with none to comfort her. Her husband, Arrowhead, had been one of the early scouts who went west to inspect the Indian Territory only to have died in a fall from his horse on his return trip.

The soldiers who must remain on the trail are anxious to get moving. They are frustrated that we are still encamped and the entire emigration is progressing so slowly. They believe that the sooner they get to the western territories, the sooner they can return to Indiana.

Meanwhile, the soldiers kill passenger pigeons for sport. The sleeping passenger pigeons are knocked out of the trees and sent to the local stores and groggeries in burlap bags. Chief Menominee fears that the indigenous bird may be removed as have his people.

Some of those who are to be discharged from duty in the morning are rejoicing. More than a few now regret ever joining the militia; privately they have vowed never again to take up a rifle or bayonet against another human being.

With all the affections of my heart, I am so attached to my good Indians; I pray that no more of their precious souls will be lost.

Petit wrote to Bishop Rosati at St. Louis.

19 September 1838

Dear Monseigneur Rosati:

Last year Monseigneur Bruté of Vincennes sent me to the Potawatomi Indians to replace Monsieur DeSeille whose death left them orphans; that mission full of vigor and growth was about to be destroyed in Indiana by the policy of the U.S. government, which seeks to remove all Indians to the west of the Mississippi River.

When soldiers forced these fervent and pious Christians off their ancestral homelands at gunpoint, Monseigneur Bruté permitted me to accompany the Indians to their new settlement so that I may reestablish their church and their mission.

I am coming west not to establish a mission in the midst of the good Indians for myself, although I am attached to them with all the affection of my priestly heart—they are my first mission and first love—am coming solely to hold this mission together so that these precious souls may not be lost until I shall be able to place in your hands or in the hands of the Jesuit Fathers this infant mission for which I would gladly consecrate my life, if obedience, which is a happiness for a priest, did not call me back to the Diocese of Vincennes.

Bishop Bruté has asked that I return by March, but in the meantime I am requesting that you grant me the privilege of exercising my priestly powers in your diocese until that time.

I beg you by all that God knows of the simplicity and the sincere piety, of the fervor and the zeal and the good will in the hearts of your new Indian flock to arrange to send them a priest so that these Christians, so eager for the reception of the sacraments, which so many others neglect, may not die of exhaustion, like abandoned children, deprived of the heavenly nourishment in which their souls find so many delights.

Your Lordship knows so much better than I can tell you how important it is for the subsequent development of the Indian missions not to let them disperse and perish by the abandonment of that Christianity fully developed which Providence sends today into the midst of the nearby tribes.

Our trip so far is a harsh experience; we have much sickness—over one hundred are ill with fever and a cough or exhaustion and heat—a dozen Indians have died thus far. Two Indians were buried today and eight others are dangerously ill. The migration cavalcade will cross into Missouri at the Mississippi River at Quincy, Illinois, and our destination is the Osage River area south of Westport near Sugar Creek.

Monseigneur, please pray God to sustain us and to bless the Christian resignation of these good Indians deprived by force of their fatherland. Accept, Monseigneur, the assurance of profound respect and of the humble submission in Jesus Christ.

Your most respectful servant,
Benjamin Petit,
Missionary Priest.

19 September

Two soldier brothers from Delphi befriended Father Petit. The two men felt quite awkward about the Indian removal. They joined the militia expecting—hoping—to battle Indian warriors. The younger one of them said, "I'd never met an Indian until I joined the militia. Now I regret ever joining, especially serving under Captain Morgan."

The oldest brother said, "Forcing them to march when it is not necessary and not allowing them to get off the road to get water is inhumane, un-American. I feel like I'm driving sheep not men. Pushing them along at bayonet's point disgusts me. They have done me no harm. Over half of them are bare-footed and even the ones with moccasins have bloody feet."

There was panic circulating amid the Indians that the blankets the Americans were giving to them might be infected with disease. General Tipton had dismissed the story as nothing more than a vicious rumor. Pepper didn't care, but Morgan hoped it was true. Some familiar with the Cherokee removal claimed the Americans' intent was to exterminate the Indian race.

Tipton believed that the separation of the races was the only way to prevent further bloodshed and establish peace among their peoples.

Petit entered the officers' tent and broached the subject of the lack of food rations with the general. "Your men are hoarding the supplies, keeping the best for themselves while my children are going hungry."

"I have been twelve days engaged in this unpleasant business of Indian removal," Tipton sharply remarked. "My militiamen expect more than the common rations that are apportioned to the Indian. If I were to allow them to have bacon, coffee, and sugar it would swell the expenses considerably. As it is, if we give them just enough it gives them an incentive to keep moving west."

"Incentive, General?"

"Yes, an incentive. Why, had I failed to effect the removal, then Indiana would be in the same situation as is Florida. The Seminole tribe there has waged war against our forces for three years. I was one of the first to introduce legislation that would establish an Indian territory. For several years it was rejected before others finally saw the wisdom of it all.

"Oh, you can disagree, but I believe with all my heart that in this removal I have prevented much bloodshed and served my country well. You may believe otherwise, and you are entitled to your opinion, but as it is, the Indians have been separated from the whites."

"What do you propose to do about the southern Negro population if slavery is ever outlawed in the South," Petit queried. "Should they be sent back to Africa or will your government carve out another western territory for Negroes?"

"You Frenchies have a way with wit, don't you?" Tipton replied.

"Some of your troops object to their mission."

"They volunteered for the mission."

"But they now believe the removal is immoral."

"They have their orders. It's their duty now as American soldiers. If they refuse to follow orders what becomes of their patriotism, not to mention their oath of office?"

"One must obey God rather than men. These soldiers now see how wrong the removal is and do not want to become murderers or accomplices to murder."

"Murder? Who are these men? They must be discharged."

"They have already asked Judge Polke to dismiss them."

"I am sure they were some of the bevy of useless characters who were merely following the emigration expecting to receive pay," Tipton said. "Listen to me, Reverend, it may be the opinion of those not well informed upon the subject of war in general, and Indian removal in particular, that this military mission was uncalled for. But I feel confident that nothing but the presence of an armed force, for the protection of the citizens of our country and to punish the insolence of the dissident Indians, could have prevented bloodshed. I have never rendered my country a better service, and I am content with the reflection that my duty was executed both with humanity and efficiency.

That's all there is to it. The Indian problem had to be resolved and I was chosen for the task. You're dismissed." He laughed to himself. "Pardon, Reverend, I thought you were one of my officers for a moment."

General Tipton later dismissed one of his men for drinking to excess. That very day James Johnson, one of the soldiers, approached Judge Polke and asked to be dismissed from duty. Officer Johnson spoke to Petit before he left the caravan. He told Petit he was sick at heart over the removal. Johnson had never known any Indians until this journey. Now that he had come to know them as fellow human beings he was convinced that their removal was both illegal and immoral.

More of the men regretted their participation in the removal and what they had witnessed and participated in.

General Tipton and his men were now free to turn back. Colonel Pepper prepared to return with them. However, fifteen soldiers decided to remain with the removal party; Captain Morgan planned to remain.

20 September

In the morning, the Indians were awakened by loud wails of lament. Some Indian mothers were carrying their dead babies in bundles of blankets and placing them in trees.

"How does one explain the meaning of this suffering to an innocent people?" Petit asked aloud in prayer.

General Tipton dismissed his volunteer army and departed, returning to Indiana, but not before he informed the remaining American militiamen that the Indians were not to be mistreated. Tipton was pleased that Petit would be accompanying the tribe west. Petit did not expect such condescension on his part.

Nanweshmah told Petit of a merciful act by General Tipton. It involved a Miami Indian named Antony Nigo. Nigo should have been allowed to remain in Indiana, but because Nigo was rounded up with all the other Potawatomi on the fourth of

September, Tipton refused to let him return for a fear that other Indians would want to leave. So, sometime on the first night while they were at Chippeway, Tipton let Nigo go free—or escape—under cover of darkness.

Petit had been riding through the encampment checking on the ill when he happened upon Tipton's farewell speech as he discharged and paid the soldiers.

"I did not feel authorized to drive these poor degraded beings from our state, but I only did what had to be done, namely to move them from the reserve, and to give peace and security to our own citizens. I am happy in being able to state that the removal of the Indians was effected without bloodshed or mal-treatment. Every attention that could be was paid to their health, comfort, and convenience.

"All along the march I was moved to see so many of you walking while allowing the sickly or infirm Indians to ride your horses. A full report will be given the governor of Indiana, whereupon your return to Indiana, you will likely be hailed as American heroes, and generations to come will speak of your valor, courage, and unselfishness in volunteering for so great a mission that forever removed the threat of terror from the red-skinned warriors for you and your posterity."

No sooner had the mothers returned from placing their dead infants in the trees did the officers fire their weapons in the camp to alert the Indians that it was time to move out. The Americans lifted the sick Indians into the baggage wagons and prodded the able-bodied to leave as they mounted their steeds, pressing the Potawatomi westward.

An elderly woman refused to rouse even after a bayonet jab from Captain Morgan. He pulled her blanket away only to discover that she was dead.

As the caravan moved on, Petit left even more graves in the shadow of the cross. Petit confided in Nanweshmah, "General

Tipton will likely be forgotten as a war hero, general, and senator. Instead he will be forever linked to the Potawatomi march of death, like that of Pontius Pilate remembered for condemning the innocent Christ to death on the gibbet of the cross."

Nanweshmah silently nodded and kept pace with Petit.

Now with General Tipton gone, Judge William Polke, as the federal conductor, chose as his assistant Chauncey Carter, a volunteer soldier from Logansport. Captain Morgan went off in a tirade against Polke for choosing Carter over him; then he began insisting that he be referred to as *General* Morgan. Polke denied him both the honor and title.

Polke and Carter were now the escorts through Illinois and across the Mississippi. They asked Petit to assist them and he agreed on condition that it be made absolutely clear that he was not in connivance with the U.S. government nor did he approve of the removal.

Petit and Nanweshmah approached Judge Polke. Both men were angry that Chief Menominee and five of the other chiefs were still shackled and handcuffed and being made to ride in the jail wagon. With the departure of Tipton and his men, Petit asked Judge Polke: "Could you please release these men and give them their freedom, the same freedom that all men should enjoy?"

Polke complied; Morgan greatly resented the action. Petit feared that Morgan might commit an act of violence.

The extreme drought and hot, humid conditions of Illinois had taken their toll upon the people. Even the horses were dehydrated. The emigration party journeyed ten miles and pitched camp at Davis' Point around three o'clock. Sadly, a ten-year-old girl fell from atop a horse and was crushed under foot by another horse. Another Indian woman died in the evening.

Kaukemazoqua, the mother of Chief Weewissa, before dying, said that General Tipton had called down a curse upon himself by enforcing the violent removal of the Potawatomi. And there was a consensus among the Indians that, because of the Indian removal, the Americans had brought down a curse upon their nation as was evidenced by the tremendous drought and spread of illness.

Paukooshuck, the young chief, gleefully prophesied that John Tipton would not live to see the summer. He had somehow obtained some whiskey and came to Petit's tent intoxicated and lamented murdering his father, but in the next breath he ranted about how much he hated his father and how his father deserved death. The act of murder was ever on his mind. Petit tried to hear his confession but he couldn't reason with him. Petit suspected that one or more of the soldiers were supplying the Indians with liquor.

Later that evening, Paukooshuck got into a fight with one of the soldiers. Paukooshuck attempted to murder the soldier for the mistreatment his people were receiving. Captain Morgan intervened. He later boasted to his soldiers that he had killed Paukooshuck. In the morning, Paukooshuck was gone. Either one of the soldiers buried him or he had somehow survived and escaped during the night.[1]

Mauri was ill and her parents were heartsick. She was barely able to walk. She was despondent from the death of her husband; they loved each other very much.

Four more Indians died this day; a total of twenty-one had died since leaving Indiana.

---

1 Paukooshuck did escape and returned to Indiana. Unfortunately he died a violent death and there is a legend that at Lake Maxinkuckee his ghost can be seen on moon-lit nights in a canoe on the water at Long Point (Willard).

21 September

The conditions continued to grow worse; the heat was nearly intolerable. The Indians soon found themselves on the grand prairies of Illinois under the extreme sun and without the benefit of one shade tree. The prairies were as vast as the ocean, and the eye sought in vain for a solitary tree. Not a drop of water could be found. It was absolute torture for the sick, some of who died each day from weakness and fatigue along the dusty trail in the miserable humidity and scorching sun.

The winds gusted and the horses, ponies, oxen, wagons, and the shifting feet of a thousand Indians stirred the dust into a veritable sandstorm. Petit tied a kerchief around his face, covered his nose and mouth, and kept his eyes squinted in the face of the gritty wind and bright sun.

Petit longed for the fluttering wings and hoarse caws of blackbirds or the shadow of an endless flock of slate blue and olive green passenger pigeons. But no insects, no birds, no animals; only a ghost-gray sky floating above a barren expanse. The lone voice of nature was the wind as it whooshed through the quivering stalks of colorless dead grass and whisked the clay of the lifeless landscape into a profane hurricane of dust. Such a cloud of minute chunks of sand and gravel was as smoke from a great forest blaze, yet there was no forest to burn. The blinding shadow wrote across the plain.

In spite of the great suffering, the Indians still offered their praise to God. Petit intoned the hymns in the Potawatomi tongue and they responded with such vigor that the American soldiers—and others who were simply curious to see the natives—marveled to witness the Indians' expression of faith in the midst of their trial. The brave native souls sang hymns and told their beads; their voices in sweet harmony, especially at the holy sacrifice of the Mass, astonishing the ears—and hearts—of all.

By afternoon, the party covered twelve miles and made it to Sidney, Illinois.

Yet there was a great tragedy today among the people. Chief Mukkose died. He was known among the Potawatomi of Menominee's village and throughout Indiana and Michigan as an honest and wise chief. Chief Mukkose had been ill for two days with diarrhea; the doctor feared it was cholera. A child also died after coming into camp. The funeral rites, chants, dance, and drums for the dead chief were impressive though melancholy.

Contrary to earlier reports, there was no water to be had. There are no woods, just a harsh, windswept valley of dead grass covered by a milky sky, seemingly evening all day. As far as the eye could see, dust and dirt stirred and spun in whirlwinds of tiny cyclones on the treeless plain.

As evening darkened into night, lightning strikes lit the clouds from behind making them ominous silhouettes as the approaching thunderstorm rolled its warning. A raw north wind wailed through the encampment, the tepees and tents moaned and thumped in the unrelenting gusts of the cold wind and heavy rain. Swift, gusting cold winds from the northwest brought enormous amounts of rain; even had there been a supply of wood, no fires could have been built due to the wet conditions. The one blessing was the fact that the humid blanket of air had lifted; however, the oppressive soldiers and their bayonets remained.

The stiff wind challenged the stark silence of God like an unanswered question.

22 SEPTEMBER

The next day, despite the constant downpour, strong headwind, and extraordinarily cool September temperatures, the caravan covered sixteen miles in a treeless prairie of Illinois. The officers finally agreed to stop at Sidoris' Grove, Illinois, forty-four miles from Danville. The natives had formed a line to a tent where a solitary candle burned. Twenty Indians sang hymns and told their beads. One of their headmen had died and was laid out in the tent. The next morning a few of the men dug a grave and Father Petit recited the prayers and blessed the grave. The body of the deceased man was wrapped in a blanket and lowered into the ground. Petit cast the first shovelful of dirt on the corpse. Afterwards, the pit was filled in and Petit marked the grave with two small twigs tied together to form a simple cross.

Some of the curious Americans had come out as if to see a spectacle; despite their prejudice against both Catholics and Indians, they were moved by these solemnities of the dead. The smirk of scorn that some of the onlookers had initially bore turned to a somber pity.

Mauri was confined to one of the wagons. She was growing worse. Save prayer there was nothing Petit could do or say to console her mother and father.

Judge Polke discharged a wagoner for drunkenness, and two intoxicated Indians were shackled and placed under guard. The Indians had been with Captain Morgan prior to the incident; Petit was growing suspicious of Morgan. The wagoner had evidently obtained liquor for some of the Indians who were despondent and wanted to forget their lot. Once he was dismissed, the man was afraid to leave because that meant he would have to travel back to Indiana alone. He had been one of those who seemed to enjoy driving the Indians weary. Now he sat and cried like a child. As for the drunken Indians they were detained until they sobered up.

The constant walk caused cramps in many of the Indians' legs, and the sores and cuts on the barefooted Indians' feet were unforgivable. The blisters on the feet of those with moccasins or shoes were so painful, but they were fortunate enough to have shoes. For Petit, the hot air, lack of wind, and direct sun on his back made his black cassock soak in every ray of sun; he was wet with sweat. Riding a horse also got tiresome, so he would walk some during the day as well.

At certain points along the way, due to the extreme heat and dry conditions one ceased to sweat and the thirst became agonizing. Many, including Petit, reeled like drunkards as they prayed for a watering hole or a solitary cloud to grant them a respite from the unforgiving sun.

There were lots of gnats and flies, especially flies—flies, flies, and more flies. The horse dung on the trail and on the feet, moccasins, and shoes of the Indians kept the flies as constant traveling companions. At night the flies gave way to mosquitoes. There was nothing one could do but cover up to prevent being bitten apart. But then the evening air was so stifling that one then burned with sweat again. There was no comfort either way.

The soldiers' constant harangue and cruel cries of, "Hurry up, injuns! Faster, faster! Come on, winter's coming! Move it!" nearly drove Petit to madness. Some of the soldiers taunted the Indians by tossing them bread, making sport of them as they scrambled for the morsels. Taking their cue from the armed men, a few of the bystanders would shout out "Dirty red-skins!" sometimes accompanied by rock throwing. The soldiers would chase them away with a mock warning.

For his part, Petit busied himself filling his two canteens every time he could, rationing out water to the thirsty. The feeling among the people was that they had traveled far enough. Some of them begged the troops to let them remain behind to die.

Chief Pepishkay elevated the peoples' fears with his questions of, "How do we even know what these soldiers tell us is the truth? Suppose they are only marching us to a certain death? What if at the end of the trail, that is, if we survive the march, we are made to dig our own graves and then the soldiers will kill us one by one beginning with the children and women to the last man, forcing the men to bury the dead."

Petit chose not to argue with the man.

Judge William Polke and Petit shared a tent at this particular stop. When Petit went to pray his breviary, he discovered that the rain had rendered his pages crinkled and uneven. The two men lay under their blankets and listened to the rain and wind beat against the tent. The sixty-three-year-old Polke seemed homesick as he reminisced of his younger days. He related to Petit his tale of being captured by Indians as a child. With such a story, one might have imagined that he had grown up hating Indians.

Petit pinched some tobacco from his pouch and lit his tobacco pipe.

"We moved to Kentucky in 1780 when I was just five," Polke described his ordeal. "We settled on Simpson's Creek in Nelson County. My father, Captain Charles Polke, was a volunteer with General George Rogers Clark to defend again the Indian raids. One day my father was away defending another settlement that was under Indian attack when Kincheloe's station, the settlement where we were staying for safety, came under attack. Most of the adults were killed. Our cabin was torched. My sister Elizabeth and I tried to run away but we were captured. She was five and I was seven. My mother was also taken prisoner; she was pregnant. All in total, there were thirty of us taken prisoner and forced to walk north through Indiana to the British garrison at Detroit, Michigan. Contrary to reports, we were treated well.

"I was adopted by one of the Indian chiefs and given the name *Young Chief of the Long Knife*. I was dressed as an Indian and learned the native tongue. A year later my father and some other men traveled north to Michigan and secured our release. I held no hatred for the Indians and even went to live among the Potawatomi at Carey Mission. I served as a missionary and teacher, but family responsibilities necessitated that I resign from the field and return to the practice of law. I then founded Chippeway Village in Fulton County, Indiana."

Petit thought it ironic that he had abandoned law for the priestly ministry and Polke had abandoned the ministry for the practice of law.[1]

Nevertheless, thought Petit, too many of the Americans, rather than allowing their Christian faith to inform their political decisions—had allowed the politics of Indian Removal to taint their Christianity; the U.S. governmental policies were first deemed proper and then the faith was utilized in supporting the government's policy. From all appearances William Polke regretted this attitude.

Petit shared his story of abandoning a law career for the priesthood. It was odd hearing the story told aloud; he was struck at how unbelievable his own story now seemed. Polke soon fell asleep, his snore keeping time with the raindrops and wind.

Meanwhile Petit had difficulty getting comfortable. He felt feverish, his throat was sore and his chest and back were still aching from the fall from his horse weeks earlier and the rock-hard ground made the pain worse. His breathing had also become labored since arriving at Danville. If the symptoms were to persist he would consult Dr. Jerolaman.

---

1 When William Polke was seventeen he was in the Battle of Fallen Timbers. He then moved to Knox County near Vincennes at Maria Creek where he practiced law. In 1810, he served as interpreter between Chief Tecumseh and William Henry Harrison, Governor of Indiana Territory. In 1811, he was wounded in the Battle of Tippecanoe. His brother-in-law, Spier Spencer, was killed in the battle. General Tipton later married Polke's sister, Spier's widow. He then served as a state senator for five terms. He joined his brother-in-law, the Rev. Isaac McCoy, at the Carey Indian Mission in Niles, Michigan, and taught the Indians from 1824-25.

That night Petit had a dream that the Indians were being allowed to turn around and return to Indiana. He awakened with a certain joy and expectation. In the dawning sunlight, he quickly realized it was but a dream and his hopes evaporated as the morning dew.

CHAPTER 27

ALIEN SOIL

23 SEPTEMBER

It is difficult to rise in the morning knowing that more of my children will likely die by nightfall. Yet I still pray: Thy will be done.

Thankfully morning came without rain. It being a Sunday, Chichipé Petit detained the troops for more than an hour for Mass with the Indians. Another Indian child died during the night. Petit performed the burial and then celebrated Sunday Mass before the journey resumed. Petit didn't want his Indians to have to travel on the Sabbath, but with winter fast approaching he acquiesced. Some of the Protestant soldiers were furious that the popery of Petit and his savages was impeding American progress.

By nine o'clock in the morning, the party was on the move. The day was windy and cold, but happily it was clear and sunny. The mid-afternoon sun warmed his chilled, wet body. The Illinois prairies were so vast that Nanweshmah told Petit he and some of the other Potawatomi feared they would never see another tree.

At mid-afternoon another Indian girl died. Petit hastily conducted a prayer service and left behind another grave: the twenty-fifth since the removal began.

After a fifteen-mile trek, the troops distributed beef and flour provisions to the Indians. The location where they were encamped was called Pyatt's Point; it was on the Sangamon River. Petit was exhausted and fell asleep after sunset.

Petit was appointed as one of the interpreters to assist Dr. Jerolaman. The measureless prairie of Illinois was a veritable torture for the sick. Petit feared more would die from weakness and fatigue; the doctor unfortunately concurred with the assessment.

The Americans, who came out in curiosity to see the sight of a vanishing race, were astonished at the piety and graciousness of the Potawatomi Tribe. It was as if the Indians were passing out of this world like the morning mist.

When the emigration party camped near a town where American Catholics lived, they would come out to see them. Often they would invite Petit to breakfast before the party's departure the next day. Many of the Catholic settlers were overjoyed at seeing a priest.

Like the Chosen People of old, the Potawatomi were a people set apart, and their example edified many who witnessed them. Through their singing and practice of religion they gave witness that even though the American government had abandoned them; their God had never abandoned them! And, they would not abandon their God.

Petit called to mind an image from Saint Paul's epistles:

In all things we suffer tribulation, but are not overwhelmed; we are bewildered, but are not destitute of hope; we suffer persecution, but are not forsaken; we are cast down, but we perish not: Always bearing about in our body the mortification of Jesus that the life also of Jesus may be made manifest in our bodies. For we who live are always delivered unto death for Jesus' sake; that the life also of Jesus may be made manifest in our mortal flesh. Knowing that he who raised up Jesus, will raise us up also with Jesus, and place us with you. For all things are for your sakes; that the grace abounding through many, may abound in thanksgiving unto the glory of God . . . For which cause we faint not; but though our outward man is corrupted, yet the inward man is renewed day by day . . . While we look not at the things which are seen, but at the things which are not seen. For the things which are seen, are temporal; but the things which are not seen, are eternal (2 Cor. 4:8-11, 14, 16-18). For now we see through a glass, darkly; but then face to face (1 Cor. 13:12).

Petit was growing more ill each day and the burden was becoming harder to deny, his people's cross of suffering was heavier to carry as they traversed ever westward. He noticed a rash of blemishes appearing on his legs, but he dismissed them as insect bites.

Bear one another's burdens; and so you shall fulfill the law of Christ . . . But God forbid that I should glory, save in the cross of our Lord Jesus Christ; by whom the world is crucified to me, and I to the world . . . From henceforth let no man be trouble-some to me; for I bear the marks of the Lord Jesus in my body (Gal: 6.2, 14, 17).

The following morning another Indian child was dead. Petit said Mass and presided at the burial. He also heard confessions today. Many of the Indians were harboring murderous thoughts against the soldiers. Petit understood the feeling fully well. Several of the young braves had disappeared, escaping in the middle of the night with several of Chief I-o-wah's horses.

Petit's fever persisted, his right eye was infected from dust and dirt and his legs pained from the strange rash of sores. Despite all this he collected himself and moved out with the caravan.

By day's end two more children had died on the way.

24 SEPTEMBER

The celebration of the Mass is always accompanied by the singing of hymns of which have the sweetest of harmony. After I fold my portable chapel, I recommend that the Indians tell their beads of the rosary along the way. On Sundays we normally do not travel in observance of the commandment. Sundays begin with Morning Prayer, a lesson from the catechism, Mass, and the recitation of the rosary; in the afternoon we assemble for a lesson, followed by vespers and a rosary. A short sermon and night prayers follow the evening meal.

The rest of the days begin with Morning Prayer and Mass. The rosary is prayed while on the march. In the afternoon, hymns are sung in the Indian tongue and I lead a brief prayer after the evening meal.

I regularly accompany the physician in his rounds to the sick. Today I met a Frenchman who had come from Vincennes. He said he knew Father Stanislaus Buteaux. I have not seen Father Buteaux since my ordination; I pray his ministry has been as fruitful as mine.

The doctor had to tend to me today. I have been feeling ill for several days; I have a fever and a cough. I believe I am simply exhausted. Everyday we are forced to march. The pain in my side has returned.

Dr. Jerolaman has warned us of the dangers of ticks and fleas. Many here—both Indians and settlers—are suffering from typhus, typhoid fever, and consumption. What little water that is here is terribly polluted. Even the contagion of dead bodies has made its way into some of the waterways. The physicians fear cholera. I fear the mosquitoes. Dr. Jerolaman has asked Judge Polke to secure more wagons for transporting the sick and dying. The horses and oxen are tiring out as well.

We advanced another fifteen miles today. Two children and one adult died on the trail today. The son of Sin-is-qua, Wash-Shing, was one of the children who died. Petit stood sentry as Sin-is-qua and her six-year-old, Nancy, remained emotionless as the frail infant boy wrapped in linen was interred in the dead earth.

Pash-po-ho, the Indian who had been imbibing to help him forget his misery, began to regain his sense of self-respect and after the day's long and dusty march, he washed, dressed in his finery and leggings with beads, ribbons, and porcupine quills, and carefully painted his face.

Due to my extreme fever, a dear Frenchman wanted to take me into his house, but I declined the invitation for fear I would not be able to catch up with the marchers.

Today is also the anniversary of my ordination to the priest-hood. None of my traveling companions realize how signifi-cant this is for me. Who but the Lord would have known all that could transpire in a year's time? Yet I believe that Providence orders all things. I am where I am called to be. Deo gratias (Thanks be to God).

With no regard for the pain in his chest and back and the difficulty in sitting erect in his saddle, Petit rode up and down the length of the caravan to see how his people were doing. Some of the clans and families had gotten separated, and Petit was trying to make sure that loved ones were reunited and allowed to stay together in the march.

Even without shoes or moccasins, many of the Indians preferred to walk the trail rather than be cramped inside the over-crowded wagon. Riding in the wagons was very rough; the roads were not smooth and the wagons were forever jolting. Unfortunately, many who walked collapsed from the dust and heat and were lifted into the wagons anyway, their feet bloody and bruised.

The Indians were fatigued with severe hunger pangs because

provisions were sparse; the food rations of salted pork and beef and dried corn were being rationed. What little bread they now had was stale, and much of their food rations were spoiled, rancid, and bug infested. Sometimes the supplies did not arrive on time or not at all.

Finally the caravan came upon some wooded areas. The natives were allowed to forage for blackberries and raspberries growing in the wild. They hunted rabbit, passenger pigeons, and quail.

The Indians hung their pots over their fires. The women pounded the corn into meal and made porridge and mush; others baked hoe cakes and bread.

Tepees, tents, and buffalo and deer hides were tied together shielding the Indians from the elements as they slept on the rocky ground; others slept in the wagons. When they would awaken, they had dirt, parched grass, and dead leaves in their hair. Some of the American landowners would come out to collect money from the Indians and charge them for camping on their land.

Petit's straw hat offered little comfort. He tried to wash the dirt, grime, and grit off of his face and hands and out of his clothes; his filthy hair clung to his head under his hat.

Though everyone was longing for rest, it was difficult to get a good night's sleep. When one finally did fall asleep, morning came all too soon. The dragoons roused the people from their pathetic slumber and forced them further westward. Their dry and dusty faces betrayed their despondency.

The natives' feet and toes were bloodied and blistered in their worn out, rotting moccasins and tattered shoes; that is, for those who were fortunate to still something that covered their feet. The natives were also dehydrated due to the lack of fresh water. What water they came across was so polluted that even the hoses would not drink it. Some of the Indians had become violently ill after drinking it.

The poor mothers, still clinging to hope, had their cradle-boards strapped to their backs; the leather straps cutting into their shoulders. Pregnant mothers were especially ill. Some had died; others were dying. Other Indians driven to rage or despair have escaped or else have turned to whiskey. For the meantime the flies appeared to be multiplying and the mosquitoes were becoming more numerous.

The tragedy of removal seems far worse than anyone ever imagined.

Chief Menominee has not spoken since being released form the jail wagon. In fact, his health was failing him, and Dr. Jerolaman thought the chief may have suffered a stroke. In Menominee's stead, and with the death of Chief Mukkose, Chief I-o-wah had ostensibly assumed leadership. However, with the presence of Chiefs Ashkum and Pepishkay, the three chiefs were clearly vying for the leadership position. Ashkum and Pepishkay were sixty years of age and believed the young Chief I-o-wah was a traitor to the tribe. Ashkum had threatened to kill I-o-wah on more than one occasion, even prior to the removal.

Judge Polke purchased Chief I-o-wah a new horse because I-o-wah has rendered him such good service. The horse cost over sixty-two dollars and the federal government paid for it. Some of the American merchantmen, taking advantage of the plight of the Indians, hiked their ferry rates and are charged high prices for basic goods and services.

Chichipé Petit hadn't shaved in over a week. He hadn't changed his shirt and trousers for just as long, and his cassock was worn to a sheen in the knees and tattered at the hem. His lone pleasure, save the companionship of the Indians, was his pipe.

The intolerable agony in his ribs and back, the bloody sores upon his legs, his persistent fever, and the infected and swollen right eye were now unbearable. On the evening of the twenty-fifth, Chichipé Petit collapsed to the cold, wet earth. "Pray for me as I pray for all of you," he said to the Indians who placed him on a cot. "I am resolved to follow His will in all things—even if I should never return. For the love of God I shall serve for no other reward but God's favor."

Dr. Jerolaman, Judge Polke, Nanweshmah, and the Chiefs I-o-wah, Ashkum, and Pepishkay argued that Petit should go ahead to Decatur in order to seek medical attention, but Petit vigorously replied, "The salvation of souls is greater than a concern for my own health or safety." For the next few days he was ill with fever and rode in one of the wagons. Despite constant pleading from Polke and Nanweshmah, he refused to leave the caravan.

Some of the Indians imbibed liquor, securing it from some of the soldiers or managing to obtain it along the way from some of the stores and groggeries in the small towns. Some horse thieves had stolen some of the Indians' ponies and horses during the night.

Yet in almost every town there was much compassion from the Americans. It begged the question: exactly who truly supported Indian removal?

Petit and the tribe found few supporters, if any, other than the soldiers driving them on and a few merchants who were gloating over the Indians as if a great victory has been won by their removal. By and large, most people came out and looked on in disbelief while others shielded their eyes and turned away in tears; the derogatory term "red-skin" was no longer heard—except from some of the volunteer militiamen.

The further west the Indians went, the less and less they were able to celebrate with their drums and song. And less and less did they talk. However, in the morning and evening, the natives still sang at their religious services. There were always a few curious onlookers who, perhaps seeking adventure, would come out to witness the disappearing children of the forests. Soldier and stranger alike commented that the sonorous strains of the natives' voices in worship were beautiful and refuted the claim that the people were savage and uncivilized.

As Petit prayed the Psalms, his heart was with his people.

I have become like a pelican in the wilderness, like an owl in a desolate place. I like awake and I moan like some lonely bird on a roof. All day long my foes revile me; those who hate me use my name as a curse. The bread I eat is ashes; my drink is mingled with tears. My days are like a passing shadow and I wither away like the grass (Ps. 102:7-10, 12).

The soldiers, smug with confidence, mounted on their steeds reminded him of other Psalms:

Put no trust in princes, in mortal man in whom there is no salvation (Ps. 146:3). God takes no delight in the strength of horses (Ps. 147:10). A king is not saved by a mighty army nor a warrior delivered by great strength. Useless is the horse for safety . . . better to trust in the Lord than to trust in mortal man in whom there is no help (Ps. 33:16-17).

For the Lord knows of what we are made, He remembers that we are dust. As for man, his days are like grass; he flowers like the flower of the field; the wind blows and he is gone and his place never sees him again. But the love of the Lord is everlasting upon those who hold Him in fear (Ps. 103:14-17).

The Lord said:

Thou art precious in my eyes . . . and I love thee. Fear not, I am with thee; from the east I will bring back thy descendants, from the west I will gather thee up (Is. 43:4-5). Thus says the Lord who made thee, thy help, who formed thee from the womb: fear not! I will pour out water upon the thirsty ground, and streams upon the dry land; I will pour out my spirit upon thy off-spring, and my blessing upon thy descendants (Is. 44:2-3).

For Petit, the suffering of the Potawatomi called to mind the passage from Isaiah concerning the suffering servant:

He was spurned and avoided by men, a man of suffering, accustomed to infirmity, one of those from whom men hide their faces, spurned, and we held him in no esteem. . . . Though he was harshly treated, he submitted and opened not his mouth. Like a lamb led to the slaughter or a sheep before the shearer; he was silent and opened not his mouth. Oppressed and condemned, he was taken away, and who would have thought any more of his destiny, when he was cut off from the land of the living? (Is. 53:3, 7-8).

After vespers with the Indians, before Petit retired for the evening, Chief Pepishkay, still a non-Christian, approached Petit. "We are being put to death. This is why we should have never left, Blackrobe. The reason your Manitou Jesus came to earth was because your people were so wicked. Now we are sharing in your misery because we listened to you. You are just as much to blame as these soldiers," Pepishkay turned and returned to his tepee.

The absence of the birds and their songs, the green forests of Indiana, croaking frogs, and the multitude of insect songs seemed an unnatural harbinger of coming desolation.

In the face of so many evils, and in spite of all the sadness, Petit was confident that Bishop Bruté's decision to send him west was an act of divine intervention. He believed he was where he should be: with his Potawatomi children, celebrating Mass, hearing their confessions, and absolving them of their sins. With so much death and uncertainty, more of the natives had come to him seeking Baptism. His flock surrounded him, cheering his heart. In his moments of doubt and illness, the Potawatomi strengthened his faith; his solace was their request for the sacrament of the Eucharist.

24–26 SEPTEMBER

The march followed the Sangamon River for the next few days. The natives waded in the cloudy waters; the thirsty plunged into the shallow river as if it was heaven. Some of the Indians were revived as was their faith. Many of those formerly sick were feeling better. Unfortunately, not all were well. Another child, Wiss-o, died on the evening of the twenty-sixth as they camped outside Decatur, Illinois.

27 SEPTEMBER

As the caravan moved through Decatur, Illinois, one child died. Dr. Jerolaman also became ill. The good news was that the day's hunt had yielded so many deer that the camp was full of venison. There was also a source of clean water as well. They encamped at Long Point, Illinois.

28 SEPTEMBER

Today was the last encampment along the Sangamon River. The Indians were reluctant to leave the waters. The caravan forded the river and traversed eighteen miles. Judge Polke promised the Indians tobacco if, as they passed through Springfield, they presented a good appearance. Father Petit questioned Judge Polke's motivation for this form of bribery.

Meanwhile, Polke placed Chief I-o-wah in charge of communicating this to all of the Indians. This only continued to confirm to Pepishkay and Ashkum that I-o-wah was in league with the Americans.

Food was in abundance, with plenty of wild berries. The horses were well fed.

29 September

The next morning, Petit collapsed to his knees in prayer when he learned that yet two more children had died during the night. He presided at their burials before the soldiers prodded the tribe to move. The Indians abided by Polke's wishes and I-o-wah's words and wore their best clothes on this morning's march.

When the party arrived at Springfield, the streets of the city were lined with eager and curious spectators. The Indians could hardly march through the street. Dr. Jerolaman became so ill he rode in a wagon. He was taken in by a Catholic doctor in Springfield and required to stay behind. That day the march traversed seventeen miles to McCoy's Mill where the people encamped at a stream with very little water.

They Indians were marched through Springfield, Illinois, the new capitol, where much building was going on. The entire city came out to see the entourage of the Potawatomi going west to their new homes. The Indians dressed in their finery so as to make a good impression. "For whom?" Pepishkay asked. Petit agreed. He challenged Polke on this point.

Polke argued that the Indians are a proud people and should be entitled to the respect they deserve. Many of the people complied with Polke's wishes because they were told that this was the capital of the state and many people would be out to see them march by.

Ashkum, Pepishkay, and Chesaugan argued that making worn out, dispirited people dress in their best clothing simply for people to gawk at was reprehensible! Petit believed it was a political stunt, carefully orchestrated so as to give the impression that removal was not as bad as some said it was and shield the public from the repugnant reality of removal.

There was not complete support from the American public for the removal; perhaps this would allay some fears that reticent Americans may have had. Among the Potawatomi the debate continued, though they did as they were asked.

A child died after the day's march.

30 September

Today was Sunday and Petit celebrated Mass and Morning Prayer. Though it was to be the Sabbath rest, due to the lack of water and uncertainty in the weather—it was an unseasonably warm, overcast, and windy day—Petit agreed with Polke's plan to march due to the extreme need for water. For three hours they marched and had yet to find fresh water. The Indians were allowed to hunt game again; large quantities were procured. The deer hide was procured for moccasins.

Though the sky threatened rain all day, none fell. All in all the party only moved westward six miles and pitched camp at Island Grove. At sunset the red and purple clouds dispersed upon the horizon revealing the hosts of heaven: the moon, Jupiter, Venus, and Mars.

That evening another volunteer militiaman was dismissed for drunkenness.

1 October

Petit rose early for Mass and prayers. Polke wanted the caravan to get to Jacksonville, Illinois, by nightfall. Tragically, along the way Me-kaw, the daughter of Chief Meteah, fell from one of the wagons and was crushed under its wheels. She lingered in terrible pain, bleeding from her ears and mouth, her legs and arms broken. Chief Meteah wept as he held her in his arms. She cried and moaned until her plea was only a whimper. Then she became unconscious. The girl died before arriving at Jacksonville. Her parents were inconsolable. Both of them continually blamed themselves for riding in the wagon. Polke ordered the march to a halt so that Me-kaw could receive a proper interment. Petit presided at the burial just east of Jacksonville.

Curious onlookers came out to see the Indians as if coming out to see a caravan of wild animals associated with a circus. However, late that night, after vespers, the encampment was serenaded by the Jacksonville band. The Indians took it as a gesture of good will, though it was music strange to their ears and sentiments.

The Indians were allowed to hunt from the region of the Illinois River to the limits of the Indian Territory. But as they neared the assigned destination, they unfortunately found that game became scarcer and scarcer. No woods were seen other than a small cluster of trees on the banks of dried up brooks, which flowed far from each other in the vast prairies.

The October leaves have dropped and all that remained were stark outlines of trees against an angry gray sky. In the meantime, the Indians were becoming more dejected. Their singing was more subdued at prayer. Many wept now instead. Some of the American soldiers, accustomed to the natives' chants, drums and reed flutes around the evening campfire, asked the Indians to sing and dance but they refused. Many of the natives who once loved to converse with Petit were deathly silent.

Psalms 136 took on new meaning. As the Israelites of old were driven into exile by their Babylonian captors, so had Petit's beloved Potawatomi been driven into exile by the Americans.

By the rivers of Babylon
there we sat and wept,
remembering Zion;
on the poplars that hung there
we hung up our harps.
For it was there that they asked us,
Our captors for songs,
Our oppressors, for joy.
"Sing to us," they said,
"one of Zion's songs."
O how could we sing
The song of the Lord
on alien soil?

2 October

On Tuesday morning, the Indians were marched into Jacksonville's town square escorted by the town's band; the citizens gave the Indians presents of apples, bread, other foodstuffs, tobacco, and pipes. The band played again and escorted them for a couple of miles out of town. The hot, dusty day ended at Exeter, a distance of sixteen miles. Water was still scarce.

Chichipé Petit fell ill again with fever and shortness of breath. An old Frenchman wanted him to rest a few days at his home, but despite his pleading, Petit refused because he didn't want to leave the Indians.

He was unable to see out of his swollen right eye, but he had yet to reveal the bleeding sores on his legs and stomach. Petit's pallid complexion was a worry to Nanweshmah and Demoskikague. Little Lizette told Blackrobe Chichipé that he looked the color of ash. Petit also had a runny nose and chapped lips. His breathing was labored with wheezing and he now walked with a noticeable limp.

Many of the Potawatomi that had embraced the Catholic faith carried their rosaries in the shameful procession. They said the beads either in meditation on the sorrowful mysteries of the Blessed Lord or else as a way to keep their mind occupied under threat of bayonet and bullet, a mental escape from the terror and torture of an unnecessary and unwanted exodus, an exodus from freedom into what many feared would be eventual annihilation.

Some of the converts began to doubt. Where was the great Blackrobe Jesus? Where was the great Christian God? Why had He allowed them to be led out to a virtual desert where so many of the children died? Why? How could a God of love allow the soldiers to treat their chiefs in such a manner? If the soldiers believed in the same God as they did, then why were they treating them in such a way? If the Christian religion taught that all men are brothers, then why were they being removed and abandoned?

Chief Pepishkay said to Petit: "Blackrobe, why don't these men just shoot us now and get it over with? They're taking us west in hopes we'll all die by the time they stop marching us. And even if some of us do survive, they're likely to kill us anyway. Can't you hear the women weeping at night? Those are the cries of anguish rising heavenward to a Christian God who does not hear because He is dead. He died on the cross, as you say, but He is as powerless now as He was when He died. Many of my people forsook the Great Spirit our ancestors worshiped for this Manitou Jesus of yours, and look what has happened? We are bereft of hope! We have not only angered our God, but we have betrayed the memory of our ancestors!"

At night the sound of weeping was accompanied by the plaintive beat of a solitary drum—either as a reminder to the people that they were still a people, or that as the people were dying, so was the heart of their nation.

Even the soldiers were exhausted and dispirited. They just

wanted the whole tragic migration, relocation, resettlement, removal, or whatever it was called, to be over and done with. Some of the soldiers regretted their involvement. They no longer drove the Indians like animals and they had long ceased poking them with their bayonets. All parties involved were ready for the march to end; no one needed any prompting to keep trudging his way westward.

One of the young American Protestant soldiers, who had abused some of the young braves at Danville, came to Petit's tent late that night. He removed his soft brimmed hat upon entering the tent fold.

"I'm not Catholic, Reverend Father, but I have been with you now for several weeks. The preacher in our church back in Indiana has always taught us that Catholics were not Christian. But you have destroyed every image I was taught about the Catholic Church being the Whore of Babylon. Certainly no one can do what you have done unless he was truly a man of God."

The young man then repented of his prejudice against the natives; he planned to ask Judge Polke to dismiss him from service.

3 OCTOBER

The soldiers roused the eight hundred Indians at daybreak and marched them nine miles. It was shortly before noon when the emigration party arrived at Naples, Illinois. Petit collapsed again, unconscious with fever and breathing problems. Mr. Craft, a Protestant gentleman and the husband of a French Catholic woman, came forward to take Petit to his house. This time Petit was so disoriented that he had no choice but to accept the kindness. The Crafts' hospitality was unparalleled. Petit could hardly stand; the sores and wounds of his legs were now severe. He took some bread and water and fell asleep at once.

The conductors and soldiers wanted the Indians across the

river from Naples so as to prevent them slipping away and going to the taverns. Naples sits upon the Illinois River and for nine hours straight the Indians forded and ferried the river on keel boats and flat boats as well as the regular ferry. Many of the Indians were able to bathe and swim; others washed their clothes. Some of the women busied themselves by making moccasins. By nine o'clock that evening, the last of the baggage wagons were ferried across.

So many of the Indians were now absolutely exhausted and some even wanted to die. How many children have to die before a people's will to live is ripped from them? No wonder some sought the inebriation of intoxication. The weather was exceedingly cold and an icy rain soaked them through. By evening the majority of the Indians had crossed the river though about a hundred remained in Naples for the night. Nearly every foot in the temporary encampment was numb and bloody. Two children died in the night.

The next morning the emigrating Indians who remained on the other side of the river opposite Naples crossed over. Meanwhile, Petit remained in bed convalescing. Polke decided to have the party remain encamped for the day to allow for much needed rest and maintenance of the wagons and wheel repairs. Meanwhile, the Indians repaired their moccasins and since they had been allowed to hunt deer they smoked some of the venison and tanned the hide for more moccasins.

5 OCTOBER

Petit remained behind in Naples at the Crafts' home. The Potawatomi traveled to McKee's creek. The only water found was in stagnant ponds.

6 OCTOBER

Petit slept through the supper hour the evening before and did not awaken until mid-morning. When he did rise he forced himself to get dressed, eat something, and take the public stage west in order to find his way to the migrating Indians. The rain turned to a mix of sleet and snow.

When his stage overtook the marchers, he was too ill to join them on foot. Instead, he rode ahead to Quincy, Illinois, in hopes of finding lodgings. On his way there, he learned there was a Catholic church at Quincy and went to meet the pastor, a German missionary priest, Father Augustus Brickwedde. The largely German-immigrant congregation received Petit with an unrivaled hospitality. Many of the American Catholics and several of the prominent Protestants welcomed him in the same manner. The priest arranged for Petit to stay at the home of Richard Montgomery Young, an Illinois state senator.

Petit began to feel better and before the Indians arrived at Quincy he had purchased boots, shoes, blankets, wine, raisins, fruit, and several pairs of goggles to protect them from the wind and dust. Father Brickwedde also gave Chichipé Petit a gift: a pipe from Germany.

The place where the Potawatomi encamped after seven hours of walking was a barren spot save some brush and tall weeds. Sadly before the camp retired, news of another child's death reverberated through the Indians' tents. This was near Liberty, Illinois.

7 OCTOBER

On Sunday morning, the choking dust had given way to rain during the night, and the air that followed was cool. They said Morning Prayer, but had no Mass due to Petit's absence. They marched twelve miles and camped at Mill's Creek.

8 OCTOBER

It was two days later when the Indians finally arrived in Quincy.

When Petit came out to rejoin them at the encampment, Judge Polke invited him to meet the Baptist preacher, Isaac McCoy.

McCoy put his hand on his heart and cried, "Ah, they are bone of my bone, flesh of my flesh! I truly feel that I love humankind! Young man, may God bless your labors among them. Make them better than they are!"

Petit assured him that he would. His impression of the Protestant minister was that McCoy was attempting to make a sensation. Petit knew of the sort of commanding enthusiasm in which the ministers of the reformers' faith were never lacking.

"The removal will preserve their people from the evil of liquor," McCoy continued. "Just keep the American traders and groggery owners from opening taverns and stores in Indian territory."

The Indians were not very receptive to Protestant ministers. The Indians believed that many of the American Protestants were the ones largely responsible for Indian removal. Petit tried to explain that not all Protestants endorsed the governmental policy. Some of the Indians didn't care.

Due to his continued fever and chills, Petit stayed at Senator Young's. Meanwhile, three more children perished.

9 OCTOBER

The Catholic Indians were permitted to attend Mass at Saint Boniface Catholic Church in Quincy on that Tuesday morning. It was the first time the Indians had ever worshiped in a brick church.

Give me again the joy of Thy help; with a spirit of fervor sustain me, that I may teach transgressors Thy ways and sinners may return to Thee. O Lord, open my lips, and my tongue shall ring out Thy goodness, my mouth shall declare Thy praise (Ps. 51:14-15, 17).

10 October Wednesday,

The natives attended Mass again on Wednesday morning before crossing the Mississippi River. The Indians also took advantage of the opportunity to wash their clothes in the river.

Before the march began, two more soldiers and a wagoner requested permission to be discharged from their duties. They had seen enough and could no longer support Indian removal. At the same time, unfortunately, more alcohol had been obtained by the Indians.

The Mississippi River was the largest river Petit and his people had seen in America. The Indians called the Mississippi "the father of waters." The process of ferrying across the river in steamboats took all day while the teams of horses worked to pull the ferries across the channel. Dr. Jerolaman finally arrived by stage; he was still in bad health. The chiefs assembled today with Polke and requested liberty to remain in camp each succeeding Sabbath for devotional exercises.

Polke agreed to accommodate the wish as much as possible.

CHAPTER 28

MISSOURI

10 OCTOBER 1838

We have crossed the great Mississippi River and are now in the state of Missouri. From the time we passed Naples, Illinois, at the Illinois River, the Americans have allowed the Indians to hunt along the way. Many deer, turkey, and pheasants were downed in this magnificent hunting ground. But as we approach the territory assigned to them we are discovering fewer and fewer deer and the rest of the game is even scarcer. The prairies are vast and there are no woods.

The further west we go, more of the young braves either sneak off to find liquor in some of the towns or flee from the emigration to return to Indiana or Michigan. Regardless, the drunkenness among the Indians and the trail of death that we have left behind brings me great anguish. We are far fewer in number than when we first embarked on the emigration.

Due to the break in the rain, but with winter already upon them, Judge Polke pressed the Potawatomi to continue westward. Thanks to the generous hospitality of Senator Young, Petit's fever subsided and he was able to ride in one of the wagons. When they arrived at camp, two more Indian children were near death. Petit said the prayers, anointed them with Extreme Unction, and gave them Viaticum.

The provisions of beef and flour were again being rationed. The only water to be had was found was in stagnant ponds; all the creeks and streams were dry. The Indians were finding alcohol wherever they could. This was causing problems for all. Guards had to watch the Indians to make sure they did not go into town to the taverns or grog shops. Meanwhile, the soldiers nearly had to kick at the Indians to wake them in the morning.

During the night, another child died as did an adult—the eldest son of one of the chiefs. The chief was not Catholic and insisted that he preside at his son's funeral, not the blackrobe.

Petit had written earlier that there was nothing as glorious as having nothing to do but work for God. With the realization of the removal and burying so many of the dead he began to experience a heavy darkness, a sadness of soul. Nanweshmah sensed the priest's dejection and reminded him of how he had once kindled his faith. Other natives gathered about Chichipé and told of happier times.

Petit remembered the scripture:

All who desire to live a godly life in Christ Jesus will be persecuted (2 Tim. 3:12). In the world you will have tribulation; but be of good cheer, I have overcome the world (John. 16:33).

A pure heart create for me, O God, put a steadfast spirit within me. Do not cast me away from Thy presence, nor deprive me of Thy Holy Spirit (Ps 51:12-13).

Polke was bothered that his soldiers had to guard against suspicious persons who followed the emigration with the intention of swindling the Indians of their ponies and property. Another important duty the dragoons performed was guarding the grogshops with which each village abounds through which they passed to prevent the intoxication of the Indians.

As the weather became cooler and frost was in the air, Polke felt compelled to purchase shoes for the elderly men and women who either had no shoes or moccasins or whose shoes were worn out. Owing to the great number of weak and infirm, Polke and Petit had also employed wagons for them.

The soldiers spent time repairing some of the wagons and shoeing their horses before moving the Indians along. The Indians busily sewed up their worn out moccasins and shoes. The soldiers had boots and rode horses, which made it easier for them to discount the Indians' complaints of how difficult the journey was becoming for those on foot.

Some of the children had loud whooping and hacking coughs that expelled dark mucus. Some were also coughing up blood as well. Unfortunately some of those children's blankets refused to stir in the morning.

The tragedy of finding a human lump under a blanket with an unblinking stare was insufferable. How does one continue to explain so much death and destruction to children? Many of them were frightened that they would be the next to die. How well Petit knew that more of them would die before they arrived at their appointed destination, and the sound of weeping and shovels digging the cold earth would resound again.

How much longer could Petit continue to tell them that all shall be well? They would think him a liar. Some already feared that he had betrayed their trust by agreeing to accompany them west. They were not completely trusting of Judge Polke, though Petit was. Some of the Indians doubted Polke's sincerity, not the least because he was an American, but because he was a Protestant minister. Petit prayed the animosity was not there, but some of the people could stand Protestants no better than the poor Irish immigrants could stand the Protestants.

11 October
Thursday

The emigrating partu encamped at Pleasant Spring near Palmyra, Missouri. Mauri seemed to be doing better. She was still unable to walk, but she was more alert and her fever had subsided. An adult Indian died today: an elderly woman. Her family cried that she had to be buried in alien soil. An accidental death of one of the boys also occurred. He was running to catch up with his father, crossed between two wagons, and was trampled underfoot by the horses.

12 October

The weather had changed drastically: extreme wind and dust, yet the air was piercingly cold and it felt as if it would soon snow. Judge Polke presented Petit with a frock coat. Petit was ill with the fever again. His right eye was inflamed and swollen from all the dust and dirt. The rash on his legs and stomach was now spreading to his chest. The itch was horrible. He informed the doctor of the symptoms; he cautioned Petit that his condition could become fatal. The young priest entrusted himself to the Mother of the Lord and her providential care.

More of the natives found liquor readily available. Their spirits were desolate, and now even their religious faith seemed to offer no comfort in the face of their removal.

A group of the braves had conspired to tomahawk the American agents and conductors but one of them came to Petit for confession. He told the brave to make Chief I-o-wah aware of the plot. Evidently the chief was able to convince the braves to abandon their plan.

Three Indians drank to excess and began to challenge Morgan and the men. The three were all placed under arrest. Captain

Morgan announced that he would resign the next day. The whisper among the soldiers was that Morgan had taken advantage of the Indians, supplying them with liquor. Another more lascivious rumor was that he had tried to seduce one of the young Indian girls.

13 October

Today was very cold and windy. They marched seventeen miles! They pitched camp at Clinton, Missouri. Chiefs I-o-wah and Ashkum had been arguing about Captain Morgan's resignation. Ashkum wanted Morgan to remain; Morgan had made promises to them that he could only keep once the caravans arrived in Indian Country.

Chief I-o-wah did not regard Ashkum as a rightful chief; I-o-wah believed Ashkum and his men should have had no say in any matter related to the tribe. I-o-wah wanted Morgan to be arrested, but if that could not be arranged, then he would be pleased with his immediate dismissal.

Morgan's behavior toward some of the Indian women was unacceptable and inappropriate, to say the least. From all indications it appeared that he gave some of them alcohol and then tried to take advantage of them.

14 October

Sunday. Cold and very windy. Polke agreed that all would remain in camp. Petit celebrated Mass for the tribe. Afterwards, he called I-o-wah and Ashkum forward in an attempt to reconcile their differences. They shook hands at Polke's tent called "headquarters."

Both chiefs demanded that Dr. Jerolman be dismissed. Jerolaman had been ill and he still had a cough. The natives no longer believed in Jerolaman's medicine since he himself was not healthy and had been absent for several days. The chiefs claimed

Jerolaman had not cared for the Indians as he had been hired to do, spending most of his time and medicine on the soldiers rather than the Indians as was promised. There was no small complaint against him for his lack of concern when so many of the Indian children were dying. Jerolaman also bled his patients for medicinal purposes. The Indians did not approve of the practice.

Petit's prayed to support his people in their darkest hour.

Christ suffered for you, leaving you an example that you should follow in His footsteps. He committed no sin, and no deceit was found in His mouth. When He was reviled, He did not revile in return; when He suffered, He did not threaten, but trusted and handed Himself over to the One who judges justly (1 Pet 2:21-23). Therefore, rejoice to the extent that you share in the sufferings of Christ, so that when His glory is revealed you may also rejoice exultantly (1 Pet. 4:13).

15 October Monday

The day brought freezing temperatures. It was difficult walking into the blowing grit and dirt. It was still twelve miles to Paris, Missouri. Polke decided that Dr. Jerolaman should be retained for the officers only. Even though Dr. Jerolaman purchased a keg of tobacco for the Indians in hopes of allaying their discontent, they still disagreed with Polke's decision; however, they did appreciate Jerolaman's gesture of kindness.

Once encamped, hay was distributed to the horses while beef, corn, and potatoes were issued to the Indians. The piercingly cold wind continued, and a hard rain mixed with sleet fell. Everyone was cold throughout their bodies: numb fingers, faces, ears, and especially feet. Their mud-covered moccasins and boots covered bloody, blistered, numb feet. For some, the holes in their moccasins made it feel as if they were barefoot. In fact, some of the natives were still barefoot and had been since leaving Indiana.

Going from such extreme heat to such extreme cold was a jolt to one's body. The icy mix became a wet, blinding snow and the dust became miry clay.

Petit gathered around one of the campfires and waited for the water to heat so he could make a hot cup of tea. He sat breathing into his hands so as to warm his fingers in hope of reviving the feeling. The moist cloud of his breath disappeared as quickly as it appeared.

Polke compromised. Dr. Jerolaman would be retained, but only for the soldiers. In an attempt to placate the Indians, Polke provided the Indians with a keg of tobacco. That night strong winds and rain pelted the encampment. The wind was so strong that some of the tents were uprooted and canvas torn. The air was cold.

16 OCTOBER

The next morning they awakened to more sleet and snow. Traveling was made difficult because the wagon wheels were clogged with ice, mud, and snow. Petit had a runny nose, and his socks were wet and frozen to his feet. As the north wind bit into Petit's face, the sleet and snow lashed him like a Roman centurion's flagellum.

Petit gave away his gloves. He then wrapped his hands in old discarded rags, breathing on his fingers and hands to rejuvenate his strength. He saw an old Indian man whose toes were protruding from his moccasins; Petit traded his shoes for the old man's moccasins. The natives' shoes and moccasins continued to rot through from the constant exposure to the rain and snow on the seemingly never-ending march. Petit's soles were soon bloody as were his heels and ankles.

As the snow fell, bloody footprints appeared, turning the virgin snow to a crimson red. Everyone's feet were now frozen whether or not one was wearing shoes. The wind worsened on the plains as they walked due west straight into the snow and wind. There were very few trees in this place. Some of the Indians prayed for death; they could go no further. Many collapsed and had to be placed in the covered wagons. Whereas some had previously died from the heat, now they died from exposure.

Petit gave his frock coat to one of the pregnant mothers. The smell of death was in the air; puddles of icy water marked the trail as the blankets soaked with rain grew heavier with each mile.

By late afternoon, the western sky was a brilliant blue and the setting sun a scarlet red, yet the mantle of snow remained frozen. The crunch of ice and snow under the thousands of feet and horse hooves and wagon wheels echoed through the white valley. When the soldiers decided upon a stopping point, the shelter for the emigrating Indians was a mere lean-to or a hastily erected tepee; the tents were rotting from the heavy rain and snow.

Petit stood near his tent and scraped snow and ice from his moccasins, blanket, and chasuble. His ears, nose, mouth, fingers and toes were numb from the driving wintry wind and sleet. The sores on his legs were foul and festering; he tried to hide his condition from everyone. His hair had grown long and his beard was unshorn.

His hooded gothic chasuble, a cloak resembling a round blanket, was very practical like a poncho. Used by a priest when he celebrated Mass, it was worn over the alb and stole to remind the faithful of the seamless garment of Christ. In this particular situation, it served to keep him from freezing even though his cough was worsening by now.

It was so cold and wet that it was almost futile to attempt to light a fire—if one could find wood at all. Nanweshmah same to Petit's tent with a report on the lack of provisions and how many of the Indians were sick or dying. Petit handed his purse to Nanweshmah. Much of the money was from Petit's mother. She said he was only to use it in case of extreme need. Such was the case. He then loaned his horse to Nanweshmah and sent him to town to secure supplies, gloves, shoes, and food.

Nanweshmah recalled the promise of an Indian prophecy: "One day there will be no more division between white men and red men; the colors of the skin will no longer matter but only the good or evil of the heart."

There was tremendous sadness of hearing the daily wail of a mother's lament from one or more tepees. He went to sleep with no assurance that he would not be one of those found in the morning bearing an unblinking stare.

17 October

The encampment awoke to more ice and sleet. Everything was frozen to the ground. A few of the natives were so hungry they ate snow and were foraging for roots and anything edible. The natives who either had no moccasins or whose moccasins had worn out dreaded the day's march.

Before Mass some of the Indians were accusing Captain Morgan of theft and drinking liquor during the night. Polke shared with Petit General Tipton's opinion of Morgan: "Morgan hangs on to his commission, but he is wholly unfit for command and without personal respect or sense of honor, he clings to the Indian removal merely for money."

Chauncey Carter told Petit, "Morgan is in the daily practice of getting intoxicated and procuring whiskey for the Indians."

One of the soldiers, Jesse Douglas, came to the tent and said that Dr. Jerolaman had been involved with Morgan in drinking and the like. Petit was surprised and saddened at this revelation. Polke, however, declined to dismiss Morgan due to his need for soldiers; the weather was increasingly bad and he needed an experienced rider like Morgan.

As they prepared to depart, more heavy snow mixed with sleet fell. The road was slippery and difficult for the Indians to stand or walk. It was miserable traveling and everyone was covered with snow and ice. Some of the Indians collapsed and had to be carried to the wagons. As the day waned, the snow turned to a cold rain. Now instead of dust, the problem was mud. The wagons slogged through the muddy trails and the frozen waters—as did the poor natives. By nightfall, many feet were numb and bloody—with or without moccasins. The party arrived at Huntsville, Missouri. It had only been a thirteen-mile walk, but it felt more like a hundred.

More sleet and snow fell that night. Very cold and wet. There was great difficulty in starting a fire once encamped. Many of the people were suffering from frostbite and exposure. The soldiers distributed straw to the Indians.

The past week has brought much sadness. Snow has fallen nearly every day and the temperature is abnormally cold. My illness has worsened. There were days where all I could do was ride in one of the wagons. I am experiencing shortness of breath and sores have now appeared all over my body. Some are bleeding. Even reading and praying has become a difficult task.

> Like the deer that yearns for running streams,
> so my soul is yearning for Thee, my God.
> My soul is thirsting for God, the God of my life;

when can I enter and see the face of God?
My tears have become my bread, by night,
by day, as I hear it said all the day long:
"Where is thy God?"

(Ps. 42:2-4).

18 October

They rose to rain and sleet. Due to such inclement weather, the party remained in camp. The Indians were given straw for their beds. It rained all day. The snow and mud was now covered with ice and it was horrendously slippery. Polke decided that the caravan would not travel owing to the flooded, snow-muddy plains. The Indians and soldiers worked at foraging enough firewood so they could rest around campfires.

By nightfall, some of the Indians were drinking with some of the soldiers. The lines of differences were blurring without Morgan around. A few of the Indians became intoxicated and they caroused most of the night. No arrests were made; either the soldiers were too tired to mess with the Indians or else they, too, were intoxicated.

Three of the Indians found to be drunk were placed under guard. Polke asked that Captain Morgan submit his resignation. He refused, so Polke dismissed him for drunkenness. Humiliated, Morgan appealed to Petit, but he could do nothing.

Polke dismissed Morgan in front of the entire tribal gathering. Morgan and his underlings left without a word of farewell to anyone.

Chief Pepishkay then became vocal with Polke. "We are being removed from our land of plenty to a desert wilderness where we will be scattered only to die!"

Petit reminded the people of God's promise in Genesis. "Have no fear, I shall provide for you and your children" (Gen.

50:21). Petit felt in his heart that the Potawatomi, like a scapegoat, had been burdened with the sins of all Indian people and led into the desert.

"The Lord found them in a wilderness, a wasteland of howling desert. The

Lord shielded them and cared for them, guarding them as the apple of His eye" (Deut. 32:10).

"You betray my people," Pepishkay said to Petit.

"How did I ever betray any of you? I love you and your people."

"*Love*? What proof have you ever given that you truly love us?"

"My *life*." Petit placed his hands to his heart; he was hurt.

Nanweshmah tried to intervene, but Petit prevented him. "My life is my witness. I have renounced all for the glory of God. In renouncing the world I have embraced you and your people. Your entire plight has become mine. I have renounced wife, children, and home for your sakes."

"Then where is your God now, Blackrobe? Still on the cross? Defeated like us?"

"Yes, still on the cross. Only to rise again. Like us. If we endure with Him, we shall reign with Him; if we die with Him, we shall also live with him."

"Many of our sons and daughters are dead! The Great Spirit is silent and the ancient ones no longer speak to me. All is a bitter desert. My wives and nine children long to die." Pepishkay pounded his walking stick into the ground, said nothing more, and walked away.

Petit lowered his head and prayed for Pepishkay and his family.

Noaquett, the full-blooded Chippewa who spoke Potawatomi and Ottawa and served as an interpreter, came to Petit's defense, as did the young chieftain, Topenebe. He had been an outspoken advocate of temperance and was one of the natives happiest to see Morgan go.

19 October

By first light the rain stopped. It was a clear day but very cold. Several times through the day the wagons were mired in mud up to the hub. Worse still was fording the Middle Chariton River. Some of the baggage was drenched as the water flowed over into the wagons. Only eleven miles were covered due to the muddy conditions as they made it to Middle Chariton, Missouri. The Indians were exhausted, some anxious to stop moving, others were anxious to reach their destination.

20–21 October

Conditions were still very, very muddy as they approached the Grand Chariton River. On this day some of the baggage, tents, and food supplies were washed away in the current. A few of the wagons sank into the soft river bed. Happily all the supplies were recovered. But the freezing temperatures made life miserable. Fortunately, the twenty-first was a Sunday and the Indians were allowed to attend Mass and rest. Father Petit and Judge Polke purchased a large amount of fresh apples and cider for the Indians.

By the following Tuesday, they had endured snow, freezing rain, sleet, frigid temperatures, and muddy and icy roads. The wagons were ferried across the Grand River while other more daring teamsters forded the channel. It was severely cold and more snow had accumulated. The wagon wheels were clogged with mud, and the natives found it a challenge to even walk.

The people's shoes, boots, and moccasins were worthless. Unbelievably, even more were going barefoot. Petit's borrowed moccasins were now so worn it was as if he was barefoot.

Everyone was tired of the same food for nearly six weeks; the Indians longed for beans and squash.

October 24

The soldiers now considered the weather too severe for the Indians to be journeying without protection for their feet so they pulled a crate from one of the wagons and opened it to reveal many pairs of shoes. Petit was furious that they had that many pairs of shoes hidden in a wagon. The soldiers explained that they wanted to keep them until it was necessary. "What?" Petit exclaimed. "When they were trudging through ice and snow in barefeet, *should shoes not then have been considered necessary?*"

Polke was equally baffled and chastised the soldiers greatly. He was not aware of the crate of shoes. Still there were only enough to shoe a small number of the Indians.

By now the people had been reduced to mournful figures wrapped in blankets. Seated before a cold fire, they stared into oblivion, a thousand thoughts in every heart. The drone of a solitary drummer pounded out a simple thump-thump every five to ten seconds, slowly beating the sound of a dirge, as if a toll bell ringing in the wilderness, announcing death.

25 October

The following morning a compassionate entrepreneur of Carrollton, Missouri, approached the emigration party and was mortified to discover that the Potawatomi had been made to walk barefooted five hundred miles through dust, rain, sleet, and snow. He left and returned with a large quantity of shoes and freely distributed them to the Indians.

The soldiers were then cautioned that there was trouble between a religious group called the Mormons and the citizens of upper Missouri. Carrollton was being heavily guarded by its citizens.

The emigration party left Carrollton in the early morning, yet the journey was made unnecessarily long because of the scarcity of water and lack of provisions and forage. Their hardships only increased as they moved over the parched prairie and the nights grew colder.

That evening, before prayers were to begin, two young Frenchmen arrived at the encampment seeking safety. Nanweshmah brought the men to Petit. They explained their situation. They had recently arrived from France and had taken the wrong steamboat, traveling north on the Mississippi to Independence, rather than south to New Orleans. They understood little English and spoke even less. They were astounded by the half-breeds speaking French and Indian. They stayed for supper and told Petit and Nanweshmah how they had gotten caught up in the crossfire among American militiamen and certain sectarians called Mormons.

The majority of the American Protestants had vowed to either expel or exterminate the Mormon sect for its unorthodox teachings and practice of polygamy. There was a frightening tale of how these Mormons had torched the town of Gallatin, Missouri. The Missouri militia was seeking to rout the Mormons from the state, and both groups were now not far from our encampment. The two Frenchmen feared they would be taken for Mormon spies, so Petit and Polke allowed them to take refuge with the emigration party.

All were awakened the following morning by artillery and rifle shots. Armed troops in formation encircled the camp. At first Judge Polke and the soldiers were unclear whether the troops were Mormons or the Missouri militiamen. To everyone's relief the armed men revealed that they were American militiamen from the town of Richmond. They had about sixty mules with them and three Mormon prisoners.

The militia's commander then approached Judge Polke and

Chauncey Carter with an audacious request for the finest Indian fighters to join their ranks. They were seeking to attack the Mormons. Polke and Carter, along with Father Petit and the Indian interpreters, immediately and wisely refused the request. Polke said it was completely out of his power and jurisdiction to agree to such a thing.

Why should Indian blood be spilled on behalf of Americans when the American government did not find the Indian worthy to live among Americans? The audacity of the militia's commander to make such a shameless appeal was hard to fathom.

Meanwhile, continual reports were that the Mormon war was raging near Carrolton, Missouri.

Petit was informed that beginning in August 1838 the Mormons and Missourians clashed in Daviess County. The Mormons petitioned Gov. Lillburn W. Boggs for protection, but the Missourians petitioned the governor to eject the Mormons from Missouri. The governor ordered the state militia to the scene to suppress the hostilities and drive the insurgents from the state.

By mid-September, the Missouri militia was sent to Daviess County, but the hostility spread into Carroll County where the Mormons were holding up in the town of De Witt, Missouri, while a force of three hundred Missourians was attempting to force their surrender.

By 15 October, a hundred Mormon men returned to Daviess County, plundering and burning the town of Gallatin. The Missouri militia was now engaging the combative Mormons.

OCTOBER 26

The emigrating party reached the Missouri River, opposite Lexington. The wagons were ferried across first, but then the women and children were carried across next in order to avoid the armed conflict between the Mormons and the Missouri militiamen. Reports were rife throughout the country of blood-shed, house burning, et cetera. The people seemed completely crazed. By sunset, all the wagons were across the river.

Petit, for his part, was preoccupied with the festering boils on his body; the rash and sores were no longer confined to his legs and feet, but were appearing all over his chest and arms. His cough now yielded much phlegm, and by week's end his cough was bloody, the dark red blood upon his lips revealing the seriousness of his condition. His hair too had ostensibly grayed overnight and he had only the use of his left eye.

27 October Saturday

From sunrise to mid-afternoon, the male Indians were ferried across. The last were hurried along to catch up with the front of the emigration. The marchers were stretched out over four miles. By evening the march had arrived at Little Schuy Creek.

28 October

On Sunday, they remained in camp. Chiefs Ashkum and I-o-wah were at each other again. Askum claimed I-o-wah did not speak for his band. The two were also arguing about annuities and money promised to the tribe. Polke explained his understanding of the annuities.

Another child died tonight, the first since 11 October. It was Petit's little White Dove; he could barely read the Mass through his tears. He left her buried beneath a mantle of newly fallen snow and a simple wooden cross. Nanweshmah and Polke had to physically remove Petit and the grieving parents from the mound of dirt covering White Dove's body. The parents were inconsolable. Petit prayed God would forgive him for being so angry, for indeed, he was angry at God.

29 October

On Monday, the party traveled through the morning ten miles

to Prairie Creek. One of the captains came with twenty-three Indians that were left behind at Logansport and Tippecanoe; he had five horses and three transport wagons.

The Indians procured wild game of deer, rabbit, squirrel, quail, and pigeon. Flour, cornmeal, beef, and pork were provided by sympathetic Americans.

30 October

On Tuesday, they traveled fourteen miles to Blue Ridge. The weather was warm and dry. Nanweshmah's wife, Demoskikiague, became ill. Nanweshmah, a devoted husband, tended to her needs.

By the end of the day Wednesday, the emigration encamped two miles south of Independence, Missouri. Happily more shoes were distributed to the natives. Unfortunately, many Indians came into camp that afternoon intoxicated.

1 November

Thursday, was the feast of All Saints. The Indians were allowed one hour for Mass before resuming the emigration. Polke confided in Petit: "It will be difficult to secure provisions from now on. This territory is almost an entire wilderness, and there are no roads." At the end of a sixteen-mile trek, they pitched camp at Blue River.

2 November

Friday, was All Souls Day. Like the poor souls in purgatory, forgotten by many, the Potawatomi caravan spread over a distance of four miles, traveling in a mist of sleet and rain lost the path. Even Polke and his men lost the way. They wandered off the path and traveled for miles in the wrong direction. Once they crossed the state line, they found themselves in the heart of a prairie with no traces to mark the route. One hundred fifty on horseback got ahead of the wagons, and in the sleet and rain, the horsemen meandered over the prairie for four hours in search of the trace of the wagons. The American conductors were furious.

When the sleet and rain lifted, they found the lost parties. They soon realized that the entire caravan had gone thirteen miles in the wrong direction and in a circle. The people were hungering and thirsting for sleep as much as they were for food. The conductors finally decided upon a stopping point at Oak Grove on the north fork of the Blue River just across the Kansas state line. Now so close to the end, many of the emigrant Indians felt dejected in the icy mist.

Demoskikiague Burnett was confined to her tent. She had ridden all day in the back of a wagon, drifting in and out of consciousness. Nanweshmah asked for the priest. Petit heard her confession, administered Extreme Unction, and gave her Viaticum. Nanweshmah remained by her side.

3 November

The following day the caravan stopped near a settlement of Wea Indians on Bull Creek. They camped at Bulltown in Kansas. The tribe seemed more anxious than eager to enter Indian Territory.

4 November Sunday

Despite Petit's condition, he forced himself to stand at a makeshift altar and celebrate Mass. His life was in danger, of that there was no doubt, but he had been sent there by God. He believed it was God's will that he be with the Potawatomi, not in relative comfort back in Indiana.

All the way west the Indians were afflicted with misery to see their devoted Father Blackrobe in the throes of a fever and bloody scabs. They covered him and shared their water with him. Yet he insisted upon mounting his horse and riding among the caravan to exhort and encourage the people—even though he knew that his decision may well hasten his death. He had taught them by campfire and candlelight with burning charity despite his own suffering. What greater love is there than this?

Though it was a Sabbath, the march moved forth after Mass since they were now so close to their intended destination, a little over twenty miles. An Indian family remained behind at Bulltown due to illness. The emigration party crossed the Osage River by two o'clock that afternoon. As they neared the destination point, the natives' eyes were sullen, their voices silent, and their hearts emotionless. Now that the peregrination was almost at an end, they were exhausted from fatigue and hunger. Many quietly mourned the loss of many of their elders and the children—especially the children. The sight of all the empty cradleboards exhausted one's emotions.

Some of the fathers who had buried their children along the way, who did not express misery, grief, or sorrow at the time, wept openly now that they were about to enter the reservation. More than forty dead. God only knows how many of the other seventy or so who escaped during the march or abandoned the tribe have died as well.

At half past three o'clock, the caravan began to arrive at their appointed destination in Indian Territory at Potawatomi Creek (so named by earlier emigration parties of Potawatomi). After nearly a two-month journey, the remnant of the Potawatomi tribe reached Potawatomi Creek with a loss of one-fifth of its original number.

Together they were greeted by other Potawatomi Indians who had been awaiting their arrival. A delegation of the resident Potawatomi and their missionary Jesuit priest, Father Christian Hoecken, greeted Petit and the Yellow River Potawatomi of Indiana. Hoecken had been ministering among the Kickapoo before being transferred to the Potawatomi reserve at the Osage River. Father Hoecken spoke both Kickapoo and Potawatomi.

The next morning the people awoke to several inches of snow. Petit's fever spiked and he was forced to remain bedridden in Father Hoecken's tent. Meanwhile, five more Indians died; Father Hoecken presided at their requiem and burials.

Chief Pepishkay lamented the living conditions and accommodations. He and others assembled at Polke's headquarters and expressed their wish to be heard: "*This* is our journey's end? We were taken from a land of milk and honey and brought to a desert to die! Your government must be satisfied now that we have been nearly exterminated" (Polke 1948, 330-334).

Judge Polke informed the Indians that he and his men would soon return to Indiana. Any further grievances they had with the removal must be taken up with the federal government.

Polke shared his journal with Petit. The 658-mile removal was recorded thus:

Plymouth, Indiana to Logansport, Indiana	40 miles
Logansport, Indiana to Quincy, Illinois	339 miles
Quincy, Illinois to Independence, Missouri	213 miles
Independence, Missouri to Potawatomi Creek	66 miles

(Willard and Campbell 2003).

CHAPTER 29
TRAIL'S END

Dear Mother,

Our long and painful journey marked by the anguish of exile and the ravages of epidemic is at an end; the Christian Indians have been relocated. Sixty-four days and 660 miles west, we have finally arrived at the Osage River two months later. My dear Potawatomi of Indiana are not the same people after their removal. They have been ripped from their beloved Indiana, and with each burial the nation was lessened along the way. Thankfully they still have their faith.

As for their number, a total of forty-three have died, and another 150 are missing, having either deserted or made their way back to Indiana or elsewhere. We started out with close to 850 Indians in the caravan. The government has now registered 650 at the Kansas reserve.

Father Hoecken has assumed the pastoral responsibilities of the Potawatomi now that we are in Kansas. I am exhausted from the trip and my cough has returned. The doctor believes I have typhus. Please pray for me, your son.

Sincerely yours,

Benjamin Petit, Catholic Missionary

at the Potawatomi village at the Osage River,

Post Office at Westport, Missouri.

6 NOVEMBER TUESDAY

The soldiers, officers, teamsters, and wagoners were all anxious to return to Indiana. Judge Polke prepared to leave as well, but not before expressing regret over the fact that the U.S. government had failed to provide homes for them as promised. "The War Department had two years to prepare for their arrival. It wasn't as if they didn't know they were coming." The Indians hoped Polke would return to see that justice was rendered to their tribe; many of them had come to respect him.

Meanwhile, the sick Indian family left behind at Bulltown came into camp. There were two less; the children had died.

Petit wrote his mother in Rennes.

10 November 1838

Polke wrote to the Honorable Carey A. Harris, the commissioner of Indian Affairs at Washington City, to inform him that the Indians had complied with the government's demands, yet the U.S. government had not abided by some of the treaty's stipulations. Polke lamented:

"Houses have not been built for them and the lands have not been cultivated. I would respectfully suggest that the promises made them both by the government and General Tipton, in regard to the improvement of their homes in the west, receive early attention. . . . I hope the Department will see the necessity of an immediate compliance with its promises."

The mid-November weather was extremely cold with lots of snow. Petit was recuperating in Andrew Goshlieu's hastily-constructed cabin. Petit hallucinated about his home in France and his mother as he fought his fever, boils, breathing problems, and swollen right eye. He wasn't sure he would ever regain sight in the eye. Though he wasn't able get out, he was still concerned that the federal government had failed to uphold its end of the treaty.

He had previously discussed with General Tipton that once the Potawatomi arrived at the western reserve, the U.S. government would pay for the building of a chapel for the Indians and build a house for a missionary priest out of the Civilization and Education funds set aside for the emigrant Indians.

26 NOVEMBER

I am unable to get up. Though my right eye is better, my fever persists and my body is now consumed with sores. The physician has been bleeding me as well. Every time I try to get up, I become even weaker. Even so, I believe that I will soon be well enough to return to Vincennes for new labors. Perhaps my health will return and permit me to minister here for a few more months. Who knows?

Abram Nanweshmah Burnett, is prepared to accompany me back to Indiana; thankfully Demoskikiague is recovering her health.

This young Christendom, in the midst of anguish and exile and the ravages of epidemic, has received the comfort of religion. The sick have been anointed, the soil, which covers the ashes of the dead, has been consecrated, and the faith and practice of religious duties has been maintained. Even in their temporal sorrows, he whom these poor people call their Father Blackrobe has had the consolation of often being able to render assistance even though such a violent blow stole them from the country where their fathers rest. I pray only for the glory of God and the salvation of souls. I sought for nothing else.

We have also learned that over 12,000 Cherokee people have been marched 1200 miles westward through Tennessee, Kentucky, Illinois, Missouri, and Arkansas to Indian Territory. Nearly 4000 of their people have died from disease, hunger, and exposure.

The Indians' lonely paths west might be called The Trail Where They Died.

Father Petit wrote Senator Tipton requesting that the promise of a house and chapel for the Catholic missionary be provided. Potawatomi Creek, Indian Country

26 November 1838

To his Honour General John Tipton, Member of the
U.S. Senate

General Tipton,

Owing to the encouragement you gave me when I was
honored with taking leave from your honor, I dare today
take the liberty of reminding you of the engagements you
have taken towards me as a Catholic missionary on behalf
of the U.S. government. It is not that I think you may
have forgotten them, but I know it is very useful for us to
call on your credit, for otherwise we cannot look for an
immediate execution of these engagements, operations
when left to themselves, going on very slow in the
Department of Indian Affairs. It would then be extremely
agreeable to us, if you would urge the execution in regard
to building a church and a dwelling for the priest here.

Now, I must also apply to you that you may be kind
to recommend to the government the propriety of an
allocation made for the support of the Catholic missionary from the Education Fund—similar allocations are
made for other denominations, and we are here in fuller
operation than any one of them which I know of—how
proper is that allocation cannot be a matter of doubt!

In this new country, a man can live only by farming but
a Catholic missionary cannot be a farmer; and while his
neighboring Protestant minister will work six days of the
week, to the improvements of his farm and to the support
of his family; the catholic priest will consecrate every
moment of every day to the instruction of his flock, to visiting the sick, or to prepare himself by studying, reading,
and learning. If, of course, the Catholic priest be not supported by his flock, and who could say that these poor

Indians are able to support him, he must necessarily live on nothing, or else, of course, give up his mission.

An allocation of $300 per annum had been made on behalf of the missionary on Yellow River; when Bishop Bruté applied to the Department that the sum would be paid, it was answered that I had been reported as opposing the action of the government, and that consequently nothing should be allowed to me (because I allegedly oppose the U.S. government). Now you know well that I have been misrepresented, for my conduct with you and among the Indians must reveal to you my true character.

I am happy to inform you, General, that I met here a Jesuit Father, Christian Hoecken, sent by the Society of Jesus, who is specially entrusted with the care of the Indian missions. He will make his residence amongst these Indians. The society has the intention to put up a school and to spare nothing for the improvement of these good Indians; for any person who is a little acquainted with the Jesuits, it is no doubt that they will be successful in their mission here, as well as anywhere else. It is in their hands that I will commit, with confidence, these Christians of whom God called me to be the pastor for a while. It is to them and for them as my successors that I claim the execution of the government's engagements and the allocation for the support of the priest.

The promising prospect of this mission deserves to be patronized by the government. If by any chance you could get the $300 allocated for the mission on Yellow River, be kind enough to direct to Bishop Bruté at Vincennes.

Hoping that you will patronize these, our just claims, I am General, of your honor, and with a high consideration.

The humble servant,
Benjamin Petit,
Missionary priest

The first week of December an ice storm hit followed by more snowfall. Petit was sick for more than three weeks. When he was finally able to return to camp he beheld a church being built. The words of Saint Paul became his own.

My eager expectation and hope is that I shall not be put to shame in any way, but that with all boldness, now as always, Christ will be magnified in [my body] me, whether by my life or by my death. For to me to live is Christ, and to die is gain. For if I go on living in the flesh that means fruitful labor for me. Yet which I shall choose I cannot tell. I am hard pressed between the two. I long to depart this life and be with Christ, for that is far better; but to remain in the flesh is more necessary for your benefit (Phil. 1:20-23).

Whatever gains I had, I count as loss for the sake of Christ. Indeed I count all as loss because of the surpassing worth of knowing Christ Jesus my Lord. For his sake I have suffered the loss of all things, and consider them as rubbish, in order that I may gain Christ and be found in Him [and] . . . may know him and the power of His resurrection, and may share in his sufferings, being conformed to His death, that if possible I may attain the resurrection from the dead (Phil 3:10-11).

I am being poured out like a libation, and the time of my departure is near. I have fought the good fight; I have finished the race; I have kept the faith. From now on the crown of righteousness awaits me, which the Lord, the just judge will award to me on that day, and not only to me, but to all who have longed for His coming (2 Tim. 4:6).

12 DECEMBER

There was plenty of snow, but no bread. Petit was sick again with the fever and the boils on his skin were infected and putrid.

O God, Thou art my God, for Thee I long;
For Thee my soul is thirsting.
My body pines for Thee
Like a dry, weary land without water
                              (Ps. 63:1).

Whom else have I in heaven but Thee? With Thee nothing on earth gives me delight. Though my flesh and my heart waste away, Thou art the strength of my heart; Thou art my inheritance forever (Ps. 73:25-26).

20 DECEMBER

Bishop Bruté wrote Petit requesting his immediate return to the diocese of Vincennes; it was essential due to the absence of one priest and the loss of another in the diocese. Father Vabret had to leave the service of the diocese due to poor health and the bishop had dispatched Monseigneur de La Hailandière to Europe in order to recruit more missionaries for the diocese and to enlist financial aid. This need for priests was another reason for Petit to want to return to Vincennes as soon as possible. He planned on taking a steamboat from St. Louis on the Mississippi River south to the Ohio River and north to Vincennes.

Before Christmas, Petit began preparing to leave Kansas, to leave his people behind for Indiana. Nanweshmah prepared to accompany Chichipé Petit on his return to Vincennes, even though they both knew that the snow and ice would inhibit their travel.

28 DECEMBER

On Christmas I was able to be with my Potawatomi children. Never have I ever celebrated a Christmas Mass that felt more like Good Friday and Easter at the same time. So many emotions have carried me these past few weeks.

The sound of the natives' voices chanting the psalms, canticles, and parts of the Mass brought tears to my eyes. I realize I may never have the privilege of hearing the praises of God rendered in the Potawatomi tongue ever again once I return to Vincennes.

My own health through December has brought me close to the cross of Christ. There were days when I believed I had breathed my last.

Alas! The Lord still has work for me.

> O Lord, Thou have been our refuge
> from one generation to the next.
> Before the mountains were born
> or the earth or the world brought forth,
> Thou are God, without beginning or end.
> Thou turn men back into dust
> and say: "Go back, sons of men."
> To thine eyes a thousand years
> are like yesterday, come and gone,
> no more than a watch in the night.
> Thou sweep men away like a dream,
> like grass which springs up in the morning.
> In the morning it springs up and flowers:
> by evening it withers and fades.
> Our life is over like a sigh.
> Our span is seventy years
> or eighty for those who are strong.
> And most of these are emptiness and pain.
> They pass swiftly and we are gone . . .
> Make us know the shortness of our life
> that we may gain wisdom of heart.

In the morning fill us with Thy love;
we shall exult and rejoice all our days.
Give us joy to balance our affliction
for the years when we knew misfortune
(Ps. 90).

2 JANUARY 1839

Maketakônia Chichipé Petit, in the company of Nanweshmah, left the mission at Bishop Bruté's order. Petit's departure was full of sadness. His heart was heavy with emotion as he embraced many of his children. Many of the Potawatomi did not want him to leave and could hardly let him go from their embrace.

He hardly knew what to say or do; he prayed with them one last time.

I know well the plans I have in mind for thee, says the Lord, plans for thy welfare, not for woe! Plans to give thee a future full of hope. When thou callest Me, when thou goest to pray to Me, I will listen to thee. When thou look for Me, thou will find Me. Yes, when thou seekest me with all thy heart, thou will find Me with thee, says the Lord (Jer. 29:11-15).

I give thanks to God at every remembrance of you, praying always with joy in my every prayer for all of you, because of your partnership for the Gospel from the first day you believed until now. I am confident that He who began a good work in you will bring it to completion until the day of the Lord Jesus Christ (Phil. 1:3-11).

Many tears accompanied his farewell.

CHAPTER 30

MAKETAKÔNIA CHICHIPÉ

6 JANUARY

I am returning to Vincennes. When I departed the Osage River Reserve, my Indian children wept; I wept as well. My Indian son, Nanweshmah, volunteered to travel with me. He has to return to Logansport on business and then travel to Rochester to close and sell his trading post. He received a letter that his post had been broken into and robbed of its contents; the sheriff knows the settler who did it.

My fever has returned, as has my exhaustion. I am wrapped in bandages due to my rash and open sores. We rode 150 miles on horseback in four days' time, but west of Jefferson City I was too weak to remain in the saddle. We secured a stage and Nanweshmah sent his horse back and he tied my horse behind the stage. We stayed in Jefferson City for a day.

The next day, Nanweshmah helped me up on my horse and then joined me in the saddle. The two of us made for Indiana. The weather was rainy and cold and the roads were frightful. My condition worsened. The sores on my backside and legs were openly bleeding.

My lungs are now full of phlegm; my mind seems to be reeling . . . .

◆━◯━◯━◆

15 January

As Petit and Nanweshmah neared St. Louis, Chichipé Petit collapsed in the saddle. Nanweshmah clutched him tightly as they entered the city. He took Petit to the Jesuit College six blocks west of the river. The white stone building of the college was on a hill overlooking Ninth Street facing the St. Charles Road, an extension of Washington Avenue. A stand of young oak trees surrounded the buildings.

The Jesuit fathers at St. Louis University cared for him like tender mothers.

Petit's cassock was frayed and torn, his head of black hair had grayed prematurely, and his face was covered with a beard. When the president of St. Louis University, Father John Elet, and the other Jesuit priests and brothers of the house realized the dying blackrobe was the young missionary, Maketakônia Chichipé Benjamin Petit, they hastened to bring him a new cassock as they all gathered about, embracing him with tears and helping him to bed. They covered him with several quilts and his own Indian blanket. Another priest soaked his eye with a warm compress. Nanweshmah remained with Chichipé Petit. That evening the priests and seminarians chanted vespers in his room.

Petit's sleep gave way to dreams. His health returned and he rode long and hard to meet with President Van Buren to argue for Indian rights. The president heard him but offered no assurances. Then Petit set sail for France. He received a hero's welcome in Paris. He had done his duty and America was no longer worthy of him. He received the same hero's welcome in Rennes, and he set out to visit his mother. When he walked into his home his mother was not there.

He opened his eyes and saw the rocking chair opposite his bed. His fever had returned and his skin burned under the many bandages. Two of the Jesuit brothers stepped into his room to attend to him.

Meanwhile he studied the cracks in the paint along the wall and in the ceiling.

The bishop of St. Louis appeared at Petit's bedside and the Jesuits told Petit that the bishop of Dubuque, Iowa, was also on his way to see him. Newspaper reporters were also seeking to interview him about the Indian Removal, but Father Elet would not allow them to bother Petit.

18 January

I am told that I lost consciousness near St. Louis. I awakened in the Jesuit University of St. Louis. The priest-professors here tell me that I have been delirious for nearly three days, though I feel that my condition is much improved. Abram Nanweshmah Burnett, my Potawatomi companion, brother, and son is here with me. He has showered his attention on me in my misery throughout my entire journey.

I have been visited by Bishop Rosati of St. Louis and Bishop Loras of Dubuque, Iowa. They have treated me as if I was Saint Francis Xavier or Saint Isaac Jogues.

18 January 1839

With great difficulty, Petit wrote Bishop Bruté.

To The Right Revd. Bishop Bruté
Vincennes, Knox County, Indiana
Care of Abram Nanweshmah Burnett,
my Potawatomi companion and son. B.P.

Dear Monseigneur Bruté,

From December 12-20 I experienced my fourth attack of the "fever." Even though you had given me until March to return to the Diocese of Vincennes, I decided that I must return to Vincennes out of obedience since one priest already had to leave the diocese due to illness and Monseigneur de La Hailandière had departed for Europe to call forth more missionaries for service in the Diocese of Vincennes. Father Hoecken concurred with my judgment though he would have preferred I remain. He hinted that I should have become a Jesuit.

Before the trip I tried to prepare myself for it as well as possible by rest and light exercise. However, after a horseback ride of 150 miles—even though I had a bearskin in the saddle—I found it impossible to continue thus on the journey; my weakness was growing worse every day. My Indian companion, Abram Nanweshmah Burnett, who is returning to Logansport, secured a stage in which for me to ride. Burnett tied my horse behind the wagon and sent his own horse back.

After coming rather painfully to Jefferson City, we sojourned there a day. Then the open wagon carried us through rain, sleet, and snow and over frightful roads to St. Louis. The good Lord permitted me to make this journey with open sores; the worse of the festering sores were on my backside, my thighs, and my legs. The rest of my body is ostensibly covered with foul sores.

I arrived at St. Louis exhausted and suffering a great deal, especially from all the sores, which had not improved much during the journey. We made our way to the University there conducted by the Society of Jesus. The Jesuit fathers welcomed us as holy pilgrims in search of solace. I was immediately taken to their medical staff and placed in their infirmary. One of the Jesuit fathers is a doctor. I was received as a brother by these black-robed scholars.

After three days of treatment and rest, I feel an improvement which Providence will, I hope, augment so that I may avail myself shortly of a steamboat, when the Wabash is open, to pay my respects to you and, by my return at your first call, to fulfill that condition of obedience under which you permitted me to make a journey so fruitful in blessings, with the provision that I employ well the favors of my Lord.

The Indian, Nanweshmah, who is the bearer of this letter, is one of my beloved children (though he is my age); he has showered tender attentions on me in my misery throughout the entire journey, both west and now east. Welcomed here like a brother and son, he will doubtless receive the same consideration from Your Fatherhood, dear Bishop. You met him at Mass at Logansport before the caravan headed west. You will likely remember him: he is not easily forgotten. The horse he rides is mine; he should leave it at Vincennes. Please have the goodness to supply him what money he needs to buy another horse so as to complete his journey north; I shall reimburse you myself later.

I have been visited by Monseigneur Loras, Bishop of Dubuque, Iowa, and Monseigneur Rosati, Bishop of St. Louis, who, knowing it was impossible for me to do them homage, did not disdain to call upon your poor priest themselves. Tomorrow a writer is coming to see me in order to get information I can give him concerning the Indians. I really feel shamed by all these visits; I am consulted concerning missions, the Indians, and a thousand other things, and I shrink from the subjects. I should like so much to be silent when I fear that importance is attached to my answers, particularly when they begin to hail me as a saint and champion of Indian rights.

I received your last letter as I was leaving the Osage River. I recognized all the tenderness and solicitude of your paternal goodness, which was already so well known to my heart.

I close, thinking that I shall be restored [to you and the diocese] in a fortnight when the Wabash opens. Then I shall have the long-denied happiness of receiving your benediction.

While awaiting that moment, accept, Monseigneur, the assurance of the respectful obedience and submission of your priest and son in Jesus and Mary.

B. Petit

Ptre. Mre. (missionary priest)

So painful were the open sores and fever and headache, Petit's body shook as he struggled to finish the letter. Nanweshmah refused to leave his blackrobe behind and remained with Petit despite his insistence that his Indian companion leave for Indiana.

Petit prayed, or tried to pray, in and through the suffering. The Jesuits tried to keep him comfortable. He would hallucinate, his mind completely incoherent, delirious, and often unresponsive, and his body rigid. His skin became bloody as more sores began to overtake his body. His previous health problems associated with his breathing and asthma returned. When he gasped for air, his whole body shivered and shook with tremors. It appeared his moments of consciousness were less and less; each breath seemingly his last.

The Indiana Senator, General John Tipton, wrote Petit to inform him that a house for a priest, a chapel, and twelve cabins would be built on the Indian mission by the U.S. government in May or June of 1839. The letter was delivered to Petit in St. Louis. Nanweshmah had sent word to Father Hoecken and the Potawatomi informing them that Petit was ill and being cared for by the Jesuits.

> Senator John Tipton,
> at Washington City,
> to Benjamin Petit
> 25 January 1839

> Reverend Sir:
>   With this letter I have the honor to enclose for your information a copy of my letter of 29 December to the Commissioner of Indian Affairs. And in reply to your letter on that subject I have to inform you that the $300 of the Civilization Fund has been transmitted to the Reverend Bishop Bruté, and steps have been taken here to comply with my promise to yourself and our Potawatomi friends, for erecting a house for your residence, a chapel, and twelve cabins in lieu of the one burned by the white settlers at Yellow River. It will be carried into effect as soon as an appropriation is made by Congress for that object, say by May or June next.
>   Wishing yourself and our Potawatomi friends peace and happiness,
>   I am sir, your most obedient servant,
>   John Tipton

Tipton had written to T. Hartley Crawford on 29 December 1838, requesting that the amount of $300 should be taken from the Indian Education Fund and be paid to Bishop Bruté and be applied to the mission; the promised buildings may be erected and paid for out of the Civilization Fund (Armstrong Robertson 1942, 788).

In early February, Petit was delirious with fever for days. The doctors told him that he hovered near death several days in a row with his health improving only to worsen.

On 2 February, Petit awoke with a request to celebrate Mass. The Jesuits were astounded that he could stand for the length of the Mass. Nanweshmah assisted Petit at the altar. Petit's joy was such that it was as if he was celebrating it for the first time; the Jesuits wondered whether it would be his last.

When Petit returned to his bed, he told Father Elet, "Forgive me, but these are days of darkness and doubt . . . but I do not believe that the Lord is finished with me yet."

Father Elet told Petit, "You have suffered much for your people."

Petit glanced at the crucifix on the wall above the foot of his bed and nodded. He opened his mouth and spoke in a raspy, belabored voice. "He has suffered much more for me . . . for all."

Father Elet removed the cross from the wall and brought it to Petit's lips for veneration. Petit smiled as he kissed the crucifix. Elet then placed it in Petit's hands.

"If it should please God to send me death," Petit breathed out, "I shall accept it in all love and submission to his amiable Providence . . . and I hope, in His mercy, at my last moment. I commend myself to Mary, now and at the hour of my death."

Nanweshmah sat at Chichipé Petit's bedside.

Petit reached for his hand and said, "Nanweshmah, you have

assisted me like a saint and cared for me in my misery like a devoted brother. You are my Potawatomi companion and beloved son. May God bless you."

Then to all in the room he wheezed out the words, "Even though I am dying, I believe that I taught the doctrine of Christ. If it is for this reason that I die, after Christ's example, I forgive my enemies. I do not hate them. I ask God to have mercy on them. Yet who will be my people's advocate in the face of all the wrongs committed upon them?"

He then asked for his rosary and he and Nanweshmah prayed it in the Potawatomi tongue.

Petit had entrusted his chalice and possessions to Nanweshmah with the instruction, "Should I not survive the trip to Vincennes I ask that you deliver my belongings to Bishop Bruté."

Petit exhorted those around him. "Following Christ means following Him into death, sharing in His passion and death so as to experience His risen glory. If we are His disciples, we too will experience the daily crosses of pain, suffering, sorrow, even death, but we will not grieve as those without hope . . . the resurrection followed the crucifixion.

"Death is swallowed up in victory. Through Christ's crucifixion, death, and Resurrection all suffering and death can be transformed into cause for hope and new life. Being plunged into the Paschal Mystery, we are united to the cross of Christ so as to enter His glory . . . .

"Our fears of violence and death are real . . . yet when Christ was faced with fear He entrusted himself to the Father . . . . When we begin to trust in God, we lose our fear . . . or the fear no longer has power over us . . . even though I should walk through the valley of death, I will not fear . . . true love casts out all fear!"

Petit was convinced that not even death could separate anyone from the love of God. "Death is not the end! It is the beginning! God will see us through and bring us peace and joy even in the midst of adversity and suffering.

"I have no desire for the mundane things of this world. My sufferings are nothing compared to the sufferings of my Potawatomi people. Imagine the anguish of the soul when one's child dies in your own arms? How does one explain the meaning of this suffering to an innocent people? The death of one's spouse or child, especially one's first born, is a great cross to bear."

Petit quietly meditated on the Scripture as he lay shivering in bed:

Naked I came forth from my mother's womb, and naked I shall go back again. The Lord gave and the Lord takes away; blessed be the Name of the Lord. If we receive happiness from God, should we not accept sorrow as well? (Job 1:21). My flesh is rotten, my skin is cracked and festering; my life is like a breath of wind (Job 7:5, 7, 9).

Petit shared his faith with the Jesuits: "Only by dying to one's carnal desires can a man learn to live; in his dying he enters into life eternal. The Potawatomi have loved me and I have loved them in return. Oh, what a wonderful exchange. I have renounced my earthly citizenship for membership in their tribe and now citizenship in heaven awaits me. I am happy to have spent myself on them though I have lost my life on account of it. Yet did not our Blessed Lord declare: 'He who wishes to save his life will lose it; he who loses his life for my sake and that of the Gospel will save it. What profit a man if he were to gain the world but lose his soul?'(Mark 8:35-37).

"And, in the end, will we not all die? It may not be today, tomorrow, or this year, but death comes for us all. Remember, we are not destined for this life. Our true home is in heaven.

"Some of my brother priests did not want the mission to the Indians because they knew the removal was inevitable. They did not want to invest themselves emotionally or spiritually in the lives of the Indians because the priests knew they would only have to part with the Indians in the end. Even though I knew I would lose my Indian children to the west, I did not fear to give my life for them. 'Without cost you have received; without cost you are to give'" (Matt. 10:8).

Petit grew worse through the week and was no longer able to hold a pen to paper. He requested that he be allowed to be near the tabernacle. "The Blessed Sacrament is my strength. In the darkness, my soul cleaves most closely to God. In the darkness, one is not lost, but learns to trust completely in Providence. 'If I say let the darkness hide me, and the light around me be night, even darkness is not dark for Thee and the night is as clear as the day' (Ps. 139:11-12a).

"'I have been crucified with Christ; yet I live, no longer I, but Christ lives in me; insofar as I now live in the flesh, I live by faith in the Son of God who has loved me and given himself up for me' (Gal. 2:19-20).

"Even though I shall die, I pray that I might make Christ known to all nations, even to the ends of the world."

Due to the fever and tremors, his thoughts and words ran together in his mind, and he wasn't certain whether he was praying or not, but he prayed nonetheless.

"God's grace has strengthened me thus far. I am content to have lost all my worldly possessions—even my health. Perhaps it is a grace that I am dying. For in dying, He has granted me His grace to bear all things patiently. These sufferings I endure may serve to release some soul from purgatory and secure graces for other souls in need. I place my life in His hands. So do not fear, little flock, nothing that happens is beyond God's will. I am confident that whatever befalls me, however evil it may seem, shall somehow serve to further His kingdom here on earth, and, in the end, benefit all of you."

On 8 February, between noon and three o'clock, Petit was burning with fever and his lungs were filling with phlegm. Petit groaned in pain while trying to smile. Bishop Rosati entered the curtained quarantine area and sat with Benjamin Petit. One would have thought that Rosati was Petit's very own dear father as he administered the Last Rites to him. Nanweshmah was at his side now like a devoted son.

Petit confessed, "I regret that I did not do more for the Potawatom . . . . They loved me more . . . more than I loved them."

For the next two days, Petit hovered in and out of consciousness. The doctor insisted on closing all the windows and keeping Petit warm with heavy blankets, propping several pillows under his head and bleeding him from the arms. Petit was languishing, his body twitched as he struggled and gasped for every breath when he wasn't coughing up blood.

The doctor explained that Petit's condition was beyond earthly hope. By evening some of the Jesuit seminarians and priests with Nanweshmah were gathered around Petit's bedside and all eyes were on his rising and falling chest, the cadence of *ave* beads increasing with each belabored exhalation and inhalation, as the men fervidly prayed the rosary, imploring the Mother of God to preserve the beloved young missionary's life.

In the middle of the rosary, Bishop Loras appeared at Petit's bedside. After the last bead of the Sorrowful Mysteries, Bishop Loras anointed him and chanted the litanies to the Sacred Heart, Mary, and Saint Joseph. With the litanies complete, the bishop intoned the *Te Deum* while Benjamin's chest sank even lower and lower, failing to rise where it had earlier in the hour. One of the sisters then handed the bishop a wet washcloth. He began stroking Petit's forehead, face, and lips. Petit wheezed loudly.

For several hours, they kept vigil by candlelight, chanting and praying aloud so as to usher him to heaven when he died.

After hours of labored breathing, Petit breathed out noisily and his chest sank. It failed to rise again. The doctor checked for a pulse, shook his head no, and determined that Benjamin Petit had, indeed, breathed his last.

It was quarter past midnight.

Bishops Rosati and Loras looked down upon the death bed. Father Elet was still holding Benjamin Petit's warm, pale hand.

Those in the room wept at the death of this young, selfless missionary.

At the office for the dead the next morning, Father Elet said of Petit. "This missionary gracefully accepted his cross. He never doubted that God's purpose would be fulfilled even in his darkest hour. His faith was deep and abiding. Even in his suffering he ministered to those around him. A dying man taught us how to live. His light burned bright till the end 'to shine on those who dwell in darkness and the shadow of death, to guide us into the path of peace' (Luke 1:79).

"Through his priesthood, he lived for God and cared for the Potawatomi people. He loved His little ones and showed them mercy. Then in his final days—even to the last—he taught all of us how to die."

Father Elet lamented to his brother Jesuits that it was regrettable that they could not claim Petit as a Jesuit, a member of the Society of Jesus. "He was a true blackrobe as in the days of old. He fulfilled the prayer of generosity of our beloved Saint Ignatius, for 'he who forgets himself for the service of God may be assured that God will not forget him.'

"Dearest Lord, teach me to be generous. Teach me to serve

Thee as Thou deserve. To give and not to count the cost; to fight and not to heed the wounds; to toil and not to seek for rest; to labor and not to ask for reward save that of knowing that I do Thy will, O my God."

Upon the death of Benjamin Petit, Father Elet wrote Bishop Bruté:

What a great loss your diocese has sustained in the death of Rev. Benjamin Petit! He arrived here on the fifteenth of January a pitiable victim of the fever; eleven putrid wounds, running sores on different parts of his body, and his person afflicted with jaundice.

God gave him without doubt strength which his poor body did not possess; for he had the consolation of coming here to end his days among his confreres, and of giving us [Jesuits] the happiness of being edified by his virtues.

What patience, what resignation, what lively gratitude to those who cared for him; but above all, what tender piety towards the mother of the Savior.

On 2 February, Petit asked my permission to celebrate Holy Mass in honor of the Mother of Goodness, who had protected him from his earliest youth and whom he had never ceased to love. His desire was so great that not withstanding my uneasiness on account of his great weakness and difficulty standing, I granted his request.

I then arranged an altar in the room next to his, made a fire, and early in the morning he said his last Mass. From this moment he suffered less, slept soundly for three nights, and felt very much relieved. But on 6 February the symptoms of his illness returned and were such as to leave us no hope.

On 8 February he received the sacraments of the dying with

angelical piety. On the evening of 10 February he told me that his end was approaching.

At ten o'clock that evening he was in agony. We recited the prayers for the dying which he followed, his eyes constantly fixed on us. He sweetly expired twenty minutes after midnight, aged twenty-seven years and ten months.

According to the custom of our society, I clothed his body in sacerdotal (priestly) vestments. On 11 February at five o'clock in the evening, all the community assembled in the chapel and recited the office of the dead. On 12 February we held the solemn Requiem Mass. All of our Fathers, the priests of the Cathedral, and Bishops Rosati and Loras assembled there. I sang Mass and Bishop Loras gave the benediction. A great number of Catholics on horseback and on foot accompanied the body to the cemetery. He was laid to rest with all the blessings of Holy Mother Church.

I will conclude, your Reverence, by praying the Father of mercies, to bless your Highness by elevating to your diocese, men as useful as he whose death we deplore; but we are all consoled by the thoughts of the merits of his life.

Many of those who came to pay their respects were unsure whether to pray for the deceased or to pray to him as a saint already in the bosom of Abraham and the communion of saints.

Among Petit's possessions that were returned to Bishop Bruté was his chalice and journal; the journal included entries of his and the Indians' two-month journey westward.

Upon Petit's death, Father Elet expressed a desire to become a missionary to the native Indians. Prior to ministering to Petit he had expressed some hesitation.

Bishop Bruté presided at vespers for the dead in the Vincennes cathedral.

> Put no trust in princes
> in mortal men in whom there is no help.
> Take their breath, they return to clay
> and their plans that day come to nothing.
> The Lord keeps faith for ever,
> who is just to those who are oppressed.
> It is He who give bread to the hungry,
> the Lord, who sets prisoners free,
> the Lord who gives sight to the blind,
> who raises up those who are bowed down,
> the Lord, who protects the stranger
> and upholds the widow and orphan.
> It is the Lord who loves the just
> But thwarts the path of the wicked (Ps. 146:3-4, 7-9).
> The Lord brings back the exile . . .
> He heals the broken-hearted,
> He binds up all their wounds . . .
> the Lord raises the lowly;
> He humbles the wicked to the dust.
> His delight is not in horses
> nor his pleasure in warrior's strength.
> The Lord delights in those who revere Him,
> In those who wait for His love (Ps. 147:2-3, 6, 10-11).
> For the Lord takes delight in His people
> He crowns the poor with salvation (Ps. 149:4).

At Petit's Requiem Mass at the Vincennes cathedral, the readings spoke of the Paschal Mystery:

Are you unaware that we who were baptized into Christ Jesus were baptized into His death? We were indeed buried with him through baptism into death, so that, just as Christ was raised from the dead by the glory of the Father, we too might live a new life [in newness of life]. For, if we have grown into union with Him through a death like his, we shall also be united with Him in the resurrection. We know that our old self was crucified with Him, so that our sinful body might be done away with, that we might no longer be a slave to sin . . . if then, we have died with Christ, we believe that we shall also live with Him. We know that Christ, once raised from the dead, will not die again; death has no more power over Him . . . He lives for God. Consequently, you too must think of yourselves as being dead to sin, but alive for God in Christ Jesus (Rom. 6:3-11).

The Bishop was assisted by the clergy of the seminary and Rev. Shawe, Petit's one-time traveling companion and fellow seminarian, now the pastor of the church at Madison, Indiana.

Bishop Bruté eulogized Petit:

This young missionary abandoned an eminent position as a successful lawyer and all his worldly hopes to come to this country, and said with the first Apostles, "Lord, we have left all things and have followed Thee."

When sent on his first mission to the poor Indians, all anticipated a long career of usefulness for that truly devoted and promising missionary—all believed that he would live many years to be an honor and a blessing to the Church; "But," says the Lord, "my thoughts are not your thoughts—as the heavens are exalted above the earth, so are My ways exalted above your ways, and my thoughts above your thoughts." The bishop then reminded the clergy and laity, but especially the young seminarians present, the first hopes of Vincennes, how necessary it is to watch and place their treasure and with it their hearts in heaven as faithfully as it was so resolutely and fervently done by Rev. Mr. Petit.

My petit Benjamin—for he was the son at my right hand, and that is what Benjamin means in Hebrew, and Petit, though *petit*, was great in the eyes of God and Man. A martyr of Charity he was. As for the Potawatomi, Indiana should no longer be called *Indiana*, the land of the Indian, for its people have been taken from the land.

Our lives were greatly enriched because of this priest. He spent his life bringing others to Christ that they might know, love, and serve Christ in this life so as to know, love and serve him forever in the next. He lived the example of Christ: No greater love is there than this, than to lay down his life for a friend. His care for others has inspired us to love as Christ loves us. Benjamin Petit's one desire in life was to grow in holiness and grace.

His life is changed, not ended. Just as Christ renounced his heavenly wealth and chose to become poor so as to make men rich, the Lord has seen fit to render his spoiled child, Benjamin, a poor beggar before the throne of Grace, a beloved servant in His kingdom.

A Prayer in Memory of Rev. Benjamin Petit

All powerful and ever-living God, Thou gavest thy servant and priest, Benjamin Petit, the courage and grace to witness to the Gospel of Christ—even to the point of giving his life. May his prayer be a source of help for us, and may his faithful example be our inspiration. By his faith and hope in Christ, help us to endure all suffering for the love of Thee; and by his exemplary charity may we seek to love Thee with all our minds, hearts, and souls and love our neighbors as ourselves, for Thou alone are the source of life. We ask this through Jesus Christ, Thy Son, Our Lord, who livest and reignest with Thee for ever and ever. Amen.

EPILOGUE

And so we lost our beloved blackrobe, Chichipé Petit. After all we'd endured to get to Kansas and after witnessing the grace he revealed as he shared in our sufferings, his death cut through us like a knife. Even those among us who hadn't been a follower of his church felt the loss keenly. We'd never felt so alone as we did when word of his passing reached us. We came to realize that for him, the journey was over, but we were beginning a new journey, in a strange and foreign place. Using his example, we reached deep into ourselves, raised our eyes to the heavens and began our new life.

One of the first decisions made on Pottawatomie Creek, where we were left following our removal, occurred when the Catholics among us expressed a desire to push on and create a separate community. Father Christian Hoecken, the priest at the mission on Pottawatomie Creek, accompanied various scouts and together they decided in favor of an area about fifteen miles south, Sugar Creek, both tributaries of the Osage River. In March of 1839, those who wished to go packed up once again and relocated. By 1847, there were three distinct bands of Potawatomi, consisting of those who had come before us, those of us on the 1838 removal, and those who followed, living in

Kansas. The Potawatomi of Indiana, the name given to the St. Joseph Band, remained on Pottawatomie Creek. The Potawattomies of the Wabash, the common name for our Band, resided at the mission at Sugar Creek. And the Pottawatomies of the Prairie lived either at one of these locations or with Kickapoo friends at the Fort Leavenworth Agency.[i] In 1840, our numbers at Sugar Creek had swelled with the addition of 526 newcomers, fifty of whom had escaped the 1838 removal of Menominee's village; they traveled under the leadership of Alexis Coquillard, accompanied by their priest Father Stanislaus Bernier, and were joined by Abram Burnett, who had gone back to Indiana to take care of some business concerns.[ii]

Slowly we began to thrive in our new home. A few weeks after our arrival at Sugar Creek, Father Hoecken wrote a letter to Senator Tipton, not having heard of his death, in which he reported that more than 30,000 rails had been split with what axes we had, land had been plowed and several cabins had been constructed. He also conveyed the information that some among us had drawn up new regulations regarding the consumption of alcohol and that those who disobeyed were subject to fines or several days' work for the good of the community.[iii]

On June 29, 1841, Mother Rose Philippine Duchesne, accompanied by Mother Lucille Mathevon and two other nuns, arrived at Sugar Creek from the Mother House of the Society of the Sacred Heart in America, located in St. Charles, Missouri. They found waiting for them a newly-constructed church and a log hut that had been built and decorated for Mother Duchesne prior to her arrival. Their new log house was readied for them by October 1841. Here they taught our children their catechism and our daughters learned to knit and to sew. In addition to teaching our children, they went out among us to minister to the sick and dying.[iv] It was almost as if Chichipé Petit walked with us once more.

By 1842, reports were sent back to the Commission on Indian Affairs stating that we had numerous acres under cultivation and good cabins. Corn and other vegetables had added to our food supplies, and by 1845, small grains had been added to the list of our crops. Father Hoecken had published several books in the Potawatomi language for use at Sugar Creek and finally the Ladies of the Sacred Heart had received funding for their school [prior to this funds for the education of the Potawatomi had been sent to the Choctaw Academy in Kentucky and several of our young men had been transported there; funds for the school at Sugar Creek came from private sources]. Mother Mathevon noted in her journal that there were 1000 Catholic Indians at the mission when she arrived, and 2000 "not yet converted." Between sixty and seventy of our young girls were able to take advantage of this opportunity for education, both in religion and in practical arts such as home-making. The boys' school was also fully functional.[v] There they learned animal husbandry as well as the latest farming techniques alongside their religious instruction.

Unfortunately alcohol continued to be a steady problem and a jail to hold miscreants had to be built, even though the fines were now half of a person's annual annuity.

All this changed when Congress started taking a serious look at Iowa's request for statehood. The new state would no longer have room for the Prairie Potawatomi living at the Council Bluffs Agency. With that in mind a delegation of our chiefs journeyed to Washington to speak with President Polk. Negotiations resulted in the ratification of a new treaty on July 23, 1846, giving the Potawatomi at Council Bluffs two years to move to a new reservation on the Kaw [Kansas] River near present-day Topeka, Kansas. Iowa's statehood followed shortly thereafter.

By the fall of 1847, most of the Prairie Potawatomi had relocated to Soldier Creek, north of the Kaw River. They were joined by the Osage Potawatomi a month later. And in November of that year, the Sugar Creek Mission was closed and Father Hoecken led us west to Mission Creek inside the borders of the newly-established Potawatomi National Reservation. Among the items we carried with us was the revered Blind Madonna statue, who we believed would always hear our prayers but could not see our faults. As we left, Father Hoecken performed his last ministerial duties, then burned the mission buildings to the ground to prevent their being desecrated.[vi] In June, 1848, even though some of us expressed concern at living so near other Potawatomi who still practiced the older religions, the Jesuit Fathers persuaded us to continue on to the new St. Marys Mission, Kansas [west of present-day Topeka],[vii] founded on land paid for from the sale of our lands in Iowa and in Kansas. We were also granted monies for resettlement with which to pay our debts and as compensation for the lands we left behind.

Our new reservation was one of gently rolling hills, rivers, creeks and, most importantly, trees. The land yielded to our plows and proved fertile; soon we were raising crops of corn, some of which had been cultivated in Indiana and been brought on the Trail of Death with us[viii], vegetables grown from seeds we'd gathered at Sugar Creek, and tobacco. With a land mass thirty miles square, or 576,000 acres, there was room for us to raise our families and prosper. We were all granted allotments according to our status in the bands and we built cabins and barns. A school soon rose from the prairies near the mission.

In keeping with the varied interests, some of us continued to farm. Others chose to become traders, still others millers. Some became true entrepreneurs, taking advantage of the travelers on the Oregon Trail by charging them fees for being ferried across rivers and buying bulky items from them only to transport them back east and resell them at profit. It is said that some of these items made the trip many times.[ix]

Continuing quarrels between the Catholics and the Prairie Band—along with the ruthless theft of land by the railroads and by unscrupulous traders who plied our people with alcohol and paid them pennies on the dollar—led to the final split on our Reservation. By this time graft was everywhere. While the Prairie Band desired to retain their lands in common, the Catholics wished to own individual allotments. Animosities developed and could not be resolved in council. Therefore, the government was once again approached and asked to draw up a treaty dividing the reservation, allowing those who wished to go to relocate on new lands in Indian Territory, now the state of Oklahoma. The treaty was ratified in 1862, settlement reached, and enrollment began. The Prairie Band chose to remain on the diminished reservation, consisting of 75,000 acres near Topeka, where they live today. Forty-one families chose to move south beginning in 1870, receiving individual allotments in what was to become Pottawatomie County. As a part of the agreement to relocate, we received citizenship, the first American Indians to do so, and became known as the Citizen Band Potawatomi. Others of us chose to remain in Kansas, where we remained on the Prairie Band Reservation. Many of us had family members who chose to remain with one band or another, and so once again our families became divided. The descendants of the Trail of Death still travel between reservations visiting friends and family or live far away from both.

But what of the people in our story? What became of them in the years following the Trail of Death? Listed among the burials at Sugar Creek, Chief Ashkum's was one of the first on September 11, 1840; he had been baptized Jacques (or James as both names are given) and his age listed as nearly seventy. Chief

Menominee was buried at the age of almost fifty on April 15, 1841. A daughter of Mas-saw and Andrew Goslin, Angelique Lizette, was buried at the age of thirteen on June 20, 1842.[x]

Abram Nanweshmah Burnett's Potawatomi wife was buried October 19, 1842. He then married a German lady, Mary Knofflock, on February 16, 1843, by whom he had six children, including a daughter who married one of the founders of Wichita, Kansas. Abram served the tribe as an interpreter prior to and during the time of the removals. A large man weighing over 400 pounds and standing 6'1" tall, he died June 14, 1870, at the age of fifty-nine and was buried near Burnett's Mound in southwest Topeka, Kansas.[xi] The mound and his grave were still well-marked when we visited around the year 2000.

We also find the names Bourassa, Bertrand, Kesis, Topash (Topach), Nadeau, Wesau (probably Wesaw), Waassessuck (probably Wahwahsuck) and Ioway in the Sugar Creek burial records, often as children or spouses of those on the Trail of Death. Many of these same names can be found on the 1863 Roll of the Citizen Band Potawatomi and quite a few of their descendants still live in Kansas and Oklahoma, as well as worldwide.

Father Christian Hoecken, while on a mission trip with Father Pierre De Smet, contracted cholera on the way to a council in the Rocky Mountains. Father De Smet recovered but Father Hoecken died on June 19, 1851. His body was buried on the Iowa side of the Mississippi River but later recovered and taken to Florissant, Missouri, where he was buried again.

Descendants of Chief Menominee include Jim Thunder, Forest County Potawatomi in Wisconsin, and his cousin Don Perrot (Neaseno), Prairie Band Potawatomi from Kansas. They work as instructors to preserve the language the Potawatomi nearly had stolen from them by the boarding schools, Catholic and Protestant alike. They also carry on the traditions of the Potawatomi from the Great Lakes area.

Mas-saw, through her daughter Elizabeth, became the great-grandmother of Jim Thorpe, ultimately to be called "the world's greatest athlete." Mas-saw's daughter Mauri was married to an employee of Ewing, Walker and Company and later to Thomas McKinney. It is unknown when they died and where they are buried.

Et-equa-ke-sec was a child on the Removal. She shared stories of Mother Duchesne with her descendants and was baptized Teresa Living ("Living" because she was one of the children who survived).[xii] She married James Slavin at the mission of St. Marys, Kansas; their descendants, among them the Pearl family who helped mark and dedicate Trail of Death sites, live in Kansas, Ohio and elsewhere.[xiii]

Chesaugan, a headman at Menominee's village was found living in a wigwam in Kansas on the Prairie Band Reservation in the late 1840s. He and his family came by wagon into Logansport, Indiana, on September 7, 1838, and removed with Menominee's band to Sugar Creek. According to records from Fort Leavenworth, Kansas, Chesaugan met up with his family after their arrival; he is presumably buried in the Vieux family cemetery outside Louisville, Kansas. His daughter Sha-note, wife of Louis Vieux, was on the 1837 removal from Wisconsin, where they operated a trading post outside Racine with his brother Jacques. They resided for the next ten years near the Council Bluffs Agency in Iowa (annuity rolls show them at Half-Breed Farms, south of Council Bluffs proper), until they were moved into Kansas and St. Marys in 1847. Sha-note, baptized Charlotte, died of illness in 1857 and is also buried in the Vieux cemetery beside her husband, Louis who died in 1872. Louis Vieux was considered a chief in Kansas and served on the business committee at the time of the 1861 split, making at least one trip to Washington D.C. on the tribe's behalf.[xiv] Vieux descendants continue as enrolled members of the Citizen Band

and many of them carry on the old traditions of the Indiana Potawatomi to this day.

Susan Campbell, Vieux descendant
Kalaheo, Hawaii
July 2006

---

i. Murphy, Rev. Joseph, O.S.B. Potawatomi of the West: Origins of the Citizen Band. Shawnee, OK: Citizen Band Potawatomi Tribe, 1988.

ii. Clifton, James A. The Prairie People. Iowa City, IA: University of Iowa Press, 1998.

iii. Robertson, Nellie A. and Dorothy Riker, eds. The John Tipton Papers, Volume 3, 1834-1839. Indianapolis, IN: Indiana Historical Bureau, 1942.

iv. Willard, Shirley and Susan Campbell. Potawatomi Trail of Death -1838 Removal from Indiana to Kansas. Rochester, Indiana: Fulton County Historical Society, 2003.

v. Murphy, Potawatomi of the West, 88-102.

vi. Hoobler, Dorothy Newcomer. The Oregon Trail, the Jesuit Mission, and the Town of St. Mary's. St. Mary's, KS: AVC Productions, 1993.

vii. Murphy, Potawatomi of the West, 136-144.

viii. Nadeau, Leo, descendant of Chesaugan, headman at Menominee's Village in 1838, signer of five treaties, and father of Sha-note. This corn continues to be grown on the Potawatomi Reservation in Kansas to this day, July 2006.

ix. Campbell, Susan. One Woman's Family and the Footprints it left behind. Kalaheo, HI, private printing, 2001. Reprint, 2005.

x. Register of Burials near the river Pottawatomie commonly called Sugar Creek 1838-1849 as recorded by Father Christian Hoecken and transcribed by Ola May Ernest, Linn County Historical Society, Pleasanton, KS.

xi. Hamilton, Tom. "Abram B. Burnett" from Willard & Campbell, Potawatomi Trail of Death: 1838 Removal from Indiana to Kansas. Rochester, IN: Fulton County Historical Society, 2003: 275-293.

xii. Pearl, Virginia C.S.J. and Robert Pearl. "Trail of Death Reflections": 268-271.

xiii. Pearl, Eileen. "Walking in Her Footsteps": 264-267.

xiv. Campbell, Susan. One Woman's Family and the Footprints it left behind.

Afterword

"The Catholic Church had labored with these people for over 150 years, oftentimes at the cost of the lives of her priests. She had seen her missions swept aside one by one until only this one remained. True to her trust, she stood by these people and used her influence to stay the hand of execution, but all in vain, all the time counseling her children to avoid shedding blood" (Stuart 1922, 259).

"Of all the names connected with this crime, there is one, Father Benjamin Petit, the Christian martyr, which stands like a star in the firmament, growing brighter and it will shine on through ages to come" (Stuart 1922, 264).

"For American Indians the scars of injustice inflicted upon them in the past are deep, painful, and, tragically, are inherited from one generation to the next. Those injustices have become ghosts in the cultural memory of a people crying out for justice. We must fully disclose the past in order to deal with the many years and generations of unresolved grief and distrust."[1]

---

1 Tom Hamilton, Warsaw, Indiana, descendant of Abram Nanweshmah Burnett and member of Citizen Potawatomi Nation, Shawnee, Oklahoma (courtesy of the Fulton County, Indiana, Historical Society).

One need not leave Indiana to learn of injustice measured out to the poor and weak by the greedy and powerful nor does one have to look far to behold a saint and martyr. The story of Benjamin Petit is a most unfortunate account in American history. Indian Removal—as well as the scourge of slavery—will forever haunt America until it comes to grips with its past.

May all who read this tale and ponder its implications strive to be an advocate for all those who suffer injustice in our world today.

John W. McMullen
14 July 2006
Feast of Blessed Kateri Tekawitha,
Lily of the Mohawks

GLOSSARY

Angelus. A traditional Catholic devotional prayer said at morning, noon, and evening to recall the Annunciation. Church bells are often rung at these three times.

Biretta. A stiff, black square cap with three ridges across the crown. A bishop's biretta has four ridges and is purple; a Cardinal's biretta is red.

Compline. The last of the canonical liturgical prayers said or sung before retiring for the night.

Dissentient. One who expresses dissent; one who has a different opinion, disagrees, or withholds assent. Dissenter and dissident are related words with similar meanings.

Gloria. The first word of the doxology, "Glory be to the Father, and the Son, and the Holy Spirit."

Métis. A person of mixed Native American and French Canadian ancestry

Pater. The first word of the Lord's Prayer. *Ave* is the first word of the Hail Mary.

Popery. A derogatory reference to the beliefs, customs, doctrines, practices, and rituals of the Roman Catholic Church; from the word *pope*.

Prie-dieu. A kneeling bench for prayer.

Rive Gauche. The left bank of the River Seine in Paris, noted for its famous Latin Quarter associated with the Lycées and universities.

Schola cantorum. A school of singers; a choir school of a monastery or cathedral

See City. The official seat and center of jurisdiction of a bishop.

Soutane. A cassock that buttons up and down the front worn by seminarians and priests.

Vespers. The sixth canonical liturgical hour of evening prayer or evensong

Viaticum. The Eucharist given to a dying person or a Catholic in danger of death; from the Latin word for traveling provisions.

Wampum. Polished shells fashioned into necklaces, belts, and jewelry; used as a form of currency in bartering.

Zucchetto. A small, round skullcap worn by bishops or abbots that vary in colors according to their ecclesiastical rank.

APPENDIX A

REVEREND BENJAMIN PETIT

Rev. Benjamin Petit was originally interred in St. Louis. Several years later, Rev. Edward Sorin, C.S.C., of the congregation of Holy Cross, and founder of Notre Dame University, had Petit's body returned to Indiana. Today, Father Petit's body rests at Notre Dame University in Badin Chapel, buried next to Father Stephen Badin and Father Louis DeSeille.

26 June 1839, four months after Benjamin Petit died, Bishop Simon Bruté died in Vincennes. He was hailed a saint at his death and in 2005 the Archbishop of Indianapolis, Daniel Buechlein, O.S.B., officially opened the canonization process for Bishop Bruté.

Rev. Celestin de La Hailandière was named Bruté's successor.

REV. STEPHEN THEODORE BADIN

Badin was called America's *proto-sacerdos*, since he was the first priest ordained by Archbishop Carroll of Baltimore. Father Badin was an adventuresome soul, very optimistic about the future of the church, yet Father Celestin de La Hailandière believed he was under the influence of liberalism and Liberal Catholicism inspired by the republican-minded apostate priest,

Feli Lamennais, and tainted with his own brand of *Theologiae Americana*. Badin permitted the use of French, English, and Potawatomi vernacular in the liturgy instead of the canonically required Latin. He also employed the use of a female interpreter in the celebration of the sacraments.

Stephen Theodore Badin was born in Orleans, France, in 1768. In 1789, he entered the seminary, but in 1791, the French government closed it. He sailed for America later that year, a refugee from the Revolution, and in January 1792, he was the first priest ordained in the United States by Bishop John Carroll. "A priest is God's surgeon and he must cut in order to cure," Badin said. He also told Bruté, "It is a lesser evil to have no priests than to have bad ones."

He served in the Diocese of Bardstown, Kentucky, from 1792 to 1818. In 1818, he returned to France due to a difference with Bishop Flaget of Bardstown, Kentucky. During this time, he preached through France about the North American missions and sent money and material to Kentucky until 1828 when he returned to the United States. In 1828, he began traveling through Ohio, Michigan, Indiana, and Illinois. It was during that time that he began his mission to the Indians, living with different tribes, but his heart was with the Potowatami Nation. He was beloved by the Potawatomi tribe and was given the Indian name *Makatekonia*. From 1828 to 1833, Badin spent himself on the Indians, even living with Chief Pokagon for some time.

He was an abolitionist and had brought many a Negro north to Indiana and set them at liberty. He had worked to convince his fellow Catholics of the need to work toward the abolishment of slavery in America. He had also caused quite a stir by advocating the abolishment of state executions of criminals. As an example to all, Badin had taken *the pledge* and many of the Indians likewise renounced the white man's *fire water*.

In 1832, Rev. Stephen Theodore Badin had originally intended to open an Orphan Asylum in St. Joseph City (in St. Joseph County) for the children of any denomination or description . . . the contemplated institution would be beneficial to society in general and to orphans in particular.

Badin then purchased from both the government and private owners about 524 acres of land in St. Joseph County upon which to establish his orphanage and school. The General Assembly of Indiana granted his request to incorporate. Two teachers were obtained from Kentucky, and a chapel and cabin were built on the site of the present University of Notre Dame in 1834. According to Thomas McAvoy, it seems probable that Badin's school was in operation for at least a brief period (McAvoy 1967, 182-183, 190). Here also is the reference to the story of the murder and Campeau's offer of her life instead of the young chief (McAvoy 1967, 183-184, 187). Badin named the spot Sainte Marie du Lac (St. Mary of the Lake).

Badin hoped his new mission at the south bend of the St. Joseph River could support a school for all races and denominations. He argued with the federal officers and land commissioners over the Indian removal policy. Badin was now nearly seventy years old.

Right Reverend Celestin de La Hailandière

Rev. Celestin de La Hailandière was named Bruté's successor. Celestin de La Hailandière grew up in Coumbourg, Brittany. As a boy, the repercussions of the Revolution were still ravaging France. His father gave sanctuary to a refugee priest who lived with his family for several years before Napoleon lifted the ban on the priesthood. This priest instructed him in the faith and educated him in the classics. When Celestin was nineteen he began his study of law and at the age of twenty-two he was admitted to the bar. He practiced law for two years, but one

Sunday at Mass, a visiting missionary priest inspired him to become a priest.

His father and mother were both opposed to his abandoning a legal career for priestly studies, so in 1822 he accepted the position of judge at the Civil Tribunal of Redon. But later that year, on the seventh of October, the feast of our Lady of the Holy Rosary, while praying the rosary, again he felt the call to become a priest. He had always had a devotion to our Blessed Mother and on that day he sensed her presence in a special way. It was then that he resolved to abandon his legal career and enter the seminary at Rennes. He finished his studies in Paris and was ordained to the priesthood at Saint-Sulpice in 1825. In the meantime, his father died. They were never reconciled though his mother had come to accept the fact that he would never give her grandchildren.

He was assigned to the Church of Saint-Germaine at Rennes, and this past year Bishop Bruté visited him and asked him if he might be interested in becoming a missionary priest. When he informed his mother of his plans to leave France, she was even more opposed to that than she was the priesthood. Instead, he had renounced the princely splendor of court life for a rugged missionary outpost. His parents had told him countless tales of horror that occurred during the Reign of Terror in 1793 and Robespierre's fanaticism in ridding France of the Church. In his own home of Brittany, his mother and their adopted abbé told and retold him the stories of how priests were hounded into exile or executed upon the scaffold of the guillotine.

He admitted that initially his pursuit of a law career was to insure that he would have a viable option should the priesthood be banned again. He had considered the priesthood since he was a small boy, but he put the idea out of his mind, partly because he feared martyrdom. Of course he knew that the blood of the martyrs was the seed of the Church, yet he didn't want it to be his blood. He asked the Lord, 'Do not give me this cross,' yet even now as a priest, whenever he tried to act with resolve and devote himself to prayer, his weak humanity would pull him down. At his ordination he had promised to be holy and zealous, yet he feared that he would become lazy and weak and give in to his desires.

At Bishop Bruté's death in 1839 he was named the second bishop of Vincennes, but in 1847 he resigned his position due to his autocratic approach to leadership. (See my book *ROMAN: Unparalleled Outrage* for a more detailed account of de La Hailandière as bishop).

APPENDIX B

GENERAL JOHN TIPTON

In February 1839 a letter was published in *The Indiana Journal*. It was a letter General John Tipton wrote Indiana Governor David Wallace to give him his account of the Potowatomi Removal from Indiana. The letter was dated September 1838 and reads as follows:

The arrival of our armed forces sufficient to put down hostile movements against our citizens affected in three days what counsel and words had failed to do in so many months.

I did not feel authorized to drive these poor degraded beings from our State, but to remove them from Indiana, and to give peace and security to our own citizens. As it was the Indians did not own one acre of land east of the Mississippi, therefore the Government was obliged to remove them to the Osage River reservation.

However, three of the self-styled chiefs, Menominee included argued that they would only listen to the advice of the priest, Benjamin Petit. He had resided with the tribe since the quarrel first began between the Indians and the whites. He left Twin Lakes and moved to South Bend shortly before the actual removal commenced.

Before we left, I invited him to join the emigration and go west. He declined at first, claiming that his bishop would not permit it; but when we arrived in Logansport, his bishop gave him permission. He finally overtook our caravan at Danville and is now with us; he will accompany the Indians west.

It is but justice to him that I should say that he has, both by precept and example, produced a very favorable change in the morals and industry of the Indians, that his untiring zeal in the cause of civilization has been and will continue to be eminently beneficial to these unfortunate Potawatomies when they reach their new abode. All of them are now satisfied, and appear eager to proceed on their journey to their new homes, where they anticipate peace, security, and happiness.

I am happy in being able to state that the removal of the Indians was effected without bloodshed or maltreatment. I see no reason for censuring any of the officers under my charge for alleged abuse. Every attention that could be, was paid to the Indians health, comfort, and convenience. When on our marches, which are sometimes very much hurried, owing to the great distance between watering places, it is not unusual to see a number of our volunteer officers walking, while their horses are ridden by the sickly or infirm Indians. I found no difficulty in raising the number of volunteer officers required, although the people of the northern portion of the State are much afflicted with sickness. I was compelled to discharge one or more every day and permit them to return, in consequence of bad health. The greatest number in service, at any one time, was ninety-seven men.

I have the honor to be, with great respect, your obedient servant,

General John Tipton,

Indiana Senator

Tipton's wife died in March. General Tipton died on 5 April 1839 after a brief one-day illness.

APPENDIX C

THE TRAIL OF DEATH MEMORIALIZED TODAY
By Shirley Willard

Saint Philippine Duchesne Memorial Park

Rose Philippine Duchesne was born August 29, 1769, in Grenoble, France, and died at St. Charles, Missouri, on November 18, 1852. She survived the French Revolution, working underground to hide priests, visiting them in prison, and teaching Catechism to neglected children. She helped found the Society of the Sacred Heart and establish its Mother House. She wanted to be a missionary to America and came to Louisiana in 1818. She helped open the first free school west of the Mississippi River at St. Charles, Missouri, where she served as the Superior of the Society of Sacred Heart in America. At St. Charles she heard the story of Father Petit and the Potawatomi Trail of Death. Her desire to be a missionary to the American Indians was finally realized in 1841 when she accompanied Mother Lucille Mathevon and two other nuns to Sugar Creek, Kansas, to set up a school for the Potawatomi children. They arrived at Sugar Creek on June 29 and from the moment the

Potawatomi first set eyes on her, they loved the old lady (age 71) who was too frail to work but prayed almost ceaselessly. They noticed her praying at night and the next morning she was in the same position still praying, and they wondered if she really prayed all night. To test her they put little pebbles on her long black robe, and the next morning they were undisturbed. So they called her "She Who Prays Always." They brought her gifts of eggs, fresh straw for her bed, wild plums, etc. Philippine grew weaker over the winter and was taken back to St. Charles exactly one year later in June 1842. She had left such an impression on all who met her, that she was never forgotten.

In 1988 Philippine Duchesne was canonized, thus becoming the first female saint west of the Mississippi River. To honor her, the Eastern Kansas Diocese bought 450 acres where the original Sugar Creek Mission had stood and created the Philippine Duchesne Memorial Park near Centerville, Kansas, in rural Linn County, about 20 miles south of Osawatomie.

The Saint Philippine Duchesne Memorial Park was dedicated in 1988. The St. Philippine Duchesne Memorial Park or Shrine is a very spiritual place to visit. Sister Virginia Pearl, C.S.J., summed it up: "There is a deep sense of presence of the holy people who walked here. It is truly holy ground." This is the end of the Trail of Death Regional Historic Trail.

TRAIL OF COURAGE LIVING HISTORY FESTIVAL

The Fulton County Historical Society (FCHS), Rochester, Indiana, founded the Trail of Death Rendezvous in 1976 as a Bicentennial event. The name of the festival was changed to Trail of Courage in 1977 in order to focus on the early 1830s when northern Indiana was still Potawatomi territory and to show a happier time more appropriate for a festival. The Trail of Courage Living History Festival is held the third weekend of September on the FCHS grounds north of Rochester.

The Trail of Courage includes historic encampments representing 1760-1840, depiction of the Western Fur Trade, Plains Indians teepees, and a Woodlands Indian wigwam village. There is also a re-creation of Chippeway Village, founded by William Polke in 1830, the first post office and American village in Fulton County.

In 2003, a memorial to Father Petit and the Trail of Death was dedicated at the Fulton County Museum. It consists of five boulders engraved with the names of the states along the Trail of Death. Plaques designed by Tom Hamilton, whose ancestor Abram Burnett was on the Trail of Death, show the map and tell the story of Father Petit and the Trail of Death. Similar memorials to Father Petit are at the Jesuit Archives in St. Louis, Missouri, in front of the Fulton County courthouse and in front of the Fulton County Museum at Rochester, Indiana.

Trail of Death Commemorative Caravan

In 1988, Shirley Willard, president of the Fulton County Historical Society, and Dr. George Godfrey, a member of the Citizen Band Potawatomi, organized the first Trail of Death Commemorative Caravan for the 150th anniversary of the 1838 forced removal of the Potawatomi Indians from Indiana to Kansas. In 1993, Mrs. Willard and Dr. Godfrey organized the second Trail of Death Commemorative Caravan. Afterwards, the Caravan members decided to work towards having the Trail of Death declared a National Historic Trail. In 1998, the Trail of Death Commemorative Committee organized a third Caravan and it was decided to seek permission to reprint the Father Petit book about the Trail of Death. That permission led to the 2003 book, *Potawatomi Trail of Death: 1838 Removal from Indiana to Kansas*, published in 2003, which is a compilation of most of the Trail of Death primary sources. The book can be purchased from the Fulton County Historical Society, Rochester, Indiana (address below).

TRAIL OF DEATH REGIONAL HISTORIC TRAIL

When Shirley Willard applied to the National Park Service to have the trail declared a National Historic Trail, she was told that the Potawatomi removal was more of regional interest and that it would cost $200,000 for research. The Trail of Death Commemorative Committee thought that would be a waste of tax dollars, since they had already done the research. So they decided to make it a Regional Historic Trail and rely on private donations.

The Indian Awareness Center, a branch of the FCHS, took this as a project. Shirley enlisted the help of the state historical societies of Indiana, Illinois, Missouri, and Kansas and contacted all the county historical societies on the Trail of Death route. She asked them to introduce the project to the state legislatures. The first one to pass it was Missouri, but because they had only one Trail of Death marker in Missouri in 1993, they wrote a resolution encouraging groups to participate in marking the route. Shirley then wrote the resolutions for the other states.

Shirley asked the Indiana Historical Society for their backing. The Trail of Death resolution was passed by the Indiana legislature in 1994 and both the Illinois and Kansas resolutions were passed in 1994. The Missouri legislature passed the declaration in 1996, having four historical markers by that time. The Trail of Death is now a Regional Historic Trail, as declared by the four state legislatures.

Potawatomi Trail of Death Association

The Trail of Death Commemorative Committee founded and organized the Potawatomi Trail of Death Association (PTDA) in 2005. For more information write to: PTDA,

Fulton Co. Historical Society, 37 E. 375 North, Rochester, IN 46975.

The PTDA hopes to erect highway signs similar to those of the Lewis & Clark Trail signs. A Potawatomi artist, David Anderson of Seattle, Washington, designed the logo. The Manitou Chapter of Daughters of American Revolution sponsored the signs needed across Fulton County, Indiana, which were erected in 2006. Each of the twenty-six counties will work on getting highway signs across their respective counties to guide motorists, bikers, and hikers to the historical markers along the original route taken in 1838. If you would like to help, contact Shirley Willard at 574-223-2352.

Now completed, the Trail of Death Regional Historic Trail has seventy-eight markers and is probably the best marked historic trail in the United States. A web site showing pictures of all seventy-eight Trail of Death historical markers has been created. It can be viewed at *www.potawatomi-tda.org*. News will be posted on this web site.

"It is our hope that people will stop to read the markers and say a prayer for peace for all mankind."

APPENDIX D

THE INDIAN REMOVAL ACT

Indian Affairs were under the president's direct control. The Secretary of War carried out the duties toward the Indians via the Office of Indian Affairs.

By the 1830s, the U.S. government was clearly pressing forth with their plans to remove the Potawatomi from Indiana. American agents were being assigned to enforce the Indian removal. Placards and bulletins were posted and circulated advertising the need for able-bodied men to help effect the Indians' removal.

Already the Black Hawk massacre of the early 1830s had so discouraged the Indians of northern Indiana that they acquiesced to the U.S. government's desire for their westward migration.

President Jackson had dared the chief justice of the Supreme Court to enforce its ruling. Alas, the power of the commander in chief resided in the executive branch of the American government. Indian removal became the policy of the nation and its enforcement would fall to President Van Buren, Jackson's successor. Jackson said of the Supreme Court's Chief Justice Marshall: "He's made his decision, let him enforce it." Henry

Clay said that Jackson's Indian policy would forever be a stain upon America's honor.

The Indiana legislature—speaking for many citizens of Indiana—believed the Indian presence was a hindrance to progress, public works and projects, and the growth of the white population. The state officials and land speculators wanted the land. Indian agents were quick to point out that since the Indians didn't farm their land like the Americans did the valuable land was actually going to waste. They also portrayed the Indians as uneducated and lacking in resourcefulness.

The agents intentionally divided the different tribes. This prevented the possibility of the Indians uniting to oppose the removal. Some corrupt traders and agents happily introduced alcohol to the Indians even though it was against the law to do so. When the Indians were intoxicated, the agents would get them to sign treaties. The treaty that had been signed by the large tribe of Potawatomi in northern Indiana had been secured by such intoxication.

The treaty policy served to protect the Indians in some ways and also to assist them in assimilating into American culture. Of course, the white culture was considered superior and civilized, whereas the Indians were regarded as savage and uncivilized. Many of the treaties gave the Indians cattle, hogs, chickens, and farm implements to further aid their enculturation in western ways of farming. Education was also part of the plans for the Indians.

However, since 1828, President Andrew Jackson had questioned the legitimacy of treaties altogether. Jackson and his administration, including his vice president, Martin Van Buren, who was later elected president in 1836, claimed that treaties were never valid since the Indian tribes were never actual sovereign states or nations. Jackson believed that God had given white Americans this land and had formed it for purposes other than Indian hunting grounds. With the advent of the Jackson administration, sweeping changes were put into place regarding the Indians. As a result, the president would have nearly unlimited power over the tribes and the tribes would have no recourse. There was national sentiment that the notion of Indian rights was anti-American.

Meanwhile, the *Cherokee Question* reverberated through the country. Some of the northern states were advocates of Indian rights—and some of their same spokesmen were advocates for slaves' rights calling for the abolition of slavery. Supporters of the Indians believed that the Indians were a sovereign nation within the United States. Some of the senators and representatives argued that it was morally wrong to displace the native peoples. Some of them sought to prick the conscience of the nation and even warned of divine retribution if the Indian removal was enforced. The adherents of Indian rights maintained that treaties were contracts between independent communities. The United States had made treaties with Indian tribes for decades, and if the Indian tribes or nations were not independent sovereign nations, then how could the United States have ever negotiated treaties? Indian rights advocates pointed out that Indian communities had been called nations since the discovery of America in the fifteenth century.

A number of the Protestant missionaries, with all due respect to their ministry, held that President Jackson was correct in his assertion that the Indians were not sovereign. They believed it was wise to remove the Indians from the states since they had no rights to the land they occupied.

Many Catholics argued for Indian rights—clergy and laity alike—but the bishops advised them to stay clear of political arguments for fear that there might be a backlash against Catholics, thereby renewing a wave of anti-Catholic persecution. In the worst scenario, it might render Catholicism illegal in America. Perhaps unfounded fears, but for those bishops who had experienced the French Revolution and its subsequent Reign of Terror where Catholics—priests and laity—were often executed simply because they were Catholic, did not wish to take any chances by giving the enemies of Catholicism any evidence of what some Americans might regard as anti-Republicanism.

Those Indian rights advocates knew that the question rested on the supposition that the Indians were not competent to enter into treaties with the United States. They argued that: if this were so, then how could one account for the great number of treaties that have been made over the course of American history? Even before the United States negotiated treaties with the Indians, the French, Spanish, and English regarded their agreements with the Indians as treaties. How then could the U.S. government say that their treaties were not treaties? The advocates of Indian rights argued that Indian removal was a blight on the national history—as was the South's institution of slavery. Both the red-skins and the Negroes were being denied their human rights to life, liberty, and the pursuit of happiness.

The Chocktaws of Mississippi, the Creek of Alabama, and the Chickasaws of Tennessee and Mississippi were removed. The government tried to remove the Seminole from Florida, but the Seminoles refused to honor the treaties they had signed and many escaped removal by hiding in the Everglades. In 1835, the United States went to war with the Seminole. *The Florida War*, as it was called, had exterminated all but a remnant of the

Seminole tribe. The Cherokee were the last to remain in the east. Many supporters of Indian rights, including those who were aware of the unnecessary carnage in the Florida War, protested Cherokee removal.

The argument against the Potawatomi removal was met with the answer that since the Potawatomi were on lands not previously held by their ancestors, that their removal could be considered simply one more migration westward. The Secretary of War, Lewis Cass, desired to remove all the Indians from Illinois, Indiana, and Missouri. The Shawnees, Delawares, Piankashaws, Weas, Peorias, Kaskaskias, and the Menominees had all been removed. The Potawatomi tribes were the only ones remaining. The northern Indian tribes had been granted several small reserves or reservations within the state, but many of the citizens of Indiana desired for the Indian removal. The tribes stood in the way of progress for the state, went the common saw.

The War Department had planned for this removal to take place later in the fall of 1838. [One might rightly wonder why the removal was planned so late. It might have extinguished the entire Potawatomi people for that would have required the Indians to walk west through late fall and the beginning of winter].

REFERENCES FOR PETIT'S JOURNAL

CHAPTER 18

Entry for 15 October (McKee 1941, 30–33). Petit in a letter to his Mother, Mme. Chauvin Petit, dated 15 October 1837.

Entry for November 1837 (ibid., 34–35, 80).

CHAPTER 19

Entry for Chichipé Outipé (ibid., 66–67, 80, 34–36, 53–54, 80).

7 December 1837 (ibid., 38–43).

13 December 1837 (McNamara 1931, 18–19).

14 December 1837 (McKee 1941, 43, 45–47).

15 December 1837 (ibid., 43–47).

26 December 1837 (ibid., 48–50).

CHAPTER 20

5 January 1838 (ibid., 51–52, 55–56).

February 1838 (ibid., 53, 55–57, 61–62, 71).

L'Arbre Croche, Crooked Tree, MI (near present day Harbor Springs, MI).

CHAPTER 21

March 1838 (McKee 1941, 59–62).

15 April 1838 (ibid., 63–68).

25 April 1838 (ibid., 65–67).

Concerning Petit's hopes that Jesuit priests would establish a mission, Jesuit Fathers Peter De Smet and Christian Hoecken had established a mission in Indian Territory by May of 1838 (ibid., 50, 107).

15 May 1838 (McKee 1941, 67–71; McDonald 1881, 30).

CHAPTER 22

1 June 1838 (McKee 1941, 72–73); Father Badin's speech can be found in Schauinger pp. 232–35.

10 June 1838 (McKee 1941, 73–76, 78).

20 June 1838 (ibid., 75–78).

24 June 1838 (ibid., 66–67).

4 July 1838 (ibid., 78–81).

14 July 1838 (ibid., 81–86).

CHAPTER 23

(McKee 1941, 81–82).

24 July 1838 (ibid., 82–86, 66–67).

4 August 1838 (ibid., 69). The continuation of the Journal of an Emigrating Party of Potawatomi Indians, 1838, and Ten William Polke Manuscripts: IMH, vol. 44, Dec. 1948: 395.

6 August (McKee 1941, 128).

20 August (ibid., 85–86).

The annals of the Propagation of the Faith. Annales de la Propagation de la foi. The Society of the Propagation of the Faith was founded in Lyons, France, in 1822, as "an endeavor to enlist the aid of all Catholics and assist all missions, without regard to situation and nationality." The Society was the chief source of support of the American Catholic missions.

28 August

Letters of John Tipton from *The John Tipton Papers, Volume III, 1834–1839* Indiana Historical Collections, Volume XXVI, compiled and edited by Nellie Armstrong Robertson and Dorothy Riker. Published by the Indiana Historical Bureau. Indianapolis, IN (1942): 679–680.

2 September 1838 (ibid., 686–87).

3 September 1838 (McKee 1941, 86–89).

There seems to be some question as to when Petit returned to the Twin

Lakes Reserve. He was at South Bend on 2 September. However, Benjamin Stuart records that Petit was present when the Indians were being rounded up and driven from their wigwams and cabins. This occurred up to 4 September (Stuart 1922, 260–61). Where and how Stuart obtained this information is unknown. I posit that Stuart is correct. Petit's devotion was so great that he likely disregarded the physician's warnings and went anyway. He ignored his own health concerns on the trail out of deference to his people.

CHAPTERS 24 AND 25

5 September (Source material for the removal: Stuart 1922, 260–262).

The Indians were resolved to fight, when, through the counsel of Father Petit and on his promise to accompany them to their new home, they promised him if the worst did come, they would submit peacefully. This averted a general massacre.

The Catholic Church had labored with these people for over 150 years, oftentimes at the cost of the lives of her priests. She had seen her missions swept aside one by one until only this one remained. True to her trust, she stood by these people and used her influence to stay the hand of execution, but all in vain, all the time counseling her children to avoid shedding blood (Stuart 1922, 259).

8 September 1838 (McKee 1941, 90–93).

9 September 1838 (ibid., 90–96).

Winter quote: (Cooke 1993, 104).

10 September 1838

"In 1838, a large emigration of the Potawatomi took place, under the direction of General John Tipton and Colonel Abel C. Pepper.... Much that is sad and touching relates to their removal westward.... It was only by a deceptive (in a moral point of view) and cunning cruel plan, they were coerced to emigrate.... By convening a special Council of the principal chiefs and head men, at the Catholic mission at the Twin Lakes, near Plymouth, under the pretense of a Council of good will, General Tipton arrived and secured the Indians as prisoners . . . a high handed act, for such it was. For its execution . . . the policy was as painful, as it was successful. Volunteers [militiamen] came crowding in from all parts of the state, in anticipation of the Indians resisting, of which at one time, there was a seeming probability.

"Very varied was this heterogeneous body of American men. Some were of the highest respectability in the state, and others, in appearance at least, vagabonds and pillagers of the lowest order, such humanity would recognize…. The white men were gathering thick around them, which was but a sad necessity for their departure. Still they clung to their homes. But the flames of the torch were applied—their villages and wigwams were annihilated. The principal chiefs were secured by the strong arm of authority and lead, or rather driven, captives out of the land at the point of the bayonet! It was truly a melancholy spectacle that awoke a deep feeling of sympathy for their unhappy fate" (Cooke 1993, 99).

CHAPTER 26

11 September 1838

"Cruelty unspeakable! Outrage infinite! Was the God of mercy still with them? May the Lord of all nations never again permit Indiana to be disgraced by such scenes as were witnessed in northern Indiana!" (Stuart 1922, 262–65).

19 September 1838

Petit's letter (McKee 1941, 93–95).

21 September (ibid., 100–106).

(Willard/Campbell 2003, 251–255).

CHAPTER 27

23 September (McKee 1941, 95, 100–106).

Pyatt's Point is now called Monticello, Illinois.

4 October (ibid., 129) (Douglas 1925, 326).

6 October; Senator Young was an Illinois senator from 1837–1843 (McKee 1941, 130).

8 October (ibid., 101).

CHAPTER 28

12 October (ibid., 108–110).

14 October (Douglas 1925, 328–29).

15 October (ibid., 329–330).

17 October (Armstrong Robertson 1942, 727, 749–56).

August 1838 the Mormons and Missourians clashed in Daviess County. The Mormons petitioned Gov. Lillburn W. Boggs for protection, but the Missourians petitioned the governor to eject the Mormons from Missouri.

The governor ordered the state militia to the scene to suppress the hostilities and drive the insurgents from the state.

On 15 September, the Missouri militia was sent to Daviess County, but the hostility spread into Carroll County, where the Mormons were holding up in the town of De Witt, Missouri, while a force of three hundred Missourians were attempting to force their surrender. The Mormons eventually gave up when their food supply ran out. They surrendered and moved to the town of Far West. Here they arrived on 12 October. On 15 October, a hundred Mormon men returned to Daviess County, plundering and burning the town of Gallatin. The militia returned and on 26 October and on 30 October the Mormons surrendered and removed to Caldwell County. In the spring of 1839, they moved to Nauvoo, Illinois (McKee 1941, 103–104).

Chapter 29

6 November

Petit's letter to his mother (McKee 1941, 105–110, 131).

Westport, Missouri, is now Kansas City, Missouri.

10 November (Polke 1948, 408).

Chapter 30

(McKee 1941, 110–112, 114–116).

Tipton wrote to T. Hartley Crawford on 29 December 1838, requesting that the amount of $300 should be taken from the Indian Education Fund and be paid to Bishop Bruté to be applied to the mission; the promised buildings may be erected and paid for out of the Civilization Fund (Armstrong Robertson 1942, 788).

Tipton's letter to Petit (ibid., 805).

Father Elet's letter to Bishop Bruté (McNamara 1931, 75–76).

The text for Bruté's eulogy of Petit ("Rev. Mr. Petit." *The Catholic Telegraph*, March 7, 1839: 102; "Obituary: the Reverend Benjamin Petit," *The Catholic Telegraph*, 21 February, 1839: 86).

BIBLIOGRAPHY PAGE

Armstrong Robertson, Nellie and Dorothy Riker, eds. *The John Tipton Papers, Volume III, 1834–1839. Indiana Historical Collections, Volume XXVI*. Indianapolis, IN: The Indiana Historical Bureau, 1942.

Brown, Mary Borromeo, S.P. *The History of the Sisters of Providence of Saint Mary of-the-Woods*. Vol. I. New York: Benziger Brothers, Inc., 1949.

Cooke, Sarah E. and Rachel Ramadhyani, comp. *Indians and a Changing Frontier: The Art of George Winter/* essays by Christian F. Feest and R. David Edmunds. Indianapolis, IN: Indiana Historical Society Press, 1993.

Douglas, J.C. "Journal of an Emigrating Party of Pottawattomie Indians, 1838." *Indiana Magazine of History*, Vol. 21 (1925): 315–336.

Edmunds, R. David. *The Potawatomis, Keepers of the Fire*. Normon, OK: University of Oklahoma Press, 1978.

Godecker, Mary Salesia, O.S.B., Ph.D. *Simon Bruté de Rémur: First Bishop of Vincennes*. St. Meinrad, IN: Abbey Press, 1931.

McAvoy, Thomas Timothy, C.S.C. *The Catholic Church in Indiana 1789–1834.* 2nd ed. New York, NY: AMS Press, 1967.

McDonald, Daniel. *The History of Marshall County, Indiana 1836–1880.* Chicago, IL: Kingman Brothers, 1881.

McNamara, Rev. William, C.S.C. *The Catholic Church on the Northern Indiana Frontier 1789–1844.* Washington, D.C.: The Catholic University of America Press, 1931.

McKee, Irving. *The Trail of Death: Letters of Benjamin Marie Petit.* Indianapolis, IN: Indiana Historical Society Press, 1941.

O'Connell, Marvin. *Edward Sorin.* Notre Dame, IN: University of Notre Dame Press, 2001.

Polke, William. "The Continuation of the Journal of an Emigrating Party of Potawatomi Indians, 1838, And Ten William Polke Manuscripts." *Indiana Magazine of History*, 44 (1948): 393–408.

Schauinger, J. Herman. *Stephen T. Badin: Priest in the Wilderness.* Milwaukee, WI: Bruce Publishing Company, 1956.

Stuart, Benjamin F. "The Deportation of Menominee and His Tribe of the Pottawattomie Indians." *Indiana Magazine of History* (1922): 264–65.

Willard, Shirley and Susan Campbell. *Potawatomi Trail of Death: 1838 Removal from Indiana to Kansas.* Rochester, IN: Fulton County Historical Society, 2003.

Winger, Otho. *The Potawatomi Indians.* Elgin, IL: Elgin Press, 1939.

"Obituary: the Reverend Benjamin Petit." *The Catholic Telegraph*, February 21, 1839: 86.

"Rev. Mr. Petit." *The Catholic Telegraph*, March 7, 1839: 102.

ABOUT THE AUTHOR

John **William McMullen,** a native of Vincennes, Indiana, holds a Master's Degree in Theological Studies from Saint Meinrad School of Theology in Indiana. He is a Third Order Benedictine Oblate; a member of the Thomas More Society of Southwestern Indiana; and a member of the Holy Cross Historical Society of Notre Dame, Indiana. He is a Theology Instructor at Mater Dei High School in Evansville, Indiana, and an adjunct Philosophy Professor at Ivy Tech Community College of Indiana.

McMullen has written numerous articles on religion and politics, a collection of short stories, and five previous novels: *ROMAN: Unparalleled Outrage; Utopia Revisited; 2084: Tomorrow is Today; Defector From Hell;* and *Poor Souls.* He is currently working on another novel. He resides in Evansville with his wife and children.

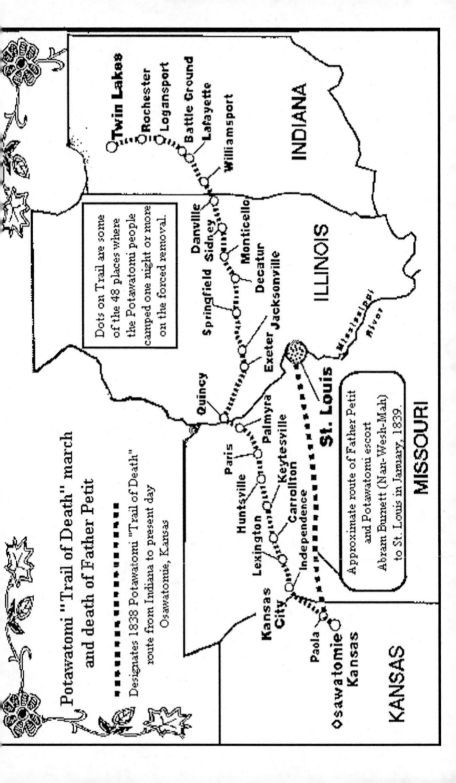

Potawatomi "Trail of Death" march and death of Father Petit

■■■■■■■■■ Designates 1838 Potawatomi "Trail of Death" route from Indiana to present day Osawatomie, Kansas

Dots on Trail are some of the 48 places where the Potawatomi people camped one night or more on the forced removal.

Approximate route of Father Petit and Potawatomi escort Abram Burnett (Nan-Wesh-Mah) to St. Louis in January, 1839.

INDIANA

Twin Lakes
Rochester
Logansport
Battle Ground
Lafayette
Williamsport

ILLINOIS

Danville
Sidney
Monticello
Springfield
Decatur
Exeter Jacksonville
Quincy

Mississippi River

St. Louis

MISSOURI

Palmyra
Paris
Huntsville
Lexington
Keytesville
Carrollton
Independence
Kansas City
Paola

KANSAS

Osawatomie Kansas